JIM MANTHORP[...] and writer, the a[...] this book. He [...] dozens of Trailb[...] years, from Lac[...] the Scottish Hig[...] love for wild places and wildl[...] filmed eagles, otters and orcas for various BBC programmes including *Springwatch*. He's also the author of *Scottish Highlands Hillwalking*, *Great Glen Way*, *Tour du Mont Blanc*, *Pembrokeshire Coast Path* and *Iceland Hiking*, all from Trailblazer.

HENRY STEDMAN (right) researched and wrote this 7th edition. He's been writing guidebooks for more than 25 years and is the author or co-author of over a dozen Trailblazer titles including *Kilimanjaro*, *Inca Trail*, *Coast to Coast Path*, *Hadrian's Wall Path*, *London LOOP* and all three books in the *South-West Coast Path* series. On most walks he's accompanied by Daisy: two parts trouble to one part Parson's Jack Russell. When not travelling, Henry lives in Battle, East Sussex, editing and arranging climbs on Africa's highest mountain through his company, Kilimanjaro Experts.

Authors

South Downs Way

First edition: 2004, this seventh edition 2022

Publisher Trailblazer Publications
The Old Manse, Tower Rd, Hindhead, Surrey, GU26 6SU, UK ⌨ trailblazer-guides.com

British Library Cataloguing in Publication Data
A catalogue record for this book is available from the British Library

ISBN 978-1-912716-23-4

© **Trailblazer** 2004, 2007, 2009, 2012, 2015, 2018, 2022: Text and maps

Editor and layout: Anna Jacomb-Hood
Cartography: Nick Hill **Proofreading**: Nicky Slade **Index**: Jane Thomas
Photographs (flora): all © Bryn Thomas except p67: red admiral © Jane Thomas;
p68: bee orchid © Tim Muddle
All other photographs: © Henry Stedman unless otherwise indicated

The maps in this guide were prepared from out-of-Crown-
copyright Ordnance Survey maps amended and updated by Trailblazer.

Dedication – to Zoë

For the wonderful company, from start to finish. Thank you darling – it was great fun!

Acknowledgements

To the other walkers we met during this update walk, thanks for your suggestions. I'm also
grateful to all those readers who wrote in with updates and recommendations, particularly
Stuart Blackburne, Anne Conchie, David Cocovini, Susan Corbett, Bea Delannoy and
Olivier, Rodney Duggua, Keith Good, Rachel and Karl-Peter Hammer, Tricia Hayne,
Andrew Hilton, Jennie Hiscock, Susie Lapwood, Richard Marshall, Jasmin McMillan, Nick
Price, Trudi & Andy Rintoul, Catherine Sharp, Danny Shone, Malcolm Simister, Sue
Tucker, and Sue Wood. Back at Trailblazer HQ, many thanks to Anna Jacomb-Hood and
Nick Hill for their stellar work on editing and mapping, to Nicky Slade for proofreading
and Jane Thomas for the index.

A request

The author and publisher have tried to ensure that this guide is as accurate and up to date
as possible. Nevertheless, things change. If you notice any changes or omissions that should
be included in the next edition of this book, please write to Trailblazer (address above) or
email us at ⌨ info@trailblazer-guides.com. A free copy of the next edition will be sent to
persons making a significant contribution.

Warning: coastal walking and long-distance walking can be dangerous

Please read the notes on when to go (pp12-16) and outdoor safety (pp54-6). Every effort
has been made by the author and publisher to ensure that the information contained herein
is as accurate and up to date as possible. However, they are unable to accept responsibility
for any inconvenience, loss or injury sustained by anyone as a result of the advice and information given in this guide.

Updated information will be available on: ⌨ trailblazer-guides.com

Photos – Front cover: Walking west towards Belle Tout. **This page**: On the Seven Sisters
looking across to Birling Gap. **Previous page**: On the Downs above Kingston-near-Lewes.
Overleaf: Marching up to Chanctonbury Ring.

Printed in China; print production by D'Print (☎ +65-6581 3832), Singapore

South Downs
WAY

64 maps & guides to 49 towns and villages
with large-scale walking maps (1:20,000)
PLANNING – PLACES TO STAY – PLACES TO EAT
Winchester–Eastbourne & Eastbourne–Winchester

JIM MANTHORPE &
HENRY STEDMAN

TRAILBLAZER PUBLICATIONS

Contents

INTRODUCTION

About the South Downs Way
History 9 – How difficult is the path? 10 – How long do you need? 11
When to go 12 – Seasons 12 – Festivals and annual events 14
Temperature 16 – Rainfall 16 – Daylight hours 16

PART 1: PLANNING YOUR WALK

Practical information for the walker
Route finding 17 – Accommodation 18 – Food and drink 21
Money 22 – Walking companies & baggage transfer 23
Information for foreign visitors 24 – Mountain biking 26
Taking dogs along the Way 27 – Disabled access 27

Budgeting 27

Itineraries
Which direction? 29 – Suggested itineraries 29 – Highlights 29
Village and town facilities 30 – Best day and weekend walks 35

What to take
Footwear 37 – Clothes 37 – First-aid kit 39 – General items 39
Camping gear 39 – Money 40 – Maps 40 – Recommended
reading 41 – Sources of further information 41

Getting to and from the South Downs Way
Getting to Britain 43 – Local transport 45 – Public transport map 48

PART 2: MINIMUM IMPACT WALKING & OUTDOOR SAFETY

Minimum impact walking
Economic impact 49 – Environmental impact 50
Access 52 – The Countryside Code 53

Outdoor safety and health
Avoidance of hazards 54 – Footcare 55
Sunburn, Hypothermia & Hyperthermia 55
Weather forecasts 56 – Dealing with an accident 56

PART 3: THE ENVIRONMENT & NATURE

Conservation of the South Downs
Government agencies 57 – Conservation organisations 59 – Geology 60

Flora and fauna
Mammals 61 – Reptiles 62 – Trees 63
Butterflies 64 – Flowers 66 – Birds 69

PART 4: ROUTE GUIDE AND MAPS

APPENDICES

Contents

This guidebook contains all the information you need. The hard work has been done for you so you can plan your trip without having to consult numerous websites and other books and maps. When you're packed and ready to go, there's comprehensive public transport information to get you to and from the trail and detailed maps (1:20,000) to help you find your way along it. It includes:

● All standards of accommodation with reviews of campsites, camping barns, hostels, B&Bs, pubs/inns, guesthouses and hotels
● Walking companies if you want an organised tour, and baggage-transfer services if you just want your luggage carried
● Suggested itineraries for all types of walkers
● Answers to all your questions: when to go, degree of difficulty, what to pack, and how much the whole walking holiday will cost
● Walking times in both directions and GPS waypoints
● Cafés, pubs, tearooms, takeaways, restaurants and food shops
● Rail, bus & taxi information for all villages and towns on the path
● Historical, cultural and geographical background information

---

❏ THIS EDITION AND THE COVID-19 PANDEMIC

This particular edition of the guide was researched during 2021, a time when the entire country was just emerging from some pretty tight restrictions. Most of the hotels, cafés, pubs, restaurants, and tourist attractions have now reopened, but some are still offering a more limited service than they were pre-pandemic.

Most **accommodation** is back open, albeit with some changes such as later checkins and earlier checkouts to allow for extra cleaning.

The majority of **pubs, restaurants and cafés** are open – though some are still operating reduced opening hours or have a limited menu. You may need to book a table in advance.

Most **train** and **bus services** were operating to reduced timetables but should now be back to normal. However, it is likely face coverings will still be required on (or in) all forms of public transport.

Museums and galleries may require booking (especially for tours) and also restrict the number of people inside at any one time.

In this book all we can do is record the opening times as they currently stand, or as the owners of the various establishments are predicting they will be by the time this is published. Do forgive us where your experience on the ground contradicts what is written in the book; please email us – **info@trailblazer-guides.com** – so we can add your information to our updates page on the website.

Hopefully, by the time you read this, Coronavirus, lockdowns and other ubiquitous words from 2020-1 will be nothing but a bad memory of a surreal year. And if that's the case, the operating hours of the establishments en route will be back to 'normal'.

For the latest information visit 🖥 gov.uk/coronavirus.

INTRODUCTION

The South Downs are a 100-mile (160km) line of chalk hills stretching from the historic city of Winchester, in Hampshire, across Sussex to the Pevensey Levels by Eastbourne. For centuries travellers and traders have used the spine of the Downs as a route from one village to the next.

For centuries travellers and traders have used the spine of the Downs as a route from one village to the next.

Today that route is still used by walkers, outdoor enthusiasts and others who simply need to escape from box-like offices in congested towns and cities. London, Brighton, Southampton and other urban areas are all within an hour or two of the South Downs, making these beautiful windswept hills an important recreational area for the millions who live in the region.

A traverse from one end to the other following the South Downs Way national trail is a great way of experiencing this beautiful landscape with its mixture of rolling hills, steep hanging woodland and windswept fields of corn. Add to this the incredible number of pretty Sussex and Hampshire villages with their friendly old pubs, thatched cottages and gardens bursting with blooms of roses, foxgloves and hollyhocks and one begins to understand the appeal of the Downs as a walking destination.

Above: A typically quaint thatched cottage in the village of Amberley.

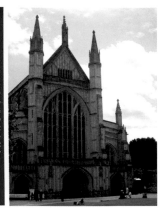

The South Downs Way begins in the cathedral city of Winchester from where it heads across rolling hills and the Meon Valley with its lazy, reed-fringed chalk-bed river and charming villages. At Butser Hill the Way reaches the highest point of the Downs with views as far as the Isle of Wight and, in the other direction, the North Downs. Continuing along the top of the ridge the Way passes through ancient stands of mixed woodland, past the Roman villa at Bignor and on towards the sandstone cottages of Amberley. Close by is the fascinating town of Arundel with its grand cathedral and even grander castle rising above the trees on the banks of the River Arun. Then it is on to Chanctonbury Ring with its fine views across the Weald of Sussex. The next stretch climbs past the deep valley of Devil's Dyke and over Ditchling Beacon to Lewes with its crooked old timber-framed buildings and the famous Harvey's Brewery. Finally, the path reaches the narrow little lanes of Alfriston with more historic pubs than one has any right to expect in such a small village. The walk's grand finale includes the meandering Cuckmere River and the roller-coaster Seven Sisters chalk cliffs – before reaching the final great viewpoint of Beachy Head, overlooking the seaside town of Eastbourne.

The official start (or end) of the South Downs Way is now the City Mill in Winchester, marked by a wooden sign outside it. Until 2017, the trail began from Winchester Cathedral (**above**) – in our opinion a much more appropriate starting point. It's well worth visiting.

The eastern end of the Way is also marked with a wooden sign (**left**), on the outskirts of Eastbourne. Most walkers will want to continue into this seaside town with its impressive Victorian pier (**below**).

Walking the Way can easily be fitted into a week's holiday but you should allow more time to be able to explore the many places of interest such as Arundel, Lewes and Winchester itself ... not to mention the lure of all those enchanting village pubs that are bound to make the trip longer than intended!

History

There has been a long-distance route running along the top of the South Downs for far longer than walking has been considered a leisure activity. The well-drained chalk hilltops high above the densely forested boggy clay below were perfect for human habitation and were certainly in use as far back as the Stone Age.

From this time onwards a complex series of trackways and paths developed across the land and it is believed that by the Bronze Age there was an established trade route along the South Downs. All along the crest of the Downs escarpment there is evidence of Iron Age hill-forts and *tumuli* (ancient burial grounds), many of them very well preserved, particularly the Old Winchester hill-fort site in Hampshire.

In more recent times the land was cleared and enclosed, and the flat hilltops were put under the plough. Although this process erased many of the lesser tracks the most significant remained; the one which ran east–west along the edge of the escarpment.

It was not until 1972, amid rapidly growing public interest in walking, that the then Countryside Commission designated the 80 miles from Eastbourne to the Sussex – Hampshire border the first long-distance bridleway in the UK. Later, the final section through Hampshire was added bringing the length of the South Downs Way to 100 miles and giving it a spectacular start in the

Above, left: Hanging on the wall in the Great Hall in Winchester is the table top said to be from King Arthur's Round Table. As it dates only from the 13th century it's too young to be genuine but still impressive at about 800 years old.
Above, right: A statue of King Alfred the Great (849-99) stands in his capital, Winchester.

Arundel Castle rises above Arundel town which is five minutes by train from Houghton Bridge.

historic city of Winchester. Today the route is growing in popularity with walkers, cyclists and horse-riders alike, all of whom tend to mingle with ease.

How difficult is the path?

The South Downs Way is one of the most accessible and easiest of Britain's long-distance paths. Those on foot will find the route usually follows wide, well-drained tracks in keeping with its designation as a long-distance bridleway, catering for cyclists, horse-riders and more recently a pony-cart wheel-chair user, as well as walkers. If anything walkers may, on occasion, crave a few more

Lewes Castle was built shortly after the Battle of Hastings in 1066.

lightly trodden paths since the route always sticks to the well-beaten track.

This 100-mile walk can be conveniently divided into sections starting and stopping at any of the numerous little villages that sit at the foot of the escarpment or in a fold in the hills. One thing to note, though, is that because the Way generally follows the high ground along the top of the South Downs, to reach

the villages offering accommodation, pubs and shops you usually have to descend steeply off the Downs and climb back onto them to continue, which can make pub lunches less attractive! When calculating the day's timings you need to bear in mind this extra walking time involved.

How long do you need?

Walkers will find that **the whole route can be tackled over the course of a week** but it is well worth taking a couple of extra days to enjoy the beautiful downland villages that are passed along the Way. It is also worth taking time to explore the former capital of Saxon England, Winchester, a historic town with a beautiful cathedral. At the other end of the walk Eastbourne is, to be polite, perhaps a little less interesting but will keep those who like to sit on a windy seafront happy for hours.

An impressive row of copper beeches to the east of Buriton.

See pp32-4 for suggested itineraries covering different walking speeds

Below: Typical rolling grassy Downs, west of Kingston-nr-Lewes.

Above: The South Downs Way has some great – and very quirky – places to eat en route, including this, perhaps our favourite, The Wildflour Café at Saddlescombe Farm. **Below**: St Pancras Church, Kingston-near-Lewes.

When to go

The south-east of England has probably the best climate in a country maligned for its fickle weather. It doesn't suffer from too much rain and enjoys more hours of sunshine than other parts of the UK. Indeed, Eastbourne proudly boasts of being the sunniest place in the UK! The route can be followed at any time of year but the chances of enjoying good weather do depend on the season.

SEASONS

Spring

A typical spring is one of sunshine and showers. From March to May a day walking on the Downs may involve getting drenched in a short sudden shower only to be dried off by warm sunshine a few minutes later. However, the weather can vary enormously from year to year, sometimes with weeks of pleasantly warm sunny weather and in other years days of grey drizzle. In general this is a great time to be on the Downs. Walker numbers are low and the snowdrops,

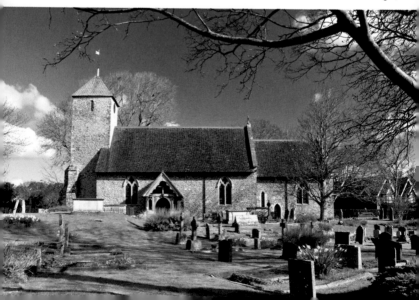

bluebells and primroses decorate the bare woodland floors.

Summer

It can get surprisingly hot and sunny from June to September but again the weather can vary from one year to the next. Always be prepared for wet weather but also be confident of enjoying some balmy summer days, too. Occasionally it can be a touch too hot for walking. This can be a problem as there is not much water on the Downs so fill up your water bottles whenever you can. Visitor numbers are high at this time of year, as you might expect, so it can be a little difficult to enjoy a solitary day on the Way. The hills are colourful in summer with wild flowers in bloom in the meadows, red poppies among the corn and fields of bright yellow oil-seed rape. Hay-fever sufferers may not agree that this is such a good thing. However, everyone seems to be in a good mood and the pubs are brimming with all sorts of folk, from fellow walkers to country gents. The big advantage of summer walking is that it remains light until well after nine in the evening so there is never any rush to finish a day's walk.

Autumn

Autumn is probably the season when you can reliably expect to be rained on. The weather from September to November tends to be characterised by low-pressure systems rolling in from the Atlantic one after another, bringing with them prolonged spells of

Right: On the Way west of Truleigh Hill

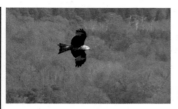

Hang-gliders, paragliders and birds of prey, such as the red kite (**above**) and the buzzard, all use the South Downs as a launchpad for riding the thermals and sea breezes.

❏ MAIN FESTIVALS & EVENTS

May/June
● **Charleston Festival** (🖥 charleston.org.uk) Held at Charleston (see p162) in the last week or two of May. Arts and literature abound.
● **Goodwood Race Course** (🖥 goodwood.com) Horse-racing takes place here **between May and October**; booking accommodation in the area can be tricky when meetings are being held, so check the website for schedules.
● **Goodwood Festival of Speed** (🖥 goodwood.com) Held over three days in late June on the Goodwood Estate a few miles south of Cocking; see box p106.
● **Viking International** (🖥 www.lta.org.uk/major-tennis-events/british-major-events/viking-international-eastbourne) women's tennis championship, a very popular pre-Wimbledon warm-up held in Eastbourne, returned at the end of June 2021.

July/August
● **Qatar Goodwood Festival** (🖥 goodwood.com) Known in horse-racing circles as 'Glorious Goodwood', this is one of the highlights of the flat-racing season and is held over five days at the end of July or start of August.
● **Winchester Hat Fair** (🖥 hatfair.co.uk) Originally a buskers' festival, now a celebration of street arts and community; all events are free but contributions are welcome – just put your money in the hat. First weekend of July.
● **Winchester Festival** (🖥 winchesterfestival.co.uk) A 10-day festival in early July which includes classical and choir music in the cathedral, folk music in the pubs, dancing in the street, art exhibitions, comedy and drama. Visit 🖥 visitwinchester .co.uk/whats-on/festivals for info and for details of the other festivals in Winchester.
● **Airbourne: Eastbourne International Airshow** (🖥 eastbourneairshow.com) Held in Eastbourne mid to late August.
● **Arundel Festival** (🖥 arundelfestival.co.uk) takes place over the last 10 days of August – folk, rock and classical music, comedy and Shakespeare plays.

September
● **Goodwood Revival** (🖥 goodwood.com) A festival of motor racing involving rare and unusual racing cars held at Goodwood over three days in mid September.

November
● **Lewes Bonfire Night Celebrations** (🖥 lewesbonfirecelebrations.com) Largest bonfire-night celebration in the country, held on 5 November unless it's a Sunday.

rain, mist and strong winds. On the positive side those who enjoy a bit of peace and quiet will find very few fellow walkers out and about at this time of year. Furthermore, it is not all rain and wind. Sometimes the weather can surprise you with a day of frost and cold sunshine that can make a day on the Way a real treat. It's important to remember that some businesses reduce their opening hours at this time of year or even close all together.

Winter

Southern England doesn't experience as many cold snowy winters as it used to some ten to twenty years ago. From December to February these days it's usually relatively mild with wet weather and occasional spells of colder, dry weather. Any snow that does

Above: A peaceful place to rest your legs: St Peter's Church, Southease.

fall is usually during January and February. It is more likely the further east you go since it is the south-east corner that gets caught by the snow showers that roll in from the North Sea, when the wind is from the north or east. Many walkers will appreciate winter walking for the wilder weather it offers and the days of solitary sauntering along the high windswept crest of the Downs. The best days are the cold, frosty ones when the air is clear and the views stretch for miles. Bear in mind that in winter some businesses, particularly in the more remote villages, are closed. It is always wise, for example, to call a pub before turning up expecting dinner.

Below: Chalk trail west of Bignor Hill.

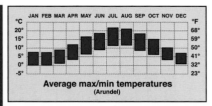

Average max/min temperatures
(Arundel)

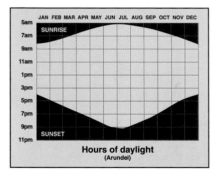

Average rainfall
(Arundel)

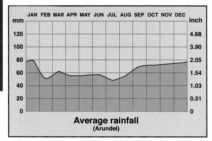

Hours of daylight
(Arundel)

TEMPERATURE

Generally, temperatures are comfortable year-round. In winter, warmer clothes will be needed as the temperature drops towards and, on occasion, just below freezing. Summer is usually pleasantly warm with temperatures around 16°C to 23°C but temperatures as high as the low 30s Celsius do occur on at least a few days during July or August which can make walking on exposed sections of the Way uncomfortable.

RAINFALL

The weather in England is affected mostly by the weather systems that come from the south-west. These are usually low-pressure systems that contain a lot of rain. Rain can and does fall in any month of the year but dry weather is usually more likely in the early summer.

DAYLIGHT HOURS

If walking in autumn, winter and early spring, you must take account of how far you can walk in the available light. Also bear in mind that, depending on the weather, you may get a further 30-45 minutes of usable light before sunrise and after sunset.

PLANNING YOUR WALK

Practical information for the walker

ROUTE FINDING

There is very little opportunity to get lost along the Way. It would be an easy route to follow even without the waymark posts, which are usually marked with the National Trail 'acorn' symbol. An acorn on a **yellow** chevron indicates that this route is a footpath, ie exclusively for pedestrians. A **blue** background indicates that the trail is a bridleway and can therefore also be used by horses and cyclists. A **purple** background quaintly adds a pony and trap. A **red** or **white** background warns that the route can also be used by motorbikes. Bear in mind that other footpaths may be indicated on the waymark posts so **follow the acorn**.

Nevertheless, it is hard to go astray and there are usually other walkers around who you can ask for directions.

Using GPS with this book

Particularly given the above, modern Wainwrights will scoff at the idea of using GPS technology for navigation on this trail but, now built into most smartphones, it's an easily accessible if non-essential aid. In no time at all a GPS receiver with a clear view of the sky will establish your position and altitude.

The maps in the route guide include numbered waypoints; these correlate to the list on pp188-92, which gives the latitude/longitude position as well as a description. Where the path is vague, or there are several options, you'll find more waypoints. You can download the complete list of these waypoints free as a GPS-readable file (that doesn't include the text descriptions) from our website: 🖥 trailblazer-guides.com (click on **GPS waypoints**).

It's also possible to buy digital mapping (see p40) to import into your phone or GPS unit, assuming that you have sufficient memory capacity, but it's not always the most reliable way of navigating and the small screen will invariably fail to put places into context or give you the 'big picture'.

Bear in mind that the vast majority of people who walk the Way do so perfectly well without GPS.

South Downs Way app

A Trailblazer South Downs Way app is now available. For more information see the Trailblazer website: 🖥 trailblazer-guides.com.

ACCOMMODATION

The South Downs lie in a populous area so there are plenty of villages and towns within easy reach of the Way, most of which offer accommodation for the walker. However, the Way generally follows the high ground along the top of the South Downs escarpment while the villages lie at the foot of the hills. This tends to leave the walker with a small detour to reach a bed at the end of each day. Bear this in mind when calculating times and distances from the maps in Part 4. As a general rule it is a good idea to allow an extra hour each day for the walk to and from your accommodation.

Camping

There is little to no opportunity for wild camping on the South Downs so campers have to rely on organised campsites. Fortunately, there are quite a few, so it is feasible to camp your way along the entire trail, though there are no campsites between Alfriston and Eastbourne. Those who do camp will certainly appreciate the experience: the pampered comforts of a B&B are outweighed by the chance to sleep under the stars and be woken by the sun, should it happen to be showing.

Refer to the itinerary charts for campers on p33 to help organise a schedule, and pay particular attention to the list below for all camping options that are right on the trail, rather than in more distant downland villages, which are a pain to get to and from with a heavy rucksack. Campsites charge between £6 and £20 per camper. Some of the more organised sites have showers and washing facilities while others are merely a place to pitch a tent in the grass. You can also camp at some YHA hostels.

Campsites right on the trail include: **Holden Farm Camping** (p84; Map 4); **Meon Springs** (pp90-1; Map 8); **The Sustainability Centre** (pp92-3; Map 9); **Bignor Farms Camping** (p115; Map 17a); **Foxleigh Barn** (p117; Map 18); **Washington Park Campsite** (pp129-30; Map 21); **White House Caravan & Campsite** (p136; Map 22); **YHA Truleigh Hill** (p140; Map 23); **Housedean Farm** (p158; Map 29); **YHA South Downs** (p163; Map 31); and **Alfriston Camping Park** (p170; Map 35).

Those who have the urge to camp in greater isolation where there is no recognised site may find it worthwhile asking a landowner for permission to set up camp.

Hostels and bunkhouses

The **YHA hostels** on the Way are both on the eastern side of the route. However, there's an **independent hostel** called South Downs Eco Lodge (p92), which is part of The Sustainability Centre near East Meon.

Despite the name, anyone of any age can join the YHA. This can be done at any hostel or by contacting the **Youth Hostels Association of England and Wales** (YHA; ☎ 01629-592700, 🖳 www.yha.org.uk). A year's membership costs £15 if paid by direct debit, £20 credit card/bank transfer. YHA hostels are easy to book, either online or by phone and you can stay even if you aren't a member though members are entitled to a 10% discount (this is valid for a

PLANNING YOUR WALK

❏ BOOKING ACCOMMODATION

You should always **book your accommodation in advance** because of the competition for beds in summer and during events such as those held at Goodwood (see box p14). It is often possible to book online but if not phone the establishment; many are now linked to online agencies, but you will get the best rate overall if you book direct. When booking **check the rate and facilities** and if walking with your children or your dog, check this won't be a problem (some B&Bs don't accept children and hostels do not allow children to stay in dormitories, for example). You may be asked to pay a **deposit**, usually 25-50%. Always let the owner know if you need to cancel so that they can free the bed for someone else.

If you are having problems finding accommodation, **tourist information centres** usually have a list of places and one or two may provide a booking service for which they may make a charge; generally a 10% deposit towards the cost of the first night's accommodation, though this then may be deducted from the bill.

member booking for up to 16 people at the same time and is applicable to the rate and meals) so it is worth joining if you expect to stay in a YHA hostel several times in a year. Note that photo ID needs to be shown at check-in but it is now possible to pay by credit card at all the hostels. They also have showers, communal space, a drying room and a fully equipped kitchen (though due to COVID the two latter weren't available at the time of research), and apart from Eastbourne they have a café-restaurant offering meals. Bedding is provided but not towels, though they can be rented.

Other cheap lodgings include: a **bunkhouse** (Houghton Bridge), **shepherd's huts** (in Chilcomb, Butser Hill, Cocking, Bury, Pyecombe and at Housedean Farm Campsite near Lewes) and **camping/land pods & bell tents** (at YHA South Downs, YHA Truleigh Hill, and also at Housedean Farm).

Bed and breakfast

Some B&Bs can be quite luxurious and come at a price, but generally speaking, all the Downs walker really wants is a warm bed and a hot bath. For this reason most of the B&Bs listed in this guide are recommended because of their usefulness to the walker and convenience to the Way, not for how many stars the tourist board has awarded them.

Bed and breakfast owners are often proud to boast that all rooms are **en suite**. This enthusiasm for private facilities has led proprietors to squeeze a cramped shower and loo cubicle into the last spare corner of the bedroom. Not having an en suite room is sometimes preferable as you may get sole use of a bathroom across the corridor and a hot bath is just what you need after a day's walking – and you will also probably save a few pounds each night.

You may find it hard to find establishments with **single** rooms. **Twin** rooms and **double** rooms are often confused but a twin room usually comprises two single beds which can either be pushed together for a couple or kept separate. A double room has one double bed. **Triple/quad** rooms are for three/four people and usually consist of a double bed and one or two single beds or bunk beds, but occasionally three/four single beds.

B&Bs do of course provide **breakfast**. Some also provide a packed lunch or an evening meal but you will need to request this in advance and there will be an extra charge. Most B&Bs, however, are close enough to a pub or restaurant and if not the owner may give you a lift to one.

B&Bs in this guide vary, usually from £35 per person (pp) for two sharing in the most basic accommodation to £60pp (or more) for the most luxurious places with en suite facilities; most charge £40-50pp. See also box below.

Guesthouses, hotels, pubs and inns

Guesthouses are usually more sophisticated than B&Bs, offering evening meals and a lounge for guests; rates are around £40-70 per person (pp) for two sharing.

Pubs and inns offer bed and breakfast of a medium to high standard and have the added advantage, of course, of having a bar downstairs and also generally offer food, so it's not far to stagger back to bed. However, the noise from tipsy punters below your room might prove a nuisance if you want an early night. Prices usually range from £30 to £60pp per night for two sharing. There are now also a few **restaurants with rooms** which are great for a treat. Expect to pay £35 to £75pp for two sharing. Generally, **hotels** tend to be more expensive, ranging from £35 to £100pp (or more) for two sharing. However, branches of chain hotels such as Travelodge (Winchester; see p75) and Premier Inn (Eastbourne; p186) can provide better value if booked in advance.

Airbnb

The rise and rise of Airbnb (🖳 airbnb.co.uk) has seen private homes and apartments opened up to overnight travellers on an informal basis. While accommodation is primarily based in cities, the concept has spread to tourist hotspots in more rural areas, but do check thoroughly what you are getting and the precise location. While the first couple of options listed may be in the area you're after, others may be far too far afield for walkers. At its best, this is a great way to meet local people in a relatively unstructured environment, but do be aware that these places are not registered B&Bs, so standards may vary, yet prices may not necessarily be any lower than the norm.

FOOD AND DRINK

Breakfast and lunch

If staying in a B&B, guesthouse or hotel you'll usually be served a full cooked

---

❑ RATES FOR B&B-STYLE ACCOMMODATION

Note that all per person (pp) rates are based on two people sharing a room. Many places do not have a single room so for single occupancy of a room they may deduct the cost of breakfast from the room rate but many places still charge the room rate. Prices can drop during the winter months and also for three or more people sharing a room. If you are on a budget you could always ask to have a room-only rate (ie no breakfast) which will usually be about £5-10 less.

breakfast which may be more than you are used to. However, some places offer a lighter continental breakfast which you may prefer first thing in the morning and some also are happy to provide vegetarian/vegan breakfasts if requested in advance; alternatively, ask to have a packed lunch instead of breakfast, particularly if you are planning an early start. If requested in advance, and for an additional cost, many places can also provide you with a packed lunch.

Alternatively, breakfast and packed lunches can be bought and made yourself; there are some great cafés and bakeries along the Way which can supply both. Remember that certain stretches of the walk are devoid of places to eat so check the information in Part 4 to ensure you don't go hungry.

Evening meals

The **pubs** that grace the pretty flint villages of the Downs rank as some of the most authentic country inns in England. Many of them date from the 14th or 15th centuries and have fascinating histories.

Food can vary from cheap traditional pub grub to high-quality cuisine served in a pub restaurant. For the serious 'connoisseur' drinker the best thing about the downland pub is the range of real ales on offer (see box p22).

While evening meals in the villages are often limited to whatever the local pub is serving, some of the larger towns such as Winchester, Eastbourne, Lewes and Petersfield are home to some quality **restaurants** with specialities ranging from fish to Italian fare.

Those on a budget, or walkers who stumble into town late in the evening, will find a number of late-night **takeaway** joints offering everything from kebabs and pizzas to Indian and Chinese and, of course, traditional fish & chips.

Self-catering supplies

If you are camping, fuel for the stove and other equipment is an important consideration. Supplies can be found at any of the outdoor shops in Winchester and Eastbourne, whilst en route there are outdoor shops in Lewes as well as hardware stores, which stock some camping-stove fuel. Some of the bigger campsites also sell camping-stove fuel, while some provide fire pits and sell bundles of kindling. Check Part 4 for more detailed information about these shops.

Drinking water

Depending on the weather you may need to drink as much as 3-4 litres of water a day. If you're feeling lethargic it may well be that you haven't drunk enough, even if you're not feeling particularly thirsty.

Although drinking directly from streams and rivers can be tempting, it is not a good idea. Streams that cross the path tend to have flowed across farmland where you can be pretty sure any number of farm animals have relieved themselves. Combined with the probable presence of farm pesticides and other delights, it is best to avoid drinking from these streams. Fortunately, there are quite a few **drinking-water taps** along the Way; we've marked them on our route maps. They are also marked on the South Downs Way trail map on the National Trails website (🖥 nationaltrail.co.uk/south-downs-way – click on 'Trail information & Map'). Also remember that, unless otherwise specified, all

PLANNING YOUR WALK

❏ **REAL ALE**

There's a plethora of local breweries for the real-ale connoisseur to get excited about. Probably the most famous Sussex brewery, and certainly the oldest, is **Harvey's** (🖳 harveys.org.uk) of Lewes (p153) which dates from 1790. Beers to look out for include their Sussex Best and Armada Ales, while in September they release their seasonal Southdown Harvest Ale which they proudly describe as the 'taste of the South Downs'.

It's also worth seeking out ales from **Long Man Brewery** (🖳 longmanbrewery .com), in Litlington. You'll find their beers in Ye Olde Smugglers Inne, in Alfriston (p171), and in the Plough & Harrow, in Litlington (p172) itself. Then there's **Riverside Brewery** (🖳 riversidebreweryltd.co.uk) in Upper Beeding who do a Beeding Best Bitter (4.2%), with a hint of liquorice, and a hoppy Sneaky Steamer (5.1%). You can try **Flowerpots Bitter** (🖳 www.theflowerpots.co.uk) right where it's brewed, at the Flower Pots Inn in Cheriton (p82). And finally, look out for beers from **Gribble Brewery** (🖳 gribbleinn.co.uk), based in Oving near Chichester, whose ales deserve awards not just for flavour but for decorating beer pumps with some of the quirkiest names. There's Pig's Ear, and the dangerously named Plucking Pheasant, but go steady on the Winter Wobbler (7.2%).

tap water in the UK, even that from the taps in public toilets, is safe to drink.

Where drinking-water taps are thin on the ground, remember that you can always ask staff in shops, cafés or pubs to fill your bottle or pouch from the tap. In England, licensed premises (ie places that serve alcohol) are required by law to provide customers with free tap water, but kind staff will sometimes be happy to help fill up your bottle even if you're not buying anything from them.

MONEY

While Eastbourne and Winchester at each end of the Way have plenty of banks and **ATMs** (cashpoints/cash machines), the villages in between do not. Bear in mind that some of these ATMs (albeit a decreasing number) charge up to £1.85 per withdrawal. However, if you find yourself without a penny on the Way it is only a short detour to some of the larger towns; banks and/or ATMs can be found in Petersfield, Midhurst, Arundel, Storrington, Steyning, Lewes and Meads.

Nevertheless, it is worth having some **cash** as small local shops may require you to pay in cash, as will some B&Bs, camping barns and campsites.

Shops that do take cards, such as supermarkets, will sometimes advance cash against a debit card (a transaction known as '**cashback**') as long as you buy something for at least £5 at the same time. Pubs sometimes do the same.

Finally, do remember that since the COVID pandemic, cash is less acceptable than it once was and many establishments now prefer you to pay by card.

Getting cash from a post office

Several banks in Britain have an agreement with the post office allowing customers with a debit card and PIN to make cash withdrawals at post office counters throughout the country. For a full list of banks that are part of this scheme contact the Post Office (🖳 www.postoffice.co.uk/branch-finder). This is a useful service particularly if no ATM is available.

OTHER SERVICES

Many villages and all the towns have at least one **food shop** and a **post office**. Post offices can be useful for sending unnecessary equipment home which may be weighing you down.

In Part 4 mention is given to services that may be of use to the walker such as **banks**, **ATMs**, **outdoor equipment shops**, **pharmacies/chemists** and **tourist information centres**, some of which can be used for finding information about accommodation among other things. **Libraries** are also shown on the maps as they sometimes offer **internet access** and **wi-fi**. **Phone boxes** are shown on the maps though it must be noted that few are still functioning as such. In some cases they are now used as mini libraries but also to house defribillators.

WALKING COMPANIES AND BAGGAGE TRANSFER

Several companies provide 'self-guided holidays' which include detailed advice and notes on itineraries, maps, accommodation booking, daily baggage transfer and transport at the start and end of your walk. If the thought of carrying a heavy rucksack doesn't appeal there is a company which will transfer your luggage to your next B&B.

Baggage transfer
● **South Downs Discovery** (☎ 01962-867728, 🖳 southdownsdiscovery.com, Cheshire) Maximum weight 20kg. Currently available April to end Sep only.

For an agreed charge some **B&B owners** may be prepared to take your luggage on to your next accommodation; it's always worth enquiring. Some **taxi companies** are also prepared to transfer luggage on an ad hoc basis.

Self-guided holidays
Note: unless specified all companies listed both offer the walk and can tailor-make a holiday in either direction.
● **Absolute Escapes** (☎ 0131-610 1210, 🖳 absoluteescapes.com, Edinburgh) Itineraries of 6-9 days.
● **British & Irish Walks** (☎ 01242-254353, 🖳 britishandirishwalks.com, Gloucestershire) Itineraries along the whole and parts of the Way.
● **Celtic Trails Walking Holidays** (☎ 01291-689774, 🖳 celtictrailswalkinghol idays.co.uk, Monmouthshire) The whole Way (west to east only) in 8-11 days' walking/9-12 nights.
● **Contours Walking Holidays** (☎ 01629-821900, 🖳 contours.co.uk, Derbyshire) Has a variety of South Downs packages from 2-day tasters to the whole walk.
● **Footpath Holidays** (☎ 01985-840049, 🖳 footpath-holidays.com, Wiltshire) Has been organising walking holidays for 35 years. A 9-night full walk, or parts of the Way using Alfriston as a base.
● **Footprints of Sussex** (☎ 01903-813381, 🖳 footprintsofsussex.co.uk, West Sussex) Has been organising SDW walks for 25 years. Offers the full Way as well as sections. Also organises an annual, supported rather than guided, walk each June (🖳 southdownsway.com).

● **Freedom Walking Holidays** (☎ 07733-885390, 🖳 freedomwalkingholi days.co.uk, Oxfordshire) A 7- to 8-day full-walk itinerary.
● **Great British Walks** (☎ 01600-713008, 🖳 great-british-walks.com, Wales) Itineraries (west to east only) with 2-10 walking days.
● **Let's Go Walking** (☎ 01837-880075, 🖳 www.letsgowalking.com, Devon) The whole path in 9 days' walking/10 nights.

🖳 INFORMATION FOR FOREIGN VISITORS

● **Currency** The British pound (£) comes in notes of £50, £20, £10 and £5, and coins of £2 and £1. The pound is divided into 100 pence (usually referred to as 'p', pronounced 'pee') which come in silver coins of 50p, 20p, 10p and 5p, and copper coins of 2p and 1p.
● **Money** Up-to-date **rates of exchange** can be found on 🖳 xe.com/currencyconverter, at some post offices, or at any bank or travel agent.
● **Business hours** If we assume that the whole COVID pandemic is behind us by the time you read this, you'll find most **shops and supermarkets** are open Monday to Saturday 7/8am-8pm (sometimes up to 15 hours a day) and on Sunday from about 9am to 5 or 6pm, though main branches of supermarkets generally open on Sunday 10am-4pm or 11am-5pm. Occasionally, especially in rural areas, you'll come across a local shop that closes at lunchtime on one day during the week, usually a Wednesday or Thursday; this is a throwback to the days when all towns and villages had an 'early closing day'.
   Main **post offices** are open at least from Monday to Friday 9am-5pm and Saturday 9am-12.30pm; branches in villages stores are often now open the same hours as the store. **Banks** typically open at 9.30am Monday to Friday and close at 3.30pm or 4pm though in some places they may open only two or three days a week and/or in the morning only; **ATMs (cash machines)** though are open all the time as long as they are outside; any inside a shop or pub will only be accessible when that place is open. Note that ATMs that charge (see p22), such as Link machines, may not accept foreign-issued cards.
   Pub hours are less predictable; although many open daily 11am-11pm; often in rural areas opening hours are Monday to Saturday 11am-3pm & 5 or 6-11pm, Sunday 11am/noon-3pm & 6 or 7-10.30pm. Last entry to most **museums and galleries** is half an hour, or an hour, before the official closing time.
● **National (bank) holidays** Most businesses are shut on 1 January, Good Friday (March/April), Easter Monday (March/April), first and last Monday in May, last Monday in August, 25 December and 26 December.
● **School holidays** State-school holidays in England are generally as follows: a one-week break late October, two weeks over Christmas and the New Year, a week mid February, two weeks around Easter, one week at the end of May/early June (to coincide with the bank holiday at the end of May) and five to six weeks from late July to early September. Private-school holidays fall at the same time, but tend to be slightly longer.
● **Documents** If you are a member of a National Trust organisation in your country bring your membership card as you should be entitled to free entry to National Trust properties and sites in the UK.
● **Entry charges** Many museums, galleries and other sights have two rates; the general rate and a higher one including a donation which is an option for UK residents who are tax payers (Gift Aid).

● **Macs Adventure** (☎ 0141 530 8886, 🖳 macsadventure.com, Glasgow) The full Way (west to east only) in 6-8 days.
● **Mickledore** (☎ 01768-772335, 🖳 mickledore.co.uk, Cumbria) Have itineraries offering the whole route in 6-10 days, or each half of the Way, and a short break 2-day circular walk.
● **Responsible Travel** (☎ 01273-823700, 🖳 responsibletravel.com, East Sussex) The whole Way in 9 nights/10 days and 10 nights/11 days.

P L A N N I N G   Y O U R   W A L K

● **EHICs and travel insurance** Until 31st December 2020 the **European Health Insurance Card** (EHIC) entitled EU nationals (on production of an EHIC card) to necessary medical treatment under the UK's National Health Service (NHS) while on a temporary visit here. However, this is not likely to be the case for EU nationals now, especially once their EHIC card has expired; check on 🖳 nhs.uk/nhs-services (click on: 'Visiting-or-moving-to-England') before you come to the UK. However, the EHIC card was never a substitute for proper medical cover on your travel insurance for unforeseen bills and for getting you home should that be necessary. Also consider getting cover for loss or theft of personal belongings, especially if you're staying in hostels, as there may be times when you have to leave your luggage unattended.

● **Weights and measures** In Britain, milk can be sold in pints (1 pint = 568ml), as can beer in pubs, though most other **liquids** including petrol (gasoline) and diesel is sold in litres. Distances on road and path signs is given in miles (1 mile = 1.6km) rather than kilometres, and yards (1yd = 0.9m) rather than metres.

The population remains divided between those who still use inches (1 inch = 2.5cm), feet (1ft = 0.3m) and yards for **distances** and those who are happy with millimetres, centimetres and metres; you'll often be told that 'it's only a hundred yards or so' to somewhere, rather than a hundred metres or so.

Most food is sold in metric weights (g and kg) but the imperial weights of pounds (lb: 1lb = 453g) and ounces (oz: 1oz = 28g) are frequently displayed too. The **weather** – a frequent topic of conversation – is also an issue: while most forecasts predict temperatures in Celsius (C), some older people continue to think in terms of Fahrenheit (F; see the temperature chart on p16 for conversions).

● **Smoking** The ban on smoking in public places relates not only to pubs and restaurants, but also to B&Bs, hostels and hotels. These latter have the right to designate one or more bedrooms where the occupants can smoke, but the ban is in force in all enclosed areas open to the public – even if they are in a private home such as a B&B. Should you be foolhardy enough to light up in a no-smoking area, which includes pretty well any indoor public place, you could be fined £50, but it's the owners of the premises who carry the can if they fail to stop you, with a potential fine of £2500.

● **Time** During the winter, the whole of Britain is on Greenwich Meantime (GMT). The clocks move one hour forward on the last Sunday in March, remaining on British Summer Time (BST) until the last Sunday in October.

● **Telephone** The international country access code for Britain is ☎ 44 followed by the area code minus the first 0, and then the number you require. Within Britain, to call a landline number with the same code as the landline phone you are calling from, the code can be omitted: dial the number only. If you're using a mobile phone that is registered overseas, consider buying a local SIM card to keep costs down.

● **Emergency services** For police, ambulance, fire or coastguard dial ☎ 999 or ☎ 112.

● **South Downs Discovery** (see also p23; ☎ 01925 914182)   South Downs Way specialists offering itineraries for 2-10 days.
● **Walkers' Britain** (formerly Sherpa Expeditions; ☎ 0800-008 7741, ☎ 020-8875 5070, 💻 walkersbritain.co.uk, London)   A 10-day itinerary in either direction; tailor-made walks west to east only.

Guided holidays
● **HF Holidays** (☎ 0345-470 7558, 💻 hfholidays.co.uk, Herts)   A long-established company which covers the whole Way in 10 days' walking/11 nights (in either direction) based at Abingworth Hall, nr Thakeham, West Sussex.
● **Secret Hills Walking Holidays** (☎ 01694-723600, 💻 secrethillswalking.co.uk; Shropshire)   Specialise in solo traveller breaks. Offer itinerary with 4½ days' walking/4 nights.

TAKING DOGS ALONG THE WAY   [see also pp192-3]

Dogs are allowed on the South Downs but should be kept on a lead whenever there are sheep around. Considering the Downs is a prime sheep-farming area this is most of the time and it is worth remembering that farmers are perfectly within their rights to shoot any dog they believe to be worrying their sheep.

❑ MOUNTAIN BIKING THE SOUTH DOWNS WAY

The South Downs Way is perfect for mountain bikers. As Britain's first long-distance bridleway it was specifically geared to horse-riders, cyclists and walkers. The entire route can be followed on two wheels on wide tracks which are, on the whole, well drained, with only a few very steep sections either side of the major river valleys. There are some sections where walkers and cyclists must follow different routes but these are well marked with blue chevrons indicating byways and yellow chevrons for footpaths.

Walk & Cycle (☎ 0844-870 8648, 💻 www.walkandcycle.co.uk/south-downs-way-cycle, Hampshire) offers 2-, 3- & 4-day **itineraries** incorporating the whole Way.

Tips for cycling the Way
● **Camp rather than stay in B&Bs** Cycling gives you the perfect opportunity to experience the joys of camping without having to carry any of your gear on your back. Strap a tent, sleeping bag and roll mat onto your bike, and off you go! See p18 for a list of campsites that are on the Way itself, rather than in the surrounding countryside far below.
● **Stick to the Way** Most of the downland villages are some distance below the Way itself, and whilst it's a joy to freewheel down to them for a pub lunch, it can be tough pulling your bike back up onto the trail afterwards. Plan accordingly; it's far better to stay on the Way at all times, if at all possible.
● **Be prepared for punctures** It hardly needs saying but don't forget your puncture repair kit (and know how to use it!) as well as your pump. Though famed for its chalk, much of the South Downs Way also contains super-sharp fragments of flint, which can cause havoc for even the sturdiest mountain-bike tyres.
● **Wet-weather gear** Chances are it will rain at some stage, and when it does the Way gets muddy; sometimes very muddy. Come prepared with wet-weather gear, including waterproof panniers, mudguards and a rag to wipe down any dirty gear.

DISABLED ACCESS

In the summer of 2016 the South Downs Way became the first fully inclusive National Trail when it was completed in its entirety by a wheelchair user using a state-of-the-art pony cart, specially developed by PonyAxeS (🖥 ponyaxes .com/south-downs-way). Unfortunately, for those without access to such carriages, some parts of the South Downs Way are still quite inaccessible to disabled people, despite many of the councils taking steps to improve access to the Sussex and Hampshire countryside.

Nevertheless, there are stretches of the Way that can be followed quite easily, particularly where roads provide direct access to the top of the hills such as at **Ditchling Beacon** (see p149). Here there are gates designed for wheelchair users and there are also plenty of benches at intervals along the path to the west of Ditchling Beacon. **Devil's Dyke** (see p142) is another good spot where access is relatively easy and the path not too rough. **Seven Sisters Country Park** (see box p175) has good facilities for the disabled both in the park and at the visitor centre and access to the beach at Cuckmere Haven is quite straightforward. Further west the easiest stretches of the Way can be found to the west of **Bignor Hill** (see p114), where there's a car park near the top, and on **Harting Down** (pp101-2) which has a relatively long stretch of gentle, level pathways. **Queen Elizabeth Country Park** (p94) has wide, level tracks and easy access.

For more information see 🖥 accessiblecountryside.org.uk/southeast.

Budgeting

CAMPING

Campsites generally charge £5-15 per person (pp) so if camping and cooking all your own food expect to need £15-25pp per day. However, it is always best to allow for more than you think necessary, to cover those occasional luxuries such as a warm bed after a day walking in the pouring rain. If you like a pint at the end of the day remember that one costing less than £4 is a rare thing in the south of England. Bearing this in mind it is worth counting on at least £20pp per day.

HOSTELS AND BUNKHOUSES

There are very few hostels and now only one bunkhouse on the Way, so you won't be able to use this type of accommodation exclusively. Combined with camping, or one or two nights in B&Bs, it can still be fairly cost-effective.

The only true **bunkhouse** on the Way, called South Downs Bunkhouse (see p117), will set you back from £26pp per night.

The YHA charges for beds in its hostels following the modern online model with lowest prices during quieter periods and rates increasing with popularity of location and date. Rooms (£29-60 for up to two sharing) are surprisingly good for such a budget price. When rooms can be used as dormitories again, expect a bed to cost around £14-22pp. All rates are 10% less if you're a YHA member. Hostels usually have a self-catering kitchen (though these were not open at the time of research) allowing you to survive on cheap food from the supermarket or local shop. However, if you want to make use of their meals, expect to pay £4.99-6.75 for breakfast, around the same for a packed lunch and £4.95-13.95 for an evening meal. Note YHAs sometimes have a kids-eat-for-free deal.

To cover the cost of a night in a private room in a hostel and the occasional bar meal and drink, count on at least £30pp per day. If the dorms have reopened, £25pp may be more accurate. If you eat out most nights this figure is likely to be £30/40pp per day (dorm/private room) or more.

B&B-STYLE ACCOMMODATION

Rates for bed and breakfast in a B&B, pub or guesthouse are usually £30-70pp (hotels are likely to be more) for two sharing a room (most places deduct about £10 from the room rate for single occupancy but some charge the full room rate). Breakfast is, of course, almost always included in the rate but you will need to allow about £5-7 for a packed lunch (more if eating in a pub or café) and about £15-20 for an evening meal. If you decide to treat yourself to quite a few meals in pubs or restaurants, drink beer and have other goodies you will probably need around £50-80pp per day.

EXTRAS

Don't forget all those little things that push up your daily bill – laundry, souvenirs, beer, ice-cream, buses here, buses there, more beer and getting to and from the Way. All these will probably add up to between £50 and £100 for the trip.

Itineraries

Part 4 of this book (the Route Guide) has been re-written for this edition so that it can be used by hikers walking the South Downs Way in either an eastward or westward direction, following a colour coding: **E➜** and **W◀**. For more details see p71. This guidebook is divided into daily stages but these are not rigid. Instead, it's structured to make it easy for you to plan your own itinerary. The South Downs Way can be tackled in any number of ways, the most challenging of which is to do it all in one go; this requires about one week. Others may prefer to walk it over a series of short breaks, coming back year after year to do a bit more. Some choose to walk only the best bits.

To help plan your walk the **colour maps** at the end of the book have **gradient profiles** and there is also a **planning map** (see opposite inside back cover). The **table of town and village facilities** (pp30-1) gives a rundown on the essential information you will need regarding accommodation possibilities and services. Alternatively, you could follow one of the **suggested itineraries** below. See p18 for details of campsites that are closest to the trail. There is also a list of recommended **day and weekend walks** (see p35) which cover the best of the path, most of which are well served by public transport. The **public transport map** is on p48.

Once you have an idea of your approach turn to **Part 4** for detailed information on accommodation, places to eat, and other services in each place on the route. Also in Part 4 you will find route descriptions to accompany the trail maps.

WHICH DIRECTION?

There are many criteria that will determine in which direction to tackle the Way. It always seems a good idea to finish a walk with something that is worth walking towards. With this in mind, although Winchester is a more attractive town to finish in than Eastbourne, the scenery improves towards the eastern end of the South Downs Way and what finer place to conclude the walk than by the sea and on top of the white cliffs of the Seven Sisters and Beachy Head. Another factor is the prevailing wind which normally comes from the south-west. Having the wind at your back is a great help so this would also suggest starting at Winchester and finishing at Eastbourne.

Although the maps in Part 4 are arranged in a west to east direction, times are given for walking in both directions so that the book can be used back to front, and for this edition we have including east-to-west route descriptions too (see p71 for further details).

SUGGESTED ITINERARIES

The itineraries are based on different accommodation types – B&B-style accommodation (p32), campsites (p33) and hostels/bunkhouses (p34) – with each divided into three categories of walking speed. They really are only suggestions and all of them can be easily adapted by using the more detailed information on accommodation found in Part 4; the distance chart on pp194-5 will also help you plan your itinerary.

Don't forget to add your travelling time from/to your accommodation both before and after the walk.

HIGHLIGHTS

There is nothing quite like taking on a long-distance path in one go but sometimes the time needed is just not available. See box p35 for suggestions of a number of day and weekend walks covering the best of the South Downs Way; these are accessible using public transport (see pp44-8) unless specified, though Sunday services may be limited or non-existent. Fitter walkers will find that the weekend walks suggested can be completed in a day.

VILLAGE AND TOWN FACILITIES
Winchester to Eastbourne – Walking East E➔

PLACE* & DISTANCE* APPROX MILES / *KM*	BANK (ATM)	POST OFFICE	INFO	EATING PLACE	FOOD SHOP	CAMP-SITE	HOSTEL BARN	B&B HOTEL
Winchester 0	✔	✔	TIC	✔✔✔	✔	✔(2¼)		✔✔✔
Chilcomb 2 / *3.2*						✔(2)		✔✔
Cheriton 4½ / *7.2* (+1.5)		✔		✔		✔		✔
Exton & Meonstoke 5½ / *8.8*		✔		✔✔	✔			✔
East Meon 5 / *8* (+1)		✔		✔✔	✔	✔		✔✔
Sustainability Centre 2 / 3.2				✔		✔	H	✔
Buriton 5½ / *8.8* (+0.5)				✔				✔
Petersfield (+2)	✔	✔	TIC	✔✔✔	✔	✔(1¼)		✔✔✔
South Harting 3½ / *5.6* (+0.5)		✔		✔	✔			✔✔
Cocking 7 / *11.2* (+0.5)		✔		✔✔	✔	✔		✔✔
Heyshott 2 / *3.2* (+0.5)				✔				
Graffham 1½ / *2.4* (+1)		mobile		✔	✔	✔		✔
Sutton & Bignor 4 / *6.4* (+1)				✔		✔		✔✔
Bury 2½ / *4* (+1)		mobile		✔				✔✔
Houghton Bridge & Amberley 1 / *1.6*		✔		✔✔✔	✔	✔	B	✔✔✔
Arundel (+5)	✔	✔		✔✔✔	✔			✔✔✔
Storrington 3 / *4.8* (+1.5)	✔	✔		✔✔✔	✔			✔
Washington 3 / *4.8* (+0.5)				✔		✔		✔
Steyning, Bramber 4 / *6.4* (+1) & Upper Beeding	✔	✔		✔✔✔	✔	✔	YHA (2½)	✔✔✔
Fulking 6½ / *10.4* (+0.5)				✔				
Poynings 2 / *3.2* (+0.5)				✔✔				✔
Pyecombe 2 / *3.2*				✔	✔	✔		✔
Clayton 1 / *1.6* (+0.5)				✔				✔
Ditchling 1½ / *2.4* (+1.5)		✔		✔✔✔	✔	✔(½)		✔✔
Plumpton 2 / *3.2* (+0.5)				✔				
Lewes 1 / *1.6* (+3)	✔	✔	TIC	✔✔✔	✔			✔✔✔
Housedean Farm 2¾ / *4.5*						✔		✔
Kingston-nr-Lewes 2¼ / *3.5* (+1)				✔				
Rodmell & Southease 4 / *6.4*				✔		✔	YHA	✔
West Firle 3½ / *5.6* (+1)		✔		✔	✔			✔
Alciston & Berwick 2½ / *4* (+1)				✔				✔
Alfriston 2 / *3.2*		mobile		✔✔✔	✔	✔		✔✔✔
Litlington 1 / *1.6*				✔✔				
Exceat/Westdean 1½ / *2.4*				✔				✔
Birling Gap 4 / *6.4*				✔				✔
Beachy Head 2¾ / *4.5*				✔				
Alternative (inland) route from Alfriston:								
Milton Street 1 / *1.6* (+0.5)								✔
Jevington 2½ / *4*				✔				✔
***End SDW** (inland)* 4½ / *7.2*	✔	✔		✔	✔			✔✔
End of SDW (Meads) 1¼ / *2*	✔	✔		✔	✔			✔✔
Eastbourne (pier) 1½ / *2.4*	✔	✔	TIC	✔✔✔	✔		YHA	✔✔✔

NOTES

***PLACE** Places in **bold** are on the path; those not in bold are a short walk off the route

***DISTANCE** = from the place above. Distances given are between places directly on the route

Bracketed distance eg (+1) shows additional distance off the route

VILLAGE AND TOWN FACILITIES
W← Eastbourne to Winchester – Walking West

PLACE* & DISTANCE* MILES / KM	BANK (ATM)	POST OFFICE	INFO	EATING PLACE	FOOD SHOP	CAMP-SITE	HOSTEL BARN	B&B HOTEL
Eastbourne (pier) 0	✔	✔	TIC	✔✔✔	✔		YHA	✔✔✔
Start of SDW (Meads) 1½ / 2.4	✔	✔		✔	✔			✔
Alternative (inland) route to Alfriston:								
Jevington 4½ / 7.2				✔				✔
Milton Street 2½ / 4 (+0.5)								✔
Alfriston (inland route) 1 / 1.6		mobile		✔✔✔	✔	✔		✔✔✔
Beachy Head 1¼ / 2				✔				
Birling Gap 2¾ / 4.5				✔				✔
Exceat/Westdean 4 / 6.4				✔				✔
Litlington 1½ / 2.4				✔✔				
Alfriston 1 / 1.6		mobile		✔✔✔	✔	✔		✔✔✔
Alciston & Berwick 2 / 3.2 (+1)				✔				✔
West Firle 2½ / 4 (+1)		✔		✔	✔			✔
Rodmell & Southease 3½ / 5.6				✔		✔	YHA	✔
Kingston-nr-Lewes 4 / 6.4 (+1)				✔				
Housedean Farm 2¼ / 3.5						✔		✔
Lewes 2¾ / 4.5 (+3)	✔	✔	TIC	✔✔✔	✔			✔✔✔
Plumpton 1 / 1.6 (+0.5)				✔				
Ditchling 2 / 3.2 (+1.5)		✔		✔✔✔	✔	✔ (½)		✔✔
Clayton 1½ / 2.4 (+0.5)				✔				✔
Pyecombe 1 / 1.6				✔	✔	✔		✔
Poynings 2 / 3.2 (+0.5)				✔✔✔				✔
Fulking 2 / 3.2 (+0.5)				✔				
Steyning, Bramber 6½ / 10.4 (+1) & Upper Beeding	✔	✔		✔✔✔	✔	✔	YHA (2½)	✔✔✔
Washington 4 / 6.4 (+0.5)				✔		✔		✔
Storrington 3 / 4.8 (+1.5)	✔	✔		✔✔✔	✔			✔
Arundel (+5)	✔	✔	TIC	✔✔✔	✔			✔✔✔
Houghton Bridge & Amberley 3 / 4.8	✔			✔✔✔	✔	✔	B	✔✔✔
Bury 1 / 1.6 (+1)		mobile		✔				✔✔
Sutton & Bignor 2½ / 4 (+1)				✔		✔		✔✔
Graffham 4 / 6.4 (+1)		mobile		✔	✔	✔		✔
Heyshott 1½ / 2.4 (+0.5)				✔				
Cocking 2 / 3.2 (+0.5)		✔		✔✔	✔	✔		✔✔
South Harting 7 / 11.2 (+0.5)		✔		✔	✔			✔✔
Petersfield (+2)	✔	✔	TIC	✔✔✔	✔	✔ (1¼)		✔✔✔
Buriton 3½ / 5.6 (+0.5)				✔				✔
Sustainability Centre 5½ / 8.8							H	
East Meon 2 / 3.2 (+1)		✔		✔✔	✔	✔		✔✔
Exton & Meonstoke 5 / 8		✔		✔✔				✔
Cheriton 5½ / 8.8 (+1.5)		✔		✔		✔		✔
Chilcomb 4½ / 7.2						✔ (2)		✔✔
Winchester 2 / 3.2	✔	✔	TIC	✔✔✔	✔	✔ (2¼)		✔✔✔

B&B/HOTEL	✔ = one place 𝒲 = two 𝒲𝒲 = three or more
BUNK/HOSTEL	YHA = YHA hostel H = independent hostel B = bunkhouse
CAMPSITE	Bracketed distance eg (½) shows distance from South Downs Way
EATING PLACE	✔ = one place 𝒲 = two 𝒲𝒲 = three or more
INFO	TIC = Tourist information centre

PLANNING YOUR WALK

PLANNING YOUR WALK

STAYING IN B&B-STYLE ACCOMMODATION – West to East

	Relaxed pace			Medium pace			Fast pace		
Night	Place	Approx distance miles	km	Place	Approx distance miles	km	Place	Approx distance miles	km
0	Winchester			Winchester			Winchester		
1	Cheriton	8	12.8	Cheriton	8	12.8	Meonstoke	12	19.3
2	Meonstoke	7	11.2	East Meon	13	20.9	South Harting	16½	26.5
3	East Meon	6	9.6	South Harting	12½	20.1	Amberley	20	32.2
4	Buriton	8½	13.6	Graffham	10½	16.9	Pyecombe	20½	33
5	Cocking	11	17.7	Amberley	9	14.4	Rodmell	15	24.1
6	Amberley	13½	21.7	Steyning	13	20.9	Alfriston	9	14.4
7	Steyning	13	20.9	Lewes*	16	25.7	Eastbourne	12½	20.1
8	Pyecombe	9½	15.2	Alfriston	17	27.3			
9	Lewes*	5½	8.4	Eastbourne	12½	20.1			
10	Rodmell	9	14.4						
11	Alfriston	8	12.8						
12	Eastbourne	12½	20.1				See Notes below		

STAYING IN B&B-STYLE ACCOMMODATION – East to West

	Relaxed pace			Medium pace			Fast pace		
Night	Place	Approx distance miles	km	Place	Approx distance miles	km	Place	Approx distance miles	km
0	Eastbourne			Eastbourne			Eastbourne		
1	Alfriston	12½	20.1	Alfriston	12½	20.1	Alfriston	12½	20.1
2	Rodmell	8	12.8	Lewes*	17	27.3	Rodmell	9	14.4
3	Lewes*	9	14.4	Steyning	16	25.7	Pyecombe	15	24.1
4	Pyecombe	5½	8.4	Amberley	13	20.9	Amberley	20½	33
5	Steyning	9½	15.2	Graffham	9	14.4	South Harting	20	32.2
6	Amberley	13	20.9	South Harting	10½	16.9	Meonstoke	16½	26.5
7	Cocking	13½	21.7	East Meon	12½	20.1	Winchester	12	19.3
8	Buriton	11	17.7	Cheriton	13	20.9			
9	East Meon	8½	13.6	Winchester	8	12.8			
10	Meonstoke	6	9.6						
11	Cheriton	7	11.2						
12	Winchester	8	12.8				See Notes below		

B&B – Notes Lewes is three miles off the trail but frequent public transport is available from Housedean Farm (see p158), very near the path, or it's a three-mile walk from trail to town. (The three miles to Lewes have not been included in the above mile counts.)

CAMPING – West to East

Night	Relaxed pace — Place	Approx distance miles	km	Medium pace — Place	Approx distance miles	km	Fast pace — Place	Approx distance miles	km
0	Winchester*			Winchester*			Winchester*		
1	Holden Farm	7	11.2	Holden Farm	7	11.2	Meon Springs	17	27.3
2	Meon Springs	10	16.1	Sustainbty Ctr	13	20.9	Manor Farm†	18	28.9
3	Butser Hill	6	9.6	Manor Farm†	16	25.7	Amberley	12	19.3
4	Manor Farm†	13	20.9	Amberley	12	19.3	Pyecombe	20	32.2
5	Graffham	3½	5.7	Truleigh Hill	14	22.5	Alfriston	22	35.4
6	Amberley	8½	13.6	Ditchling	9	14.4	Eastbourne*	12½	20.1
7	Washington	7	11.2	Southease	11	17.7			
8	Truleigh Hill	8	12.8	Alfriston	8	12.8			
9	Pyecombe	6	9.6	Eastbourne*	12½	20.1			
10	Housedean Fm	8	12.8						
11	Southease	7	11.2	† Manor Farm is on the Way (just south of Cocking)					
12	Alfriston	8	12.8						
13	Eastbourne*	12½	20.1				See Notes below		

CAMPING – East to West

Night	Relaxed pace — Place	Approx distance miles	km	Medium pace — Place	Approx distance miles	km	Fast pace — Place	Approx distance miles	km
0	Eastbourne*			Eastbourne*			Eastbourne*		
1	Alfriston	12½	20.1	Alfriston	12½	20.1	Alfriston	12½	20.1
2	Southease	8	12.8	Southease	8	12.8	Pyecombe	22	35.4
3	Housedean Fm	7	11.2	Ditchling	11	17.7	Amberley	20	32.2
4	Pyecombe	8	12.8	Truleigh Hill	9	14.4	Manor Farm†	12	19.3
5	Truleigh Hill	6	9.6	Amberley	14	22.5	Meon Springs	18	28.9
6	Washington	8	12.8	Manor Farm†	12	19.3	Winchester*	17	27.3
7	Amberley	7	11.2	Sustainbty Ctr	16	25.7			
8	Graffham	8½	13.6	Holden Farm	13	20.9			
9	Manor Farm†	3½	5.7	Winchester*	7	11.2			
10	Butser Hill	13	20.9						
11	Meon Springs	6	9.6	† Manor Farm is on the Way (just south of Cocking)					
12	Holden Farm	10	16.1						
13	Winchester*	7	11.2				See Notes below		

Camping – Notes In some cases it is necessary to walk up to a mile for the campsite but see p18 for a list of campsites directly on the trail.

* No campsites at places marked with an asterisk. For Winchester consider Morn Hill Caravan Club Campsite: it is two miles north-east of Chilcomb and 1½ miles north of the Cheesefoot Head car park (both Map 2), or 2¼ miles from Winchester but accessible by bus from Winchester bus station. For Eastbourne stay in the YHA, or catch the last train home.

PLANNING YOUR WALK

PLANNING YOUR WALK

STAYING IN HOSTELS/BUNKHOUSES – West to East

	Relaxed pace			Medium pace			Fast pace		
		Approx distance			Approx distance			Approx distance	
Night	Place	miles	km	Place	miles	km	Place	miles	km
0	Winchester*			Winchester*			Winchester*		
1	Cheriton*	8	12.8	Cheriton*	8	12.8	East Meon	18	28.9
2	East Meon	13	20.9	East Meon	13	20.9	Buriton*	9	14.4
3	Buriton*	9	14.4	Sth Harting*	12½	20.1	Bignor*	19½	31.3
4	Cocking*	11½	18.5	Bignor*	16	25.7	Truleigh Hill	20	32.2
5	Bignor*	9	14.4	Truleigh Hill	20	32.2	Southease	21	33.8
6	Washington*	12½	20.1	Ditchling*	10½	16.9	Eastbourne	20½	33
7	Truleigh Hill	8½	13.6	Southease	13½	21.7			
8	Ditchling*	10½	16.9	Alfriston*	8	12.8			
9	Southease	12	19.3	Eastbourne	12½	20.1			
10	Alfriston*	8	12.8						
11	Eastbourne	12½	20.1						

* No hostels/bunkhouses at places marked; alternative accommodation available

STAYING IN HOSTELS/BUNKHOUSES – East to West

	Relaxed pace			Medium pace			Fast pace		
		Approx distance			Approx distance			Approx distance	
Night	Place	miles	km	Place	miles	km	Place	miles	km
0	Eastbourne			Eastbourne			Eastbourne		
1	Alfriston*	12½	20.1	Alfriston*	12½	20.1	Southease	20½	33
2	Southease	8	12.8	Southease	8	12.8	Truleigh Hill	21	33.8
3	Ditchling*	12	19.3	Ditchling*	13½	21.7	Bignor*	20	32.2
4	Truleigh Hill	10½	16.9	Truleigh Hill	10½	16.9	Buriton*	19½	31.3
5	Washington*	8½	13.6	Bignor*	20	32.2	East Meon	9	14.4
6	Bignor*	12½	20.1	Sth Harting*	16	25.7	Winchester*	18	28.9
7	Cocking*	9	14.4	East Meon	12½	20.1			
8	Buriton*	11½	18.5	Cheriton*	13	20.9			
9	East Meon	9	14.4	Winchester*	8	12.8			
10	Cheriton*	13	20.9						
11	Winchester*	8	12.8						

* No hostels/bunkhouses at places marked; alternative accommodation available

❏ THE BEST DAY AND WEEKEND WALKS

Day walks

Exton to Buriton   **12 miles/19.3km (see pp88-97)**
The best of the East Hampshire downland, passing over Old Winchester Hill and its magnificent hill-fort remains and Butser Hill, the highest hill on the Downs, with far-reaching views over the Meon Valley and Queen Elizabeth Country Park.

There are no bus services at Exton but there are to East Meon so if you need to use public transport it is easiest to start there.

Amberley to Steyning   **13 miles/20.9km (see pp126-34)**
Starting in one of the prettiest villages on the Way and ending in one of the most beautiful towns, this walk provides extensive views from the spine of the Downs, taking in the famous local landmark of Chanctonbury Ring.

Devil's Dyke to Ditchling Beacon   **5 miles/8km (see pp142-9)**
Possibly the most spectacular dry valley on the Downs, Devil's Dyke is the magnificent starting point of this short section that continues by climbing over the isolated Newtimber Hill before ending at the beauty spot of Ditchling Beacon. There are seasonal bus services (Sat, Sun & public holidays only) to both Devil's Dyke and Ditchling Beacon.

Kingston-near-Lewes to Southease   **5 miles/8km (see pp159-61)**
One of the quieter stretches of the Downs with fine views of Mount Caburn on the other side of the Ouse Valley and a little bit of literary history to be had at Rodmell, once the home of Virginia Woolf.

Exceat to Eastbourne via Cuckmere Haven   **9 miles/14.4km (see pp172-8)**
Arguably the finest day of walking anywhere between Winchester and Eastbourne, following the rollercoaster tops of the Seven Sisters chalk cliffs to the high point of Beachy Head high above Eastbourne.

Alfriston to Eastbourne via Jevington   **10 miles/16km (see pp181-3)**
This inland route is not as spectacular as the coastal route to Eastbourne but equally enjoyable, encompassing the beautiful Cuckmere Valley, the ramshackle timber-framed houses of Alfriston and the curious Long Man of Wilmington chalk figure.

Weekend walks

Buriton to Amberley   **23½ miles/38km (see pp97-120)**
Stopping off in either Cocking or Midhurst for the night, this section takes in the fine wooded sections close to Buriton and the airy Harting Down on the first day, followed by Rignor Hill with its Roman road, Stane Street, on the second day.

Amberley to Pyecombe   **20½ miles/33km (see pp120-46)**
Extensive views and the curious, enchanted Chanctonbury Ring are the highlights of the first day with a wide choice of places to stay in historic Steyning, or Bramber with its castle. The second day follows the open top of the Downs all the way to the impressive valley of Devil's Dyke.

Circular walk (Eastbourne, Alfriston, Cuckmere Haven)   **19 miles/30.5km**
The Exceat to Eastbourne and Alfriston to Eastbourne walks (see p171 & p181) can be combined to make a wonderful circular walk and can be started and finished anywhere on the circuit. You'll pass through the beautiful villages of Jevington, Alfriston, Litlington and Westdean as well as walking the entire coastal section from Cuckmere Haven to Eastbourne.

PLANNING YOUR WALK

What to take

Deciding how much to take with you can be difficult. Experienced walkers know that you really should take only the bare essentials but at the same time you need to ensure you have all the equipment necessary to make the trip safe and comfortable.

KEEP YOUR LUGGAGE LIGHT

Carrying a heavy rucksack really can ruin your enjoyment of a good walk and can also slow you down a great deal, turning an easy 7-mile day into an interminable slog. Be ruthless when you pack and leave behind all those little home comforts that you tell yourself don't weigh that much really. Always pack the essentials, of course, but try to leave behind anything that you think might 'come in handy' but probably won't. This advice is even more pertinent to campers who have the added weight of camping equipment to carry.

HOW TO CARRY IT

The size of the **rucksack** you should take depends on where you are planning to stay and how you are planning to eat. If you are camping and cooking for yourself you will probably need a 65- to 75-litre rucksack which can hold the tent, sleeping bag, cooking equipment and food. All the hostels on the Way provide bedding (though not towels) and have cooking facilities (though due to COVID they may not be open), so if staying in these a 40- to 60-litre rucksack should be sufficient. If you have gone for the B&B option you will probably find a 30- to 40-litre daypack is more than enough to carry your lunch, clothes, camera and guidebook. If you've booked a self-guided holiday, or are using a baggage-transfer service (see p23), you could even just take a suitcase, although a backpack is still probably better for the beginning and end of your trip where you may have to carry your luggage.

Whatever size your rucksack is, ensure it has a stiffened back and can be adjusted to fit you comfortably; this will make carrying the weight much easier. Rucksacks are decorated with seemingly pointless straps but if you adjust them correctly it can make a big difference to your personal comfort while walking. Make sure the hip belt and chest belt (if there is one) are fastened tightly as this helps distribute the weight; most of it should be carried on your hips.

When packing the rucksack make sure you have all the things you are likely to need during the day – this guidebook (of course!), a map, a water bottle, waterproofs, packed lunch – near the top or in the side pockets. A good habit to get into is always to put things in the same place and memorise where they are. There is nothing more annoying than pulling everything out of your pack to find that lost banana when you're starving or that camera when there is a butterfly basking briefly on a nearby rock.

Even though most rucksacks come with their own rain cover, it is still a good idea to keep everything inside it in **canoe bags**, **waterproof rucksack liners** or strong plastic bags (or bin-liners). If you don't it's bound to rain.

If you are using a baggage-transfer service you will need a small **bum bag** or **day pack** for the essentials for the day.

FOOTWEAR

Boots versus trainers Your footwear is arguably the most important item of gear that can affect the enjoyment of your hike. In summer you can get by with a light pair of running trainers or trail shoes, especially if you're carrying only a small pack, although this is an invitation for wet, cold feet if there is any rain and they don't offer support for your ankles. On the plus side, lightweight running trainers dry off after a rainstorm much more quickly than big heavy hiking boots. Some of the terrain can be quite rough and wet, though, so many people prefer a pair of good walking boots. If going down this route, remember they must fit well and be properly broken in: it is no good discovering that your boots are slowly murdering your feet two days into a one-week walk.

Socks The traditional wearing of a thin liner sock under a thicker wool sock is no longer necessary if you choose a high-quality sock specially designed for walking. A high proportion of natural fibres makes them much more comfortable. Three pairs are ample, although you may need more if it rains a lot.

Extra footwear Some walkers like to have a second pair of shoes to wear when not on the trail. Trainers, sport sandals, or flip flops are all suitable as long as they are light. Flip flops are certainly useful for wearing in the shower blocks at campsites.

CLOTHES

Experienced walkers will know the importance of wearing the right clothes. Always expect the worst weather even if the forecast is good. Modern technology in outdoor attire can seem baffling but it basically comes down to the old multi-layer system: a base layer to transport sweat away from your skin; a mid-layer to keep you warm; and an outer layer or 'shell' to protect you from the rain.

Underwear and base layer As with socks, two or three changes of your normal **underwear** is fine. Cotton absorbs sweat, trapping it next to the skin which will chill you rapidly when you stop exercising. A thin lightweight **thermal top** made from a synthetic material is better as it draws moisture away, keeping you dry. It will be cool on its own in hot weather and warm when worn under other clothes in cooler conditions. A spare would be sensible. Also bring a **shirt** or top for wearing in the evening.

Mid layers In the summer a woollen jumper or mid-weight polyester **fleece** will suffice. For the rest of the year you will need an extra layer to keep you warm. Both wool and fleece, unlike cotton, have the ability to stay reasonably warm when wet.

Outer layer A decent **waterproof jacket** is essential year-round and will be much more comfortable (but also more expensive) if it's also 'breathable' to prevent the build up of condensation on the inside. This layer can also be worn to keep the wind off.

Leg wear Whatever you wear on your legs it should be light, quick-drying and not restricting. Many British walkers find **polyester tracksuit bottoms** comfortable. Poly-cotton or microfibre trousers are excellent. Denim jeans should never be worn; if they get wet they become heavy, cold and bind to your legs. A pair of **shorts** is nice to have on sunny days; many hikers wear **'zip-off' trousers** – ie trousers where the lower part of each leg is attached to the rest of the garment by a zip, so you can convert them into shorts if preferred – and these are the most versatile, and thus the most suitable option for the South Downs. Thermal **long-johns** or thick tights are cosy if you're camping but are probably unnecessary even in winter.

    Waterproof trousers are necessary most of the year. In summer a pair of windproof and quick-drying trousers is useful in showery weather.

    Gaiters are not really necessary but may come in useful in wet weather, when the vegetation around your legs is dripping wet.

Other clothes A **warm hat** and **gloves** should always be kept in your rucksack; you never know when you might need them. In summer you should also carry a **sun hat** with you, preferably one which covers the back of your neck. For cooling off on beaches, or in local swimming pools, take a **swimsuit**.

TOILETRIES

Take only the minimum: unless staying in B&Bs, you'll need a small bar of **soap** or small bottle of **shower gel**, either of which can also be used instead of shaving cream and for washing clothes; a tiny tube of **toothpaste** and a **toothbrush**; and one roll of **loo paper** in a plastic bag. If you are planning to defecate outdoors you will also need a **lighter** for burning the paper and a lightweight **trowel** for burying the evidence (see p51 for further tips).

    You'll also need a **towel** (if camping or staying in a hostel though at the latter they can usually be rented), **razor**, **deodorant**, **tampons/sanitary towels** and a high-factor **sunscreen** and/or **lip balm**.

FIRST-AID KIT

Medical facilities in Britain are excellent so you need only take a small kit to cover common problems and emergencies. A basic kit will contain a pack of **aspirin** or **paracetamol** for treating mild to moderate pain and fever; **plasters/ Band Aids** for minor cuts; '**moleskin**', '**Compeed**' or '**Second skin**' for blisters; a **bandage** for holding dressings, splints or limbs in place and for supporting a sprained ankle; an **elastic knee support** for a weak knee; a small selection of different-sized **sterile dressings** for wounds; **porous adhesive tape**; **antiseptic wipes**; **antiseptic cream**; **safety pins**; **tweezers** and a small pair of **scissors**. Pack the kit in a waterproof container.

GENERAL ITEMS

Essential

The following should be in everyone's rucksack: a **water bottle/pouch** (holding at least one litre); a **torch** (flashlight) with spare bulb and batteries in case you end up walking after dark; **emergency food** which your body can quickly convert into energy; a **penknife**; a **watch** with an alarm; and a **bag** for packing out any rubbish you accumulate. A **whistle** is also worth taking. It can fit in a pocket and although you are very unlikely to need it you may be grateful of it in the unlikely event of an emergency (see p56). **Face masks** may no longer be essential but it would probably be worth having some.

Of course, a **smartphone** can do the job of some of the above (torch, watch, alarm), as well as being a **GPS**, **map**, **camera**, **compass** – oh, and a phone too. As such, most people will regard them as an essential bit of kit. However, they're only any good if they're charged up. Otherwise, they're just 150g or so of dead (but precious) weight. So another bit of essential kit you'll need is a **power/battery pack**, to reduce the chances of it running out of power while you're walking. Oh, and don't forget to bring the appropriate **leads** too so that you can connect battery pack and phone – and the **chargers** for both phone and battery pack. (Phone reception on the South Downs, by the way, is generally good.)

Useful

The quality of the camera on a smartphone these days is impressive, though most serious photographers would still prefer to use an **SLR**. That said, it can be liberating to travel without one once in a while; a **notebook** can be a more accurate way of recording your impressions (but remember to take some **pens**). Other items include a **book** to pass the time on train journeys; a pair of **sunglasses**; **binoculars** for observing wildlife; **walking poles** to take the strain off your knees and a **vacuum flask** for carrying hot drinks. Although the path is easy to follow a 'Silva' type **compass** could be a good idea.

CAMPING GEAR

Campers need a decent **tent** (or bivvy bag if you enjoy travelling light) that's able to withstand wet and windy weather; a two- to three-season **sleeping bag** (but obviously in winter a warmer one is a good idea and on hot summer nights you could get away with a one-season bag); a **sleeping mat**; a **stove** and **fuel** (there is special mention in Part 4 of which shops stock fuel); a **mug**; a **spoon**; a wire/plastic **scrubber** for washing up; and a pan or **cooking pot**. One pot is fine for two people; some pots come with a lid that can be used as a plate or frying pan. You can also buy camping pot sets that pack away neatly into one pot.

MONEY

There are not many banks along the Way so you will have to carry most of your money as **cash**. A **debit card** is the easiest way to withdraw money either from banks or ATMs and a debit or **credit card** can be used to pay in most larger shops, restaurants and hotels. There are still B&Bs that don't accept cards, so you may need to pay cash. Alternatively ask if your B&B accepts a bank transfer.

MAPS

The **hand-drawn maps** in this book cover the trail at a scale of 1:20,000 – plenty of detail and information to keep you on the right track; the **colour maps** at the back of the book are at a smaller scale covering the surrounding area.

To explore even further afield you might be interested in Ordnance Survey maps (OS; 💻 ordnancesurvey.co.uk). The best maps for walkers are the 1:25,000 OS Explorer Maps (orange cover). The relevant numbers for the South Downs Way are Nos 3 (Meon Valley), 8 (Chichester), 10 (Arundel & Pulborough), 11 (Brighton & Hove), 25 (Eastbourne & Beachy Head) and 32 (Winchester). **Note that these maps were renumbered in 2015**: OL 3 used to be 119, OL 8 was 120, OL 10 was 121, OL 11 was 122, OL 25 was 123 and OL 32 was 132. If you're exploring by car, the pink-covered OS Landranger maps at a scale of 1:50,000 are perhaps better: Nos 185, 197, 198 & 199 cover the trail and beyond. All OS maps listed here are £8.99 each, though occasionally they are on sale at £20 for three. OS also offers **digital maps** (see below), which come free with the paper map or you can download them separately for a fee.

The *AZ Adventure Series South Downs Way map* (💻 collins.co.uk/pages/a-z-maps-atlases; £8.95) includes the relevant section of the OS maps at a scale of 1:25,000 and also has an index.

There's also a single-sheet Harvey's *South Downs Way Map* (Harvey Maps, £14.50, 💻 harveymaps.co.uk) at a scale of 1:40,000.

❏ DIGITAL MAPPING

Most smartphones have a GPS chip so you can see your position overlaid onto a digital map on your phone. There are numerous software packages that provide Ordnance Survey (OS) maps for a smartphone, tablet, PC or GPS unit. Maps are downloaded over the internet, then loaded into an app, also available by download, from where you can view them, print them and create routes on them.

It is important to ensure any digital mapping software on your smartphone uses pre-downloaded maps stored on your device, and doesn't need to download them on-the-fly, as this may be expensive and will be impossible without a signal. Note that battery life will be significantly reduced, compared to normal usage, when you are using the built-in GPS and running the screen for long periods.

Many websites have **free routes** you can download for the more popular digital mapping products; anything from day walks to complete Long Distance Paths. **Memory Map** (💻 memory-map.co.uk) currently sell OS 1:25,000 mapping covering the whole of the UK for £166. They also have annual subscriptions from £25.

For a subscription of £2.99 for one month, or £23.99 for a year (on their current offer) **Ordnance Survey** (see above) will let you download and then use their UK maps (1:25,000 scale) on a mobile or tablet without a data connection for a specific period.

Harvey Maps sell their digital South Downs Way map for £20.49 for use on any device.

A Trailblazer **South Downs Way app** is now available; for more information see the Trailblazer website 💻 trailblazer-guides.com.

RECOMMENDED READING

Many bookshops and most of the tourist information centres along the South Downs Way stock many of the following books.

An excellent read recounting **one person's experience** of his walk is *The South Downs Way* (Mainstream, 2002) by Martin King. Other books worth considering are: *Alone on the South Downs Way: one woman's solo journey from Winchester to Eastbourne* by Holly Worton (Tribal, 2016); *The South Downs Way* by Belinda Knox (Frances Lincoln, 2008), a photographic based guide, or *Whan That Aprille: For the Curious: An Exploration of the South Downs Way in Hampshire*, Heather Lacey (Redback Publishing; 2016).

For **bird identification** there are plenty of books to choose from including the *Collins Bird Guide* by Lars Svensson et al (2010) and the *New Birdwatcher's Pocket Guide to Britain and Europe* by Peter Hayman and Rob Hume (Mitchell Beazley, 2002). The RSPB's *Pocket Guide to British Birds* by Simon Harrap (Bloomsbury Wildlife, 2018) is also recommended; birds are identified by their plumage and song.

⨆ SOURCES OF FURTHER INFORMATION

Tourist Information

● **Tourist/Visitor Information Centres** (TICs) are based in towns throughout Britain; they provide all manner of locally specific information and a few offer accommodation booking. However, some are staffed by volunteers who can help with information but not book accommodation; they also generally have limited opening hours. The following TICs lie on or near the Way: **Winchester** (see p75); **Petersfield** (see p98); **Lewes** (see p153); **Eastbourne** (see p184).

In addition there are some **visitor centres** such as the ones at Queen Elizabeth Country Park (see p96) and Seven Sisters Country Park (see box p175). Visitor centres generally only have information about the actual attraction.

● **Friends of the South Downs** (South Downs Society) See p61.

Organisations for walkers

● **Backpackers' Club** (💻 backpackersclub.co.uk) Aimed at people who are interested in lightweight camping through walking and other activities. Membership costs £20/30 per year for an individual/family and includes a quarterly magazine and a comprehensive advisory & information service; they also organise weekend trips.

● **The Long Distance Walkers' Association** (💻 ldwa.org.uk) Membership includes a journal (Strider) three times per year with details of challenge events and local group walks as well as articles on the subject. Membership costs £18/25.50 a year for individuals/families (£15/22.50 if paying by direct debit).

● **Ramblers** (💻 ramblers.org.uk) A charity that looks after the interests of walkers throughout Britain and promotes walking for health. Annual membership costs from £36.60/49 (concessionary £25.60/34), and includes their quarterly Walk magazine as well as access to their app and their library of walking routes plus walks arranged by the various regional groups.

One of the best field guides to **flora** is *The Wild Flowers of Britain and Ireland* by Marjorie Blamey et al (Bloomsbury Natural History, 2013). Now sadly out of print, but used copies may be available online, the best guidebook specifically aimed at the **wildlife of the region** is the hardcover *Downland Wildlife – A Naturalist's Year in the North & South Downs* by John S Burton, illustrated by John Davis (George Philip, 1992).

The Field Studies Council (🖳 field-studies-council.org) publishes a series of **fold-out charts** in the form of laminated sheets (£4 each) showing commonly found birds, trees, flowers etc. The series includes *Features of the South Downs Way*.

There are also numerous **fieldguide apps** for both iPhone and Android, for identifying flowers, butterflies and birds by their song as well as by their appearance. One to consider for birds is: 🖳 merlin.allaboutbirds.org.

Getting to and from the South Downs Way

It could not be easier to reach the South Downs from London as there are numerous road and rail links not just to Winchester and Eastbourne, the start and finish of the walk, but to many other points along the Way. Most parts of the South Downs Way are no more than 1½-2 hours from the capital. Access from other parts of Britain often involves going via London but there are rail services to Winchester and Southampton via Reading. The rail line running across the south coast goes from Dover to Ashford International, then to Hastings and along the coast to Eastbourne and Brighton; from Brighton there are services to Portsmouth and Southampton.

See box opposite for routes from continental Europe to south coast of England.

NATIONAL TRANSPORT

By rail

The two main rail operators for services to locations along the South Downs are Southern (from London Victoria to the south coast) and SouthWest Trains (from London Waterloo stopping at Winchester and Petersfield). Other providers are: Thameslink (from Bedford to Brighton via Luton Airport and St Pancras International) and Cross Country (from Manchester/Birmingham to Bournemouth and calling at Winchester). See the box p44 and map on p48 for contact and service details.

Timetables, ticket and fare information can be found on the rail operators' websites, apps or through **National Rail Enquiries** (☎ 03457-484950, 🖳 www.nationalrail.co.uk, app available); you can purchase tickets through the relevant rail operator's website. Note, it is much cheaper if you book tickets in advance and especially if you can travel on trains at a specific time. It may also

❏ GETTING TO BRITAIN

● **By air** The nearest international airport to Winchester is Southampton Airport (🖳 www.southamptonairport.com) on the south coast. The alternative would be to fly to London's Gatwick (🖳 gatwickairport.com) or Heathrow airports (🖳 heathrow.com), both of which serve destinations worldwide. Further away but with a direct rail connection to Brighton is Luton Airport (🖳 www.london-luton.co.uk); Gatwick also has a direct train connection to Eastbourne (via Lewes), see box p44.

Another option is London City Airport (🖳 londoncityairport.com); the Docklands Light Railway is connected to the airport terminal and from there take a train to Canning Town and transfer to the Jubilee line (underground) for Waterloo Station.

● **From Europe by train** Eurostar (🖳 eurostar.com) operates a high-speed passenger service via the Channel Tunnel between Paris/Brussels and London. The Eurostar terminal in London is at St Pancras International station; services to Ashford International (and Ebbsfleet International) stopped in 2020 due to COVID and there are no plans to restart this service until 2022 at the earliest.

For information about the various rail services to Britain from the continent contact your national rail service provider, or visit 🖳 railteam.eu.

● **From Europe by coach** Eurolines (🖳 eurolines.de/en) have a huge network of long-distance coach services connecting over 500 cities in 25 European countries to London. However, these tickets often don't work out that much cheaper than flying the same route with a budget airline which is also far quicker (although less environmentally friendly, of course). **Megabus** (🖳 uk.megabus.com) is part of the Stagecoach group and it operates low cost coach services from a number of destinations in Europe to London and other cities.

● **From Europe by car** Eurotunnel ('le shuttle'; 🖳 www.eurotunnel.com) operates a shuttle **train** service for vehicles via the Channel Tunnel between Calais and Folkestone, taking an hour between the motorway in France and the motorway in England. There are many **ferry** routes between France (Caen, Calais, Cherbourg, Dieppe, Dunkerque, Le Havre and St Malo) and the south coast ports of England such as Dover, Newhaven, Poole and Portsmouth. There are also services from Spain (Bilbao and Santander) to Portsmouth. Look at 🖳 directferries.com for a full list of companies and services.

PLANNING YOUR WALK

be worth looking at 🖳 www.thetrainline.com to see if you can get an even cheaper fare.

It is also often possible to book train tickets that include (discounted) bus travel to your ultimate destination; enquire when you book your train ticket or look at Plus Bus's website (🖳 plusbus.info).

By car

The south of England is overrun with dual carriageways and bypasses so there is no shortage of 'A' roads to follow down to the Downs. On holiday weekends, however, be prepared for long tailbacks as everyone heads for the coast. There are main roads from London passing through Winchester, Petersfield, Cocking, Amberley, Arundel, Washington, Pyecombe, Lewes, Brighton and Eastbourne.

By air

Although there are local airports, such as Brighton City Airport at Shoreham, the easiest way to fly to the South-East from other corners of the UK is to get a flight to Gatwick or Southampton; see box p43. Bear in mind the environmental

[see map p48]

❏ USEFUL RAIL SERVICES

Note: not all stops are listed here, nor are all shown on the map. Check the relevant operator's website for full details.

Also note that timetables may change following completion of the upgrade works (scheduled to be 2023) at Gatwick Airport.

At the time of research some services were still operating on a COVID timetable.

Southern (🖳 southernrailway.com, **Southern On Track app**)
(**Note**: services from London Victoria usually also stop at Clapham Junction, East Croydon and Gatwick Airport)
● London Victoria to Horsham via Three Bridges & Crawley, Mon-Sat 2/hr, Sun 1/hr
  At Horsham the trains divide:
    to Bognor Regis via Christ's Hospital (1/hr), Billingshurst, Pulborough, Amberley & Arundel, Mon-Sat 2/hr, Sun 1/hr
    to Portsmouth & Southsea via Barnham, Chichester & Havant, daily 1/hr
    to Southampton Central via Barnham, Chichester & Havant, daily 1/hr
● London Victoria to Brighton via Gatwick Airport & Haywards Heath, daily 2/hr
● London Victoria to Littlehampton via Haywards Heath, Hassocks, Hove, Shoreham-by-Sea & Worthing, daily 1-2/hr
● London Victoria to Eastbourne/Hastings/Ore via Haywards Heath, Wivelsfield, Plumpton (1/hr), Lewes, Glynde (1/hr), Berwick (1/hr), Polegate, Hampden Park, Eastbourne, daily 2/hr (1/hr to Hastings & Ore)
● Hastings to Brighton via Eastbourne, Berwick, Glynde, Lewes & Falmer, daily 1-2/hr
● Portsmouth to Brighton via Havant, Chichester, Barnham & Shoreham, daily 1/hr
● Southampton to Brighton via Havant, Chichester, Barnham & Shoreham, daily 1/hr
● Brighton to Seaford via Moulsecoomb, Falmer, Lewes, Southease (1/hr) & Newhaven Town, daily 1-2/hr

South Western Railway (🖳 southwesternrailway.com, **SWR app**)
● London Waterloo to Weymouth via Clapham Junction, Winchester, Southampton Airport, Southampton & Bournemouth, daily 1/hr
● London Waterloo to Portsmouth Harbour via Guildford, Haslemere & Petersfield, daily 2/hr
● London Waterloo to Southampton Airport & Southampton Central via Woking (1/hr), Basingstoke (1/hr) & Winchester, daily 2/hr

Thameslink (🖳 thameslinkrailway.com, **On Track app**)
● Bedford to Brighton via Luton/Luton Airport, London St Pancras International, East Croydon, Gatwick Airport, Three Bridges & Haywards Heath, daily 1-2/hr
● Cambridge to Brighton via Stevenage, London St Pancras International, East Croydon, Gatwick Airport, Three Bridges & Haywards Heath, daily 1-2/hr

Cross Country Trains (🖳 crosscountrytrains.co.uk, **CrossCountry app**)
● Manchester to Bournemouth via Birmingham, Reading, Winchester & Southampton, COVID timetable daily 2-3/day, normal timetable additional services

cost of flying, details of which can be found here: 🖳 chooseclimate.org.

By coach

Coach travel is generally cheaper but takes longer than the train. **National Express** (🖳 nationalexpress.com, National Express Coach app) is the principal coach (long-distance bus) operator in Britain and has services to a number of destinations on or near the Way; see box opposite.

LOCAL TRANSPORT

❏ **USEFUL COACH SERVICES**

Note: not all stops are listed – contact **National Express** for full details.
025 London VCS to Brighton via Gatwick Airport North Terminal, 4/day
032 London VCS to Southampton via **Winchester**, 5/day
205 Heathrow Airport to Poole via **Winchester** & Bournemouth, 4/day
727 Norwich to Brighton via Stansted, Heathrow & Gatwick airports, 5/day

Hampshire, West Sussex and East Sussex have good local transport networks which make getting to and from the Way and planning linear day and weekend walks fairly easy.

The public transport map on p48 summarises all the useful routes; see the box on pp46-7 for details (though not all stops are listed). Where school bus services may be of use to walkers they are mentioned in the relevant place in the route guide. The tourist information centres along the Downs can provide, free of charge, a comprehensive local transport timetable for their particular region.

Most bus companies permit up to two **dogs** on a bus but it is also up to the discretion of the driver and dogs must be on a lead, well behaved and sitting under the seat or on their owner's lap; definitely not actually on a seat.

PLANNING YOUR WALK

❏ **GETTING CHEAPER TRAIN TICKETS**

You probably already know that the **earlier you buy your train ticket, the cheaper it will be.** But did you also know you could save money by '**splitting your ticket**'? Because of Britain's complex rail system, it can often be cheaper to buy two separate tickets that cover your whole journey rather than pay just one single fare. For example, if you're travelling from A to C, rather than just buying a single ticket for the journey it might be cheaper to buy two separate tickets, one from A to B, which is one of the stops en route, and then from B to C. Note that paying two separate fares in this way doesn't make any difference to the actual journey. Just because you have two tickets for the journey doesn't mean you have to change trains. But the savings can be large. The rail companies say that there are plans afoot to alter the price structure of rail fares to ensure that there is no financial advantage to fare splitting – but at the moment, it's still worthwhile investigating the possibility.

For further information the website 🖳 www.moneysavingexpert.com has a good article on fare splitting, and there are websites that help you find the cheapest price for your journey – sites such as 🖳 www.mytrainpal.com and 🖳 www.traintickets .com. Note that none of these are ideal – the sites don't always find the best fare, or are slow, or charge commission – but they will at least point you in the right direction to help you split the fare yourself.

PLANNING YOUR WALK

LOCAL BUS SERVICES

[see map p48]

Note: not all stops are listed for all routes.

No	Operator	Route and frequency details
1	bluestar	Southampton to **Winchester**, Mon-Sat 4/hr, Sun 2/hr
1	Stagecoach	**Midhurst** to Worthing via Petworth, Pulborough, **Storrington**, **Washington** & Findon, Mon-Sat 1/hr, Sun 6/day
2	B&H	Rottingdean to **Steyning** via Brighton, Shoreham, **Upper Beeding** & **Bramber**, daily 1/hr (3/hr R'dean to Shoreham)
3/3A/4	Stagecoach	**Foot of Beachy Head** to **Eastbourne** via **Meads**, Mon-Sat 2/hr, Sun 1/hr, plus Meads to Eastbourne, Mon-Sat 3/hr
12/12A	B&H	(Coaster) Brighton to Eastbourne via Rottingdean, Newhaven, Seaford, **Exceat** (Seven Sisters Park Centre), East Dean & YHA Eastbourne (12 only), Mon-Sat 3/hr, Sun 4/hr (Note the No 12 provides a more direct service than the 12A)
12X	B&H	(Coaster) Brighton to **Eastbourne** as for No 12 but fewer stops at places in between, Mon-Sat 3/hr
13X	B&H	Brighton to **Eastbourne** via Rottingdean, Newhaven, Seaford, **Exceat** (Seven Sisters Park Centre), **Birling Gap**, **Beachy Head** & YHA Eastbourne, Sun & public holidays only, 2/hr
23	Metrobus	Crawley to Worthing via Horsham, Ashington & **Washington**, Mon-Sat approx 1/hr, Sun & public hols 5/day
28	B&H	Brighton to **Lewes** via Falmer station & **Housedean Farm** (A27), Mon-Sat 4/hr, Sun 1/hr (to Uckfield)
29	B&H	Brighton to Tunbridge Wells via Falmer station, **Housedean Farm** (A27), **Lewes** & Uckfield, Mon-Sat 2/hr, Sun 1/hr
37	Stagecoach	Havant to **Petersfield** via Waterlooville, Clanfield, **Queen Elizabeth Country Park** (request stop), Mon-Fri 1/hr, Sat 8/day (services connect with No 38)
38	Stagecoach	Alton to **Petersfield**, Mon-Fri 4/day (connects with No 37)
47	CCB	Cuckmere Valley Rambler: **Berwick** Station circular route via **Alfriston**, Seaford, **Exceat**, **Seven Sisters Country Park**, **Litlington** & **Lullington**, late Mar to late Oct Sat, Sun & public hols 1/hr
54	Stagecoach	**Petersfield** to Chichester via **South Harting** & **Uppark**, Mon-Sat 5/day
60	Stagecoach	Chichester to **Midhurst** via **Cocking**, Mon-Sat 2/hr, Sun 1/hr
64	Stagecoach	Alton to **Winchester** via Alresford & Morn Hill, Mon-Sat 2/hr, Sun & public hols 1/hr
67	Stagecoach	**Winchester** to **Petersfield** via Alresford, **Cheriton**, Bramdean, West Meon & **East Meon**, Mon-Fri 4-6/day, Sat 4/day
69	Compass	Alfold to Worthing via **Pulborough**, **Bury**, **Houghton** & **Arundel**, Tue & Fri 1/day
70	Stagecoach	**Midhurst** to Guildford via Haslemere station, Mon-Sat 1/hr
71	Compass	**Storrington** to Chichester via **Pulborough**, **Bury** & **Houghton**, Wed 1/day
74/74A/74B	Compass	Horsham to **Storrington**, Mon-Fri 1/day, Tue & Thur 3/day (one afternoon service continues to Amberley railway station and Houghton on school days)
77	B&H	Brighton to **Devil's Dyke**, mid June to mid Sep daily 1-2/hr, mid Sep to mid June Sat, Sun & public hols only, 7/day
79	B&H	Brighton (station) to **Ditchling Beacon**, late Apr to mid Sep Sat, Sun & public holidays 1/hr

85	Compass	Chichester to **Arundel**, Mon-Fri 3/day
85A	Compass	Chichester to **Arundel** via Barnham, Mon-Fri 2/day
91	Stagecoach	**Midhurst** to **Petersfield** via South Harting, Mon-Sat 1/day
92/93	Stagecoach	**Midhurst** to **Petersfield**, Mon-Sat 6-7/day
94	WD	**Petersfield** to **Buriton**, Mon-Fri 4-5/day
99	Compass	Chichester to Petworth via Upwaltham (no other stops unless prebooked ☎ 01903-264776; bookable stops include Goodwood, Graffham Down, Graffham, Sutton & Bignor), Mon-Sat 6/day except public holidays*
100	Compass	Burgess Hill to Horsham via Henfield, **Upper Beeding, Bramber, Steyning, Washington & Storrington** & Pulborough, Mon-Sat approx 1/hr
119	Compass	Seaford to **Alfriston**, Mon-Sat 1-2/day
123	Compass	Newhaven to **Lewes** via **Southease, Rodmell & Kingston-near-Lewes**, Mon-Fri 6/day, Sat 5/day
125	Compass	**Lewes** to **Eastbourne** via **Glynde, Charleston, Berwick, Alfriston & Wilmington**, Mon-Fri 2/day
126	CCB	**Berwick** to **Seaford** via **Alfriston**, Mon-Sat 1-2/day
143	Compass	**Lewes** to **Hailsham**, Mon-Fri 5/day
166	Compass	**Lewes** to Haywards Heath via **Plumpton** & **Wivelsfield**, Mon-Fri 5/day
270	Metrobus	East Grinstead to Brighton via Burgess Hill, Hassocks & Pyecombe, Mon-Sat approx 1/hr, Sun & public hols 3/day
271	Metrobus	Crawley to Brighton via Burgess Hill, Hassocks & Pyecombe, Mon-Fri 9/day, Sat 5/day, Sun 4/day
273	Metrobus	Crawley to Brighton via Hickstead, Hassocks & Pyecombe, Mon-Fri 5/day, Sat: 4/day

Note: Services not shown on the map: CCB (operated solely by volunteers) also operate some **limited-frequency services** which stop where it is safe. These include: **25** Lewes to **Eastbourne** via **Glynde, Charleston, Berwick, Alfriston & Wilmington**, Sat 3/day plus 1/day Alfriston to Eastbourne (see also Compass Travel No 125 above); **26** Seaford to **Eastbourne** via **Alfriston, Berwick** (Drusillas), **Wilmington**, Polegate & Willingdon, Sun & public hols 4/day plus 1/day **Berwick** to **Eastbourne** (see also Compass Travel service 119/125 above); **40** Seaford to Berwick via Exceat, Westdean, Charleston, Litlington, Lullington, Wilmington & Alciston, Tue & Fri 1/day; **42** Hailsham to Berwick circular route via Alciston & Alfriston Wed 1/day; **43** Eastbourne to Berwick via Hailsham and Polegate, Mon 1/day; **44** Berwick to Eastbourne via Polegate, Tue 2-3/day (also via Wilmington). Thur 2-3/day (services also call at Alciston & Wilmington)

Operator contact details: bluestar (☎ 01202-338421, 🖳 bluestarbus.co.uk); **Brighton & Hove Buses (B&H);** ☎ 01273-886200, 🖳 buses.co.uk; Brighton & Hove Buses app); **Compass Travel (ComT;** ☎ 01903-690025, 🖳 www.compass-travel.co.uk, myTrip app); **Cuckmere Community Bus (CCB;** ☎ 01323-870920, 🖳 cuckmerebuses.org.uk); **Metrobus** (☎ 01293-449191, 🖳 metrobus.co.uk); **Stagecoach** (🖳 stagecoachbus.com; Stagecoach Bus app); **Wheel Drive (WD;** ☎ 01730-892052)

PLANNING YOUR WALK

South Downs Way

PUBLIC TRANSPORT
Not all services or stops are shown for all routes

NOT TO SCALE
CCB services 25, 26, 40, 42, 43 & 44 not shown

ENGLISH CHANNEL

ISLE OF WIGHT

Ferry to Dieppe
Ferry to Cherbourg
Ferry to Le Havre

Tunbridge Wells
Uckfield
Berwick
Hailsham
Wilmington
Hastings & Ashford International
Eastbourne
Beachy Head
Exceat
Seaford
Alfriston
Kingston-near-Lewes
Rodmell/Southease
Newhaven
Rottingdean
Brighton
Hove
Lewes
Plumpton
Hassocks
Haywards Heath
Falmer Station
Ditchling Beacon
Pyecombe
Burgess Hill
Crawley
Henfield
Storrington
Washington
Steyning, Bramber & Upper Beeding
Devil's Dyke
Shoreham
Worthing
Horsham
Ashington
Pulborough
Sutton/Bignor
Grafham
Bury
Houghton/Amberley
Barnham
Arundel
Littlehampton
Petworth
Cocking
Chichester
Bognor Regis
Haslemere
Midhurst
South Harting
Havant
Petersfield
East Meon
Buriton
Queen Elizabeth Country Park
Clanfield
Portsmouth
Alresford
Cheriton
Winchester
Southampton Airport Parkway
Southampton
Cowes

To Gatwick Airport & London Victoria; also to St Pancras International, Luton Airport & Bedford
To Gatwick Airport & London Victoria
To Alton & to Guildford
To Alton
To London Waterloo
To Alton
To Reading & Birmingham

29
143
125
47
125
125
47/125/126
123
A27
28-29
79
166
991
270 271 273
274-273
77
100
74A/74B
74, 7, 71
69-71
66
54
91
92, 93
94
37
67
67
64, 67
1
2
2
69
85A
85
70
90
38

MINIMUM IMPACT & OUTDOOR SAFETY

Minimum impact walking

Walk as if you are kissing the Earth with your feet

Thich Nhat Hanh *Peace is every step*

The popularity of the 'Great Outdoors' as an escape route from the chaos of modern living has experienced something of a boom over the last couple of decades or so. It is therefore important to be aware of the pressures that each of us as visitors to the countryside exert upon the land. The South Downs are particularly vulnerable, situated as they are in the most populous corner of the British Isles. Thousands of people explore the network of trails that criss-cross these historic chalk hills.

Minimum impact walking is all about a common-sense approach to exploring the countryside, being mindful and respectful of the wildlife and those who live and work on the land. Those who appreciate the countryside will already be aware of the importance of safeguarding it. Simple measures such as not dropping litter, keeping dogs on leads to avoid scaring sheep and leaving gates as you find them will already be second nature to anyone who regularly visits the countryside. However, there are several other measures that are not quite so well known and are worth repeating here.

ECONOMIC IMPACT

Buy local

Rural businesses and communities in Britain have been hit hard in recent years by a seemingly endless series of crises, most recently COVID. In addition, they have to compete with the omnipresence of chain supermarkets that are now so common in towns across Britain.

Faced with such competition local businesses struggle to survive. Visitors to the countryside can help these local businesses by 'buying locally'. It's a fact of life that money spent at local level – perhaps in a market, or at the greengrocer, or in an independent pub – has a far greater impact for good on that community than the equivalent spent in a branch of a national chain store or restaurant. It's perhaps a step too far to advocate that walkers should boycott the larger supermarkets, which after all do provide local employment, but it's worth remembering that businesses in rural communities rely heavily on visitors for their very existence.

If we want to keep these shops and post offices, we need to use them. The more money that circulates locally and is spent on local labour and materials, the greater the impact on the local economy.

Encourage local cultural traditions and skills

No two parts of the countryside look the same. Buildings, food, skills and language evolve out of the landscape and are moulded over hundreds of years to suit the locality. Discovering these cultural differences is part of the pleasure of walking in new places. Visitors' enthusiasm for local traditions and skills brings awareness and pride, nurturing a sense of place; an increasingly important role in a world where economic globalisation continues to undermine the very things that provide security and a feeling of belonging.

ENVIRONMENTAL IMPACT

By choosing a walking holiday you are already minimising your impact on the environment. Your interaction with the countryside and its inhabitants, whether they be plant, animal or human, can bring benefits to all. The following are some ideas on how you can go a few steps further in helping to minimise your impact on the natural environment while walking the South Downs Way.

Use public transport whenever possible

Both Sussex and Hampshire have a good public transport system (see pp44-8). There are plenty of options to get the walker to the Downs, making driving there unnecessary, and also various bus services linking the Way with nearby towns and villages as well as offering convenient start and finish points for day walks.

Never leave litter

Leaving litter shows a total disrespect for the natural world and others coming after you. As well as being unsightly, litter kills wildlife, pollutes the environment and can be dangerous to farm animals. Please take your rubbish with you so you can dispose of it in a bin in the next village. It would be very helpful if you could pick up litter left by other people, too.

● **Is it OK if it's biodegradable?** No. Apple cores, banana skins, orange peel and the like are an eyesore, encourage flies, ants and wasps and ruin a picnic spot for others. They also promote a higher population of scavengers such as carrion crows and magpies, an explosion of which can have a detrimental effect on rarer bird species. Those who use the excuse that orange peel is natural and biodegradable are simply fishing for an excuse to clear their conscience. Biodegradable? Yes, but surprisingly slowly. Natural? The South Downs have never been known for their orange groves.

● **The lasting impact of litter** A piece of orange peel left on the ground takes six months to decompose; silver foil 18 months; a plastic bag 10 years; clothes 15 years; and an aluminium can 85 years.

Erosion

● **Stay on the main trail** The effect of your footsteps may seem minuscule but when they are multiplied by several thousand walkers each year they become rather more significant. Avoid taking shortcuts, widening the trail or taking more than one path; your boots will be followed by many others. This is particularly pertinent on the South Downs where there is such a huge volume of visitors.

● **Consider walking out of season** Unfortunately, most people prefer to walk in the spring and summer which is exactly the time of year when the vegetation is trying to grow. Walking on the South Downs in the autumn and winter can be just as enjoyable and eases the burden on the land during the busy summer months. The quieter season also gives the walker a greater chance of a peaceful walk away from the crowds and fewer people are competing for accommodation.

Respect all wildlife, plants and trees
If you come across wildlife keep your distance and don't watch for too long. Your presence can cause considerable stress, particularly if the adults are with young or in winter when the weather is harsh and food is scarce. Young animals are rarely abandoned. If you come across young birds keep away so that their mother can return. Never pick flowers – leave them for others to enjoy too – and try to avoid breaking branches off or damaging trees in any way.

The code of the outdoor loo
As more and more people discover the joys of the outdoors, issues like toilet business rapidly gain importance. How many of us have shaken our heads at the sight of toilet paper strewn beside the path or, even worse, someone's dump left in full view? Human excrement is not only offensive to our senses but, more importantly, can infect water sources.

● **Where to go** Wherever possible **use a toilet**. Public toilets are marked on the trail maps in this guide and you will also find facilities in pubs, cafés and campsites along the Way. If you do have to go outdoors choose a site at least **30 metres away from running water** and 200 metres from any high-use areas such as hostels and beaches, or from any sites of historic or archaeological interest. Carry a small trowel and dig a small hole about 15cm (6") deep in which to bury your excrement. It decomposes quicker when in contact with the top layer of soil or leaf mould. Use a stick to stir loose soil into your deposit as well, as this speeds up decomposition even more. Do not squash it under rocks as this slows down the composting process. If you have to use rocks to cover it make sure they are not in contact with your faeces.

● **Toilet paper and tampons** Toilet paper takes a long time to decompose whether buried or not. It is easily dug up by animals and may then blow into water sources or onto the path. The best method for dealing with it is to **pack it out**. Put the used paper inside a paper bag which you then place inside a biodegradable bag. Then simply empty the contents of the paper bag at the next toilet you come across and throw the bag away. You should also pack out **tampons** and **sanitary towels** in a similar way and for the same reasons.

Wild camping
There is very little opportunity for wild camping along the length of the Downs. Most of the land is private farmland and much of this is arable cropland. If the urge to camp away from an organised site is too much to resist always ask the

landowner first. If the opportunity for wild camping is there, take it. Camping in such an independent way is an altogether more fulfilling experience than camping on a designated site.

Remember that by camping off the beaten track you accept added responsibilities. By taking on board the following suggestions for minimising your impact the whole experience of wild camping will be a far more satisfying one.

● **Be discreet** Camp alone or in small groups and spend only one night in each place. Pitch your tent late in the day and leave as early the next day as you can.

● **Never light a fire** The deep burn caused by camp fires, no matter how small, seriously damages the turf and takes years to recover. Use a camp stove instead.

● **Don't use soap or detergent** There is no need to use soap; even biodegradable soaps and detergents pollute streams. Wash up without detergent; use a plastic or metal scourer, or failing that some bracken, grass or grit.

● **Leave no trace** Enjoy the skill of moving on without leaving any sign of having been there. Before heading off check your campsite and pick up any litter (even if not left by you), so leaving the place in a better state than you found it.

ACCESS

The south-eastern corner of England is the most populated area of the British Isles and is criss-crossed by some of the busiest roads in the country. Thankfully, there are also countless public footpaths and rights of way for the large local population and visitors alike. But what happens if you want to explore some of the local woodland or tramp across a meadow? Most of the land on the South Downs is agricultural land and, unless you are on a right of way, it's off limits. However, the 'Right to Roam' legislation (see opposite) opened up some previously restricted land to walkers.

Rights of way

As a designated National Trail the South Downs Way is a public right of way – this is either a footpath, a bridleway or a byway; the South Downs Way is made up of all three. Rights of way are theoretically established because the owner has dedicated them to public use. However, very few rights of way are formally dedicated in this way. If the public has been using a path without interference for 20 years or more the law assumes the owner has intended to dedicate it as a right of way. If a path has been unused for 20 years it does not cease to exist; the guiding principle is 'once a highway, always a highway'.

On a public right of way you have the right to 'pass and repass along the way' which includes stopping to rest or admire the view or to consume refreshments.

> ❏ **LAMBING**
>
> Most of the Way passes through private farmland, some of which is pasture for sheep. Lambing takes place from mid March to mid May when dogs should not be taken along the path. Even a dog secured on a lead is liable to disturb a pregnant ewe. If you should see a lamb or ewe that appears to be in distress contact the nearest farmer.

You can also take with you a 'natural accompaniment' which includes a dog, but obviously could also be a horse, on bridleways and byways. All 'natural accompaniments' must be kept under close control.

Farmers and land managers must ensure that paths are not blocked by crops or other vegetation, or otherwise obstructed, and the route is identifiable and the surface is restored soon after cultivation. If crops are growing over the path you have every right to walk or ride through them, following the line of the right of way as closely as possible. If you find a path blocked or impassable you should report it to the appropriate highway authority as they are responsible for maintaining public rights of way. Along the Way the highway authorities are Hampshire, West Sussex and East Sussex county councils. The councils are also the surveying authority with responsibility for maintaining the official definitive map of public rights of way.

❑ THE COUNTRYSIDE CODE

Respect everyone
● Be considerate to those living and working in the countryside
● Leave gates and property as you find them
● Take special care on roads without pavements
● Follow local signs and keep to marked paths, even if they're muddy.

Protect the environment
● Take all your litter home
● Do not light fires
● Always keep dogs under control and in sight.
● Care for nature – do not cause damage or disturbance

Enjoy the outdoors
● Check your route and local conditions
● Follow advice and local signs
● Make no unnecessary noise

For more information visit:
⌨ www.gov.uk/government/news/ new-countryside-code-launched-to- help-people-enjoy-the-outdoors

---

Right to roam

For many years groups such as the **Ramblers** (see box p41) and the **British Mountaineering Council** (⌨ thebmc.co.uk) campaigned for new and wider access legislation. This finally bore fruit in the form of the Countryside & Rights of Way Act of November 2000, colloquially known as the CRoW Act or 'Right to Roam'. It came into full effect on 31 October 2005 and gave access for 'recreation on foot' to mountain, moor, heath, down and registered common land in England and Wales. In essence it allows walkers the freedom to roam responsibly away from footpaths, without being accused of trespass, on about four million acres of open, uncultivated land. The areas of access land open to walkers are shown on OS Explorer maps. 'Right to Roam' does not mean free access to wander over farmland, woodland or private gardens, and much of the true chalk grassland of the South Downs has long since been ploughed up. Along with this, most of that which remains is already annexed as national and local nature reserves where access is relatively unrestricted anyway, so the results of the CRoW Act on the South Downs Way might not be quite as liberating as expected.

For those who wish to get off the beaten track and away from the crowds there are plenty of lesser-known rights of way. Follow any of these and you are likely to spend the whole day alone, which is not an easy thing to do in this part of England. However, if you want to leave the path entirely and beat your own trail through the woods and fields always check with local landowners.

Those who do exercise their 'right to roam' should remember that this added freedom comes with the responsibility to respect the immediate environment. This is particularly pertinent on the South Downs where most of the land is worked by farmers and is the home to a variety of wildlife. Always keep this in mind and try to avoid disturbing domestic and wild animals.

Outdoor safety and health

AVOIDANCE OF HAZARDS

Walking does not come much more hazard-free than on the South Downs. However, these low southern hills should be given as much respect as their loftier counterparts. Good preparation is just as important here as it is on the northern mountains. The following common-sense advice should ensure that those out for a day trip as well as those embarking on the whole route enjoy a safe walk. Always make sure you have **suitable clothes** to keep you warm and dry, whatever the conditions, as well as a spare change of inner clothes.

Take more **food** than you expect to eat. High-energy snacks such as chocolate, fruit, biscuits and nuts are useful for those last few gruelling miles each day. With the Downs being made of permeable chalk there is a distinct lack of running water so make sure you have at least a one-litre **water bottle** or **pouch** that can be refilled when the opportunity arises. You need to drink plenty of water when walking; 3-4 litres per day depending on the weather. There are a few drinking water taps placed conveniently along the path; these are marked on the maps in Part 4. If you start to feel tired, lethargic or get a headache it may be that you are not drinking enough. Thirst is not always a good indicator of when to drink; stop and have a drink every hour or two, even if you're not feeling thirsty. A good indicator of whether you are drinking enough is the colour of your urine – the lighter the better. If you are not needing to urinate much and your urine is dark yellow you may need to increase your fluid intake.

You should always take a torch, whistle, simple first-aid kit (see p38) and compass, though the latter may not be necessary as the trail is clear. A whistle is also unlikely to be used due to the close proximity of people and villages. The **emergency signal** is six blasts on the whistle or six flashes with a torch.

It is a good idea to be aware of where you are throughout the day. **Check your location** on the map or phone regularly. Getting lost on the Downs is unlikely to be a major cause for concern but it can turn a pleasant day's walk into a stressful trudge back in the dark, praying that the pub chef has not gone home. If you do get lost it is unlikely to be long before someone passes by who does know their Downs from their Bottoms (the name given to the interior valleys of the Downs).

If you are walking alone you must appreciate and be prepared for the increased risk. It is always a good idea to leave word with somebody about where you are going; you can always ring ahead to book accommodation and let them know you are walking alone and what time you expect to arrive. Don't forget to contact whoever you have left word with to let them know you've arrived safely. Carrying a mobile phone can be useful though you cannot rely on a strong signal, or your phone's battery life.

Be aware that, because much of the South Downs Way is on a chalk ridge high above the surrounding countryside, there may be a steep climb down to, and back up from the adjacent towns and villages.

To ensure you have a safe trip it is well worth following this advice:

● Keep to the path – avoid steep sections of the escarpment and old quarries
● Be aware of the increased possibility of slipping over in wet or icy weather, especially where the chalk is exposed
● Whether you choose to wear hiking boots, trainers or even hiking sandals, be sure that your footwear has good grip and is well worn-in before you start
● Be extra vigilant with children
● Take extra care when leading dogs through areas of grazing animals
● In an emergency dial ☎ 999.

FOOTCARE

Caring for your feet is vital; you're not going to get far if they are out of action. Wash and dry them properly at the end of the day, change your socks every day and if it is warm enough take your boots and socks off when you stop for lunch to allow your feet to dry out. It is important to 'break in' new boots or shoes before embarking on a long walk. Make sure they are comfortable and try to avoid getting them wet on the inside. If you feel any 'hot spots' stop immediately and apply blister plasters (eg Compeed) and leave them on until the area is pain free or the tape starts to come off. If you have left it too late and a blister has developed it's still worth putting on a blister plaster (or a regular one if you don't have any blister plasters) to protect it from abrasion. Popping it can lead to infection. If the skin is broken keep the area clean with antiseptic and cover with a non-adhesive dressing material held in place with tape.

SUNBURN, HYPOTHERMIA, HYPERTHERMIA & HEATSTROKE

Sunburn can happen, even in England and even on overcast days. The only surefire way to avoid it is to stay wrapped up but that's not always an option. What you must do, therefore, is to always wear a hat, preferably a wide-brimmed one, and to smother yourself in sunscreen (with a minimum factor of 15, although higher is much better) and apply it regularly throughout the day. Don't forget your lips, nose, the back of your neck and even under your chin to protect you against rays reflected from the ground.

Hypothermia, also known as exposure, occurs when the body can't generate enough heat to maintain its normal temperature, usually as a result of being wet, cold, unprotected from the wind, tired and hungry. The risk of hypothermia while walking on the Downs is extremely small. However, it is worth being aware of the dangers. Hypothermia is easily avoided by wearing

MINIMUM IMPACT & OUTDOOR SAFETY

suitable clothing, carrying and eating enough food and drink, being aware of the weather conditions and checking the morale of your companions.

Early signs to watch for are feeling cold and tired with involuntary shivering. Find some shelter as soon as possible and warm the victim up with a hot drink and some chocolate or other high-energy food. If possible give them another warm layer of clothing and allow them to rest until feeling better.

If allowed to worsen, strange behaviour, slurring of speech and poor co-ordination will become apparent and the victim can quickly progress into unconsciousness, followed by coma and death. In the unlikely event of a severe case of hypothermia, quickly get the victim out of wind and rain, improvising a shelter if necessary. Rapid restoration of bodily warmth is essential and best achieved by bare-skin contact: someone should get into the same sleeping bag as the patient, both having stripped to their underwear with any spare clothing under or over them to build up heat. Send urgently for help.

Hyperthermia occurs when the body generates too much heat, eg heat exhaustion and heatstroke. Not an ailment that you would necessarily associate with England, heatstroke is a serious problem nonetheless. Symptoms of **heat exhaustion** include thirst, fatigue, giddiness, a rapid pulse, raised body temperature, low urine output and, if not treated, delirium and finally a coma. The best cure is to drink plenty of water. **Heatstroke** is another matter altogether, and even more serious. A high body temperature and an absence of sweating are early indications, followed by symptoms similar to hypothermia (see above) such as a lack of co-ordination and convulsions. Coma and death will follow if treatment is not given instantly. Sponge the victim down, wrap them in wet towels, fan them, and get help immediately.

WEATHER FORECASTS

The South Downs is one of the driest parts of what is a notoriously wet island. However, the weather can still change from blazing sunshine to a stormy wet gale in the space of a day. The wind, in particular, can be surprisingly severe along the top of the Downs. Couple this with rain and a nice walk can turn into a damp battle against the elements. For detailed local weather outlooks online log on to 🖥 www.bbc.co.uk/weather, or 🖥 www.metoffice.gov.uk.

DEALING WITH AN ACCIDENT

● Use basic first aid to treat the injury to the best of your ability.
● Try to attract the attention of anybody else who may be in the area. The emergency signal is six blasts on a whistle, or six flashes with a torch.
● If possible leave someone with the casualty while others go to get help. If there are only two people, you have a dilemma. If you decide to get help leave all spare clothing and food with the casualty.
● Telephone ☎ 999 and ask for the ambulance service (or coastguard if relevant). They will assist in both offshore and onshore incidents. Be sure you know exactly where you are before you call. Report the exact position of the casualty and their condition.

THE ENVIRONMENT & NATURE

Conservation of the South Downs

Ever since the Industrial Revolution and the rapid development over the last 200 years the English countryside has been put under a great deal of strain. The South Downs were once wooded hills, home to wolves, wild boar and other species that have long since departed. The need to feed an increasing population led to much of the countryside being cleared and ploughed. The result of this is the landscape we see today, although the traditional patchwork pattern of fields and hedgerows has been replaced in some parts of the Downs by much larger fields, the hedgerows having been torn out.

The South Downs is, then, a man-made landscape; even the woodland has been coppiced and the meadows ploughed at one time or another. This is not necessarily a bad thing, however. The resulting habitat is a rare one that provides an essential niche for endangered species, most notably the butterflies for which the Downs are famous.

Although the Downs, positioned in a populous corner of England, continue to be put under pressure from road and housing projects, the increasing awareness of the value of our natural (or perhaps semi-natural) heritage has resulted in greater efforts in the conservation. There are several groups, on a local and national scale and on both a voluntary and government basis, who help protect the species, habitats and buildings of the Downs. They also help visitors to get the most out of their trip whilst at the same time trying to ease the pressure brought by the increase in tourist numbers.

Now that the South Downs have National Park status (see box p58) the effort to conserve the area should become less of a struggle owing to the increased environmental protection and financial benefits that the designation brings.

GOVERNMENT AGENCIES AND SCHEMES

Natural England

Natural England (🖳 gov.uk/government/organisations/natural-england) is the single government body responsible for identifying, establishing and managing National Parks, Areas of Outstanding Natural Beauty, National Nature Reserves, Sites of Special Scientific Interest, and Special Areas of Conservation.

❏ HOW THE SOUTH DOWNS BECAME A NATIONAL PARK

The South Downs almost became one of the first designated national parks back in the 1950s but the proposal was rejected on the grounds that the area did not offer sufficient recreational possibilities for the public. This seems rather surprising today when you consider the number of walkers, cyclists, horse-riders and paragliders who use the hills. National Park status is not just about providing an area of fun for outdoor enthusiasts, however. It is about protecting the area from harmful development such as road building, a real problem in the South-East, and preserving the natural and cultural heritage of the area.

In 1999 the Department of the Environment, now Department for Environment, Food and Rural Affairs (DEFRA), proposed that the Countryside Agency, now part of Natural England, designate the South Downs a National Park. A Designation Order was published in late 2002 and in November 2003 a public inquiry began, to hear the views of those likely to be affected by the change. In 2006 a report was passed to the Secretary of State. After several more delays and legal wrangles, in 2009 it finally was announced that the South Downs would receive National Park status, and the newly appointed **South Downs National Park Authority** (🖳 southdowns.gov.uk) officially assumed responsibility for it on 1st April 2011.

Although at 1648 sq km it is not the largest in area (that distinction going to the Lake District National Park at 2292 sq km), being only an hour from London it encompasses several large towns including Petersfield and Lewes, and is by far the most densely populated of all the National Parks.

The highest level of landscape protection is the designation of land as a **National Park** which recognises the national importance of an area in terms of landscape, biodiversity and as a recreational resource. This designation does not signify national ownership and they are not uninhabited wildernesses, making conservation a knife-edged balance between protecting the environment and the rights and livelihoods of those living in the park. In April 2011 the South Downs became England's ninth National Park, and its most densely populated. Some 85% of the land within the South Downs National Park is agricultural, so this balancing act is particularly critical here.

The next level of protection within the National Park includes **National Nature Reserves (NNRs)** and **Sites of Special Scientific Interest (SSSIs)**. The **NNRs** along the course of the South Downs Way (SDW) include: Beacon Hill (see p86), just before the village of Exton; Old Winchester Hill (see p88), just after Exton; and Butser Hill (see p93) several miles further along the path. Though there are no NNRs near the Way in West Sussex, in East Sussex Lullington Heath (p180) lies right on the trail, and Castle Hill and Lewes Downs (ie Mount Caburn; see p156) both lie very near to it too.

SSSIs range in size from little pockets protecting wild flower meadows, important nesting sites or special geological features, to vast swathes of upland, moorland and wetland. They are a particularly important designation as they have some legal standing. They are managed in partnership with the owners and occupiers of the land who must give written notice before initiating any operations likely to damage the site and who cannot proceed without consent from

❑ **NATIONAL TRAILS**

The South Downs Way is one of 15 National Trails (💻 nationaltrail.co.uk) in England and Wales. These are Britain's flagship long-distance paths which grew out of the post-war desire to protect the country's special places, a movement which also gave birth to National Parks and AONBs. The Pennine Way was the first to be created.

National Trails in England are designated and largely funded by Natural England and are managed on the ground by a National Trail Officer. They co-ordinate the maintenance work undertaken by the local highway authority and landowners to ensure that the trail is kept to nationally agreed standards.

Natural England. SSSIs along the SDW include: Cheesefoot Head (see p81), Butser Hill (see p93), Heyshott Down (see pp108-9), Chanctonbury Hill (see p133) and Seaford to Beachy Head.

Special Areas of Conservation (SACs) are designated by the European Union's Habitats Directive and provide an extra tier of protection to the areas that they cover. Along the SDW Butser Hill NNR and SSSI is also a SAC.

See Natural England's website for further information about all of these.

Historic England

Created in April 2015 as a result of dividing the work previously done by English Heritage (see below), Historic England (💻 historicengland.org.uk) is now the name for the government department responsible for looking after and promoting England's historic environment and is in charge of the listing system, giving grants and dealing with planning matters.

CAMPAIGNING AND CONSERVATION ORGANISATIONS

The **National Trust** (NT; 💻 nationaltrust.org.uk) is a charity which, through ownership, aims to protect threatened coastline, countryside, historic houses, castles, gardens and archaeological remains for everyone to enjoy. It manages large sections of the Downs including an area of chalk grassland on the Seven Sisters between the hamlet of Crowlink and Birling Gap (see p176), Harting Down (p102), Devil's Dyke and Newtimber Hill (see pp143-4 for both). It also owns various properties on the Way, such as Monk's House (p160) in Rodmell and Alfriston Clergy House (p167), its first-ever property, bought in 1896.

English Heritage (💻 english-heritage.org.uk) has been a charitable trust since April 2015 (see Historic England, above). It cares for over 400 historic buildings, monuments and sites in England; Bramber Castle (see p138) is one of the properties it manages.

The **Wildfowl & Wetlands Trust** (WWT; 💻 wwt.org.uk) is the biggest conservation organisation for wetlands in the UK; their centre at Arundel (see p122) is well-known and very popular with visitors year-round.

The Wildlife Trusts (💻 wildlifetrusts.org) undertake projects to improve conditions for wildlife and promote public awareness of it as well as acquiring land for nature reserves to protect particular species and habitats. The Sussex

Wildlife Trust (🖳 sussexwildlifetrust.org.uk) manages: the Amberley Wild Brooks network of ponds and marshland; Ditchling Beacon; and Malling Down, Lewes. The Hampshire and Isle of Wight Wildlife Trust (🖳 hiwwt .org.uk) manages St Catherine's Hill, Winchester.

The **Royal Society for the Protection of Birds** (RSPB; 🖳 rspb.org.uk) was the pioneer of voluntary conservation bodies and although it doesn't have any reserves directly on the South Downs Way, there is one near Pulborough, a couple of miles north of Storrington. The wet grassy meadows here attract ducks, geese, swans and wading birds.

Butterfly Conservation (🖳 butterfly-conservation.org) was formed to prevent the decline in the number of butterflies and moths. The two branches relevant to the SDW are Hampshire and the Isle of Wight (🖳 hantsiow-butter flies.org.uk) and Sussex (🖳 sussex-butterflies.org.uk). Sites along the SDW where butterflies are likely to be found include Beachy Head, Cissbury Ring and Malling Down.

There are also smaller conservation groups such as **Murray Downland Trust** (🖳 murraydownlandtrust.org.uk) which manages five reserves (Heyshott Escarpment, Heyshott Down, Buriton, Under Beacon, and The Devil's Jumps) in West Sussex and East Hampshire. The Trust's main objective is to 'rescue and enhance neglected areas of unimproved chalk downland' but it also looks after some ancient monuments in the area such as the Bronze Age archaeological site (see p110). Access to the Trust's sites is permitted except when the area should be left undisturbed for conservation reasons. The trust relies on volunteers to help clear the land in its care and sheep are often brought

---

❏ **GEOLOGY OF THE DOWNS**

How the chalk Downs were formed

It helps to examine the geology of the region as a whole in order to understand how the South Downs reached their present-day form. South-East England is made up of three bands of rock and sediment, the deepest layer being sandstone, the one above clay and the top layer chalk. Over time these layers were pushed up, probably due to tectonic plate movements, with Africa nudging into Europe. Through the ensuing millennia the soft chalk was eroded through weathering, exposing first the clay and then the more resistant sandstone. The North and South Downs are all that remains of the chalk that lies over the deeper clay and sandstone layers. They are still being eroded.

One interesting feature of the Downs is the lack of streams. Chalk is highly permeable so streams flow only very briefly during periods of very heavy rainfall. It is worth remembering this when walking on a hot day.

Flint

Flint is a mineral found in bands within chalk and has played a big part in the history of the Downs. When man first found the ability to make tools the folk who lived on the Downs used flakes of flint to make arrowheads and knives. It was also found to be a very useful stone for starting fires. Today flint can be seen in local village architecture, being a very versatile building brick. The traditional Sussex Downs house and barn would not be the same if it were not for flint.

in during the winter months to eat the scrub that threatens the grassland.

The Friends of the South Downs (🖥 friendsofthesouthdowns.org.uk), formerly the South Downs Society, campaigns specifically for the conservation and enhancement of the landscape of the South Downs. It was formed in 1926 and is supported entirely by donations and subscriptions (membership costs £25/35 individual/joint members). In 2017 they successfully campaigned against Eastbourne Borough Council's plans to sell off four downland farms located in the South Downs National Park behind Beachy Head, stating that 'there is no substitute for benign ownership if landscape, wildlife, recreation and cultural heritage are to be conserved and enhanced'. Their current projects include replacing stiles with kissing gates throughout the park, to enable those walkers who are unable to climb stiles to still enjoy the Downs, and introducing benches along the route of the South Downs Way. They also arrange a programme of strolls and walks, on and around the Downs, throughout the year.

Flora and fauna

The South Downs region is essentially a man-made landscape. Centuries of farming have shaped these rolling hills and left a unique habitat for a variety of common and not-so-common species. Left alone the South Downs would revert to scrub and woodland. This may not appear to be a great tragedy. However, the habitat that would be lost is a much scarcer one that provides sanctuary to a variety of endangered species which rely on the unique chalk grassland environment. The Downs are not free of trees either. The plough never reached the steep scarp slope that runs along the northern edge of the Downs. Indeed there is a healthy balance between the open grassland of the high ground and the deciduous beech woodland which can claim to be some of the oldest and most undisturbed woodland in Britain.

MAMMALS

The well-drained soil of chalk downland is ideal habitat for the **badger** (*Meles meles*), a sociable animal with a distinctive black-and-white-striped muzzle. Badgers live in family groups in large underground 'setts'. They are rarely spotted since they tend to emerge after dark to hunt for worms in the fields. Sadly, they are more commonly seen dead on the road: after hedgehogs they are the most inept at crossing roads. The **fox** (*Vulpes vulpes*) is another common mammal on the Downs. Although they prefer to come out at night they are not exclusively nocturnal; particularly in summer they may be out in broad daylight in some of the quieter corners of the hills though the best time to spot a fox is at dusk when you might see one trotting along a field or woodland edge.

The **rabbit** (*Oryctolagus cuniculus*) is seemingly everywhere on the Downs. The well-drained, steep grassland is ideal for their warrens.

The **grey squirrel** (*Sciurus carolinensis*) was introduced from North America at the end of the 19th century. Its outstanding success in colonising Britain is very much to the detriment of other native species including the red squirrel. Greys are bigger and stockier than reds and to many people the reds, with their tufted ears, bushy tails and small beady eyes, are the far more attractive of the two. Sadly there are no red squirrels anywhere on the Downs.

The **roe deer** (*Capreolus capreolus*) is a small, native species of deer that tends to hide in woodland. They can sometimes be seen, alone or in pairs, on field edges or clearings in the forest but you are more likely to hear the sharp dog-like bark made when they smell you coming.

If the Downs were made for any one species it is probably the **brown hare** (*Lepus europaeus*) which, if you are observant, can be seen racing across the fields on the hilltops. Hares are bigger than rabbits, with longer hind legs and ears, and are far more graceful than their prolific little cousins. Some other small but fairly common species to keep an eye out for include the carnivorous **stoat** (*Mustela erminea*), its smaller cousin the **weasel** (*Mustela nivalis*), the **hedgehog** (*Erinaceus europaeus*) and a number of species of **voles**, **mice** and **shrews**.

At dusk **bats** can be seen hunting for moths and flying insects along hedgerows, over rivers and around street lamps. All 17 species in Britain are protected by law. The commonest, and smallest, species is the **pipistrelle** (*Pipistrellus pipistrellus*). Although only about 4cm long it can eat up to 3000 insects in one night. You may also be lucky enough to see the slighter larger **Daubenton's bat** (*Myotis daubentonii*) hunting for mosquitoes over rivers and ponds.

REPTILES

The **adder** (*Vipera berus*) is the only poisonous snake in Britain. It is easily recognised by the distinctive zigzag markings down its back and a diamond shape on the back of its head. On summer days adders bask in sunny spots, such as on a warm rock or in the middle of a path so watch your step. Adders tend to move out of the way quickly but should you be unlucky enough to inadvertently step on one and get bitten, sit still and send someone else for help. Their venom is designed to kill small mammals, not humans. A bite is unlikely to be fatal to an adult but *is* serious enough to warrant immediate medical attention, especially in the case of children. Nevertheless, the likelihood of being bitten is minuscule. Walkers are far more likely to frighten the adder away once it senses your footsteps.

The **grass snake** (*Natrix natrix*), an adept swimmer, is a much longer, slimmer snake with a yellow collar around its neck. It's non-venomous but does emit a foul stench should you attempt to pick one up. It's much better for you and the snake to leave it in peace.

The **common lizard** (*Lacerta/Zootoca vivipara*) is a harmless creature which can often be seen basking in the sun on rocks and stone walls. About 15cm long, it is generally brown with patterns of spots or stripes. However, you are far more likely to hear them scuttling away through the undergrowth as you approach.

A curious beast, looking like a slippery eel or small snake, is the **slow worm** (*Anguis fragilis*) which, despite the name, is neither a worm nor indeed an eel or snake but a legless lizard. Usually a glossy grey or copper colour, they can be seen on woodland floors and in grassland. They are completely harmless and usually slip away into the leaf litter when they hear footsteps.

TREES

Over the last few hundred years the once-extensive forest cover in southern England has been fragmented into a patchwork of copses and coppiced woodland. Trees were felled for fuel and for shipbuilding and, in the case of the South Downs, to clear land for agricultural needs. In more recent times many of the hedgerows that helped create the familiar patchwork landscape have been grubbed up to create much larger fields.

Nevertheless, there are parts of the Downs that have survived the threat from axe and chainsaw. The north-facing scarp slope was, and still is, too steep for clearing and too inaccessible for ploughing. Consequently, this is where most of the trees are found. Although there are still areas of semi-natural or ancient mixed woodland, much of the remaining woodland has been coppiced, an old method of promoting growth of more numerous and narrower trunks by cutting a tree at its base. Coppicing was common in hazel stands and the resulting product used in constructing fences and making furniture. Although coppicing is no longer widespread it is still practised in some parts by enthusiasts of old woodland crafts and also by conservationists who recognise that coppiced woodland can be beneficial to certain species.

Most of the woodland on the Downs is mixed deciduous, made up largely of beech and ash but there are many other species to look out for.

Tree species

The **beech** (*Fagus sylvatica*) with its thick, silvery trunk is one of the most attractive native trees. It can grow to a height of 40 metres with the high canopies blocking out much of the light. As a result the floors of beech woodlands tend to be fairly bare of vegetation. They favour well-drained soil, hence their liking for the steep scarp slope. In autumn the colours of the turning leaves can be quite spectacular. One species that does survive the shady floor of beech woodland is the distinctive **common holly** (*Ilex aquifolium*) with its dark waxy leaves which have sharp points. Holly varies in size, usually growing as a sprawling bush on the woodland floor or in hedgerows but also as a tree when established in more isolated locations.

Famous for its longevity, lasting for well over a thousand years in some cases, the **common yew** (*Taxus baccata*) is abundant in churchyards but there are also natural stands on the scarp slope and among beech woodland. The dark glossy needles are quite distinctive as is the flaky red bark of the often gnarled and twisted old trunks and branches. Do not be tempted to eat the bright red berries; they're poisonous. Another tree with red berries is the **hawthorn** (*Crataegus monogyna*). It has small leaves and is usually found in hedgerows

THE ENVIRONMENT & NATURE

but can also grow as a small tree. In early autumn the berries provide food for woodland birds and are particularly popular with blackbirds.

BUTTERFLIES

The Downs are famous for their butterflies. Many of the national nature reserves in the area were set up specifically because of the variety and number of butterflies. One of the most prevalent is the **meadow brown** (*Maniola jurtina*), a very common species, dusty brown in colour with a rusty orange streak and dark, false eyes. They can be seen in meadows all across the Downs. The small **gatekeeper** (*Pyronia tithonus*) likes similar habitat and is also widespread throughout the Downs. They are identified by their deep orange and chocolate-brown markings.

The **peacock** (*Inachis io*) is surely Britain's most beautiful butterfly; it's quite common in this area. The markings on the wings are said to mimic the eyes of an animal to frighten off predators. Also common is the impressive **red admiral** (*Vanessa atalanta*). Owing to climate change it is now starting to over-winter in Britain and appears to be thriving.

The **brimstone** (*Gonepteryx rhamni*) is also widespread, though well camouflaged as its wings look very like leaves; the **white admiral** (*Limenitis camilla*), however, is declining in numbers but may still be seen in some woodland sites. Although it has also recently been in decline in other parts of the country, the **small tortoiseshell** (*Aglais urticae*) is still widespread here and also in towns and villages.

Other very common butterflies include the **small white** (*Pieris/Artogeia rapae*) and the **large white** (*Pieris brassicae*); both can travel large distances, some migrating from continental Europe each year.

Along many of the country lanes and tracks the **speckled wood** (*Pararge aegeria*) can be seen basking on hedgerows. It is a small dark butterfly with a few white spots and six small false eyes at the rear.

There are several butterflies that are synonymous with chalk downland, notably the butterflies known as blues. The **holly blue** (*Celastrina argiolus*) and **chalkhill blue** (*Polyommatus/Lysandra coridon*) are similar in appearance, being very small and pale blue in colour, although the chalkhill blue has a dark strip on the edge of each wing. The **common blue** (*Polyommatus icarus*) is even smaller and as the name suggests is the most common of the blues. The underside of its wings is a dusty brown colour with small orange and white spots.

A rare downland butterfly is the **Duke of Burgundy fritillary** (*Hamearis lucina*) which you may be lucky enough to see on Beacon Hill or Old Winchester Hill. It has pale orange spots on small dark wings.

Another rarity that relies on chalk grassland is the **silver spotted skipper** (*Hesperia comma*), a diminutive yellow butterfly with small white flashes on the undersides of the wings.

Finally, the **brown argus** (*Aricia agestis*), a small dark butterfly with distinctive orange spots along the edges of each wing, is another that is restricted to chalk grassland; it can sometimes be seen flying close to the ground.

Common Blue
Polyommatus icarus

Peacock
Inachis io

Small
Tortoiseshell
Aglais urticae

Silver-washed
Fritillary
Argynnis paphia

Small Garden/Cabbage White
Pieris rapae

Chalkhill Blue
Lysandra coridon

Painted Lady
Cynthia cadui

Large
Garden/
Cabbage White
Pieris brassicae

Small
Copper
*Lycaena
phlaeas*

Small
Heath
*Coenonympha
pamphilus*

Red Admiral *Vanessa atalanta*

White Admiral
Limenitis camilla

Meadow
Brown
*Maniola
jurtina*

Common Poppy
Papaver rhoeas

Tormentil
Potentilla erecta

Scarlet Pimpernel
*Anagallis
arvensis*

FLOWERS

Many of the flowering meadows that once covered large stretches of downland farmland have been destroyed by modern farming techniques. However, in places, efforts are being made to revive these by encouraging farmers to employ more flower-friendly methods.

Meadows

The dominant grass found in fields all over the Downs is the appropriately named **sheep's fescue** (*Festuca ovina*) which was cultivated specifically for pastureland and is the grass of choice for downland sheep. Of far greater interest are the likes of the **common poppy** (*Papaver rhoeas*) with its spectacular deep red petals. They often colonise arable fields and path edges, preferring well-disturbed soil. Entire fields turn red in the flowering season in late summer.

Earlier in the season walkers are likely to come across the **cowslip** (*Primula veris*) and its head of pale yellow flowers. The flowers flop down in small bunches earning the plant the old nickname 'bunch of keys'.

Perhaps one of the most beautiful of the downland flowers is the **round headed rampion** (*Phyteuma orbiculare*). Its striking dark blue flowers have earned it the local name 'The Pride of Sussex'.

The tiny yellow flower of **tormentil** (*Potentilla tormentilla*) can be seen hugging the ground in short grassland. It gets its name from an age when it was used as a medicinal remedy for diarrhoea and haemorrhoids: the taste is so foul that it tormented whoever took it. Another tiny flower that's found close to the ground is the **scarlet pimpernel** (*Anagallis avensis*), a member of the primrose family. The flowers are just 5mm in diameter but stand out from their grassy background thanks to their light red colour.

Many people assume orchids to be so rare as to be nearly impossible to find. In truth there are several fairly common species that may readily be seen flowering on the Downs,

Rowan (tree)
Sorbus aucuparia

Ramsons (Wild Garlic)
Allium ursinum

Common Hawthorn
Crataegus monogyna

Common Centaury
Centaurium erythraea

Common Ragwort
Senecio jacobaea

Cowslip
Primula veris

Yarrow
Achillea millefolium

Foxglove
Digitalis purpurea

Bird's-foot trefoil
Lotus corniculatus

Meadow Buttercup
Ranunculis acris

Marsh Marigold
(Kingcup)
Caltha pulustris

Herb-Robert
Geranium robertianum

Primrose
Primula vulgaris

St John's Wort
*Hypericum
perforatum*

Dog Rose
Rosa canina

Honeysuckle
*Lonicera
periclymemum*

Ox-eye Daisy
Leucanthemum vulgare

Common Knapweed
Centaurea nigra

Red Admiral butterfly (*Vanessa atalanta*) on
Hemp Agrimony (*Eupatorium cannabinum*)

Pyramidal Orchid
*Anacamptis
pyramidalis*

Bee Orchid
*Ophrys
apifera*

usually around mid-summer. These include the **early purple orchid** (*Orchis mascula*) which can be seen in rough grassland. It stands about 10-15cm tall and has an elongated head of pinky-purple flowers. Also quite common are the **pyramidal orchid** (*Anacamptis pyramidalis*) and the **common spotted-orchid** (*Dactylorhiza fuchsii*).

There are of course some species that do fit the rare orchid label including the **fly orchid** (*Ophrys insectifera*) with flowers resembling small insects. These cleverly designed flowers attract wasps which pick up the pollen and take it on to the next insect-shaped flower they see. Another orchid with the same tactic is the **bee orchid** (*Ophrys apifera*) whose flowers are shaped like, well, bees.

Apart from the orchids, one of the most endangered and also one of the most striking flowering plants that may be seen, particularly on the Downs above Eastbourne, is **pheasant's-eye** (*Adonis annua*) with its blood red petals and large seed head.

Bluebell
*Hyacinthoides
non-scripta*

Early Purple Orchid
Orchis mascula

Common Spotted-Orchid
Dactylorhiza fuchsii

Rosebay Willowherb
Epilobium angustifolium

Gorse
Ulex europaeus

Forget-me-not
Myosotis arvensis

Common Dog Violet
Viola riviniana

Old Man's Beard
Clematis vitalba

Red Campion
Silene dioica

In overgrown areas thorny **gorse** (*Ulex europeous*) bushes brighten up the summer with their small yellow flowers that burst open from February until June, filling the air with a coconut-like scent.

Woodland and hedgerows

There are several flowering plants associated with open woods and woodland edges. In May the pink flowers of the slightly inaccurately named **red campion** (*Silene dioica*) come into view along woodland edges and at the foot of hedgerows while deeper into the woods the floor becomes covered with **bluebells** (*Hyacinthoides non-scripta*) in the early spring. Other common woodland flowering plants include the **wood anemone** (*Anemone nemorosa*) with its round white flowers which cover forest floors in a similar way to bluebells. A more isolated flower, although sometimes seen growing in small groups, is the cheerful yellow **primrose** (*Primula vulgaris*).

Bramble (*Rubus fruticosus*) is a common woodland and hedgerow species with small sharp thorns. It spreads rapidly, engulfing everything in its path. In its favour, blackberries appear on the branches in the autumn to provide sustenance for hungry birds and peckish walkers. In hedgerows and along woodland edges you'll see the distinctive feathery climber, **old man's beard** (*Clematis vitalba*), also known as traveller's joy. The feathery part of the plant is actually the fruit. The **foxglove** (*Digitalis purpurea*) is a very tall and graceful plant with white or purple trumpet-like flowers. It is commonly spotted along hedgerows, roadside verges and in shady woodland. Other fairly common woodland species that are just as comfortable on hedgebanks include the **forget-me-not** (*Myosotis arvensis*) which has very small blue flowers and **cow parsley** (*Anthriscus sylvestris*), a tall plant with a head of white flowers.

Perhaps the most unusual and to some eyes the ugliest of plants, found in dark corners of beech woodland, is the pale yellow **bird's nest orchid** (*Neottia nidus-avis*), so-called because of its nest-like root system that intertwines across the ground.

BIRDS

The chalk grassland of the Downs is ideal for a variety of bird species but the grassy hillsides are not the only habitat on the Downs. There are many woodland species in the beech forests on the steep scarp slope, freshwater species on the rivers and sea birds by Cuckmere Haven and the Seven Sisters' cliffs. The following list gives just a few of the birds that may be seen while walking on the Downs.

Scrubland and chalk grassland

One of the most attractive birds the Downs walker might spot, usually seen feeding on open arable farmland, is the **lapwing** (*Vanellus vanellus*), also known as the peewit. It has long legs, a short bill and a distinctive long head crest. Sadly, this attractive bird is declining in numbers. The name comes from its lilting flight, frequently changing direction with its large rounded wings. It is also identified by a white belly, black and white head, black throat patch and distinctive dark green wings.

Towards dusk **barn owls** (*Tyto alba*) hunt for voles along field and woodland edges. To see a barn owl, with its ghostly white plumage, is a real treat but their dwindling numbers make such a sighting increasingly rare. The colourful little **stonechat** (*Saxicola rubicola*) with its deep orange breast and black head is among the more commonly sighted of Downland birds. They are easily identified by their habit of flitting from the top of one bush to another, only pausing to call out across the fields. The stonechat's call sounds much like two stones being struck together, hence the name. The **yellowhammer** (*Emberiza citrinella*), also known as the yellow bunting, can sometimes be seen perched on the top of gorse bushes. Most field guides to birds along with some old romantic country folk claim that the distinctive song of the yellowhammer sounds like the bird is saying the phrase: 'a little bit of bread and no cheese'. At a push they are right, but the yellowhammer is certainly no talking parrot.

The call of the **skylark** (*Alauda arvensis*) can probably be considered the sound of the Downs. This small, buff-coloured, ground-nesting lark is usually heard but not often seen. The characteristic flight pattern, rising steadily upwards on rapid wingbeats whilst twittering relentlessly, is what makes the skylark such a distinctive little bird. However, the skylark is difficult to see against the blue sky but if you look carefully you might just spot one way up high.

Woodland

A common raptor that is often heard before it's seen is the **buzzard** (*Buteo buteo*), a large broad-winged bird of prey which looks much like a small eagle. It is dark brown in appearance but slightly paler on the underside of its wings. It has a distinctive mewing call and can be spotted soaring ever higher on the air thermals or sometimes perched on the top of fenceposts. Buzzards are less common towards the eastern end of the Downs where the woodland cover is not so great. They are far easier to spot above the dense woodland on the West Sussex Downs and around the Meon Valley in Hampshire.

The **kestrel** (*Falco tinnunculus*), a small falcon, is much smaller than the buzzard. It hovers expertly in a fixed spot above grassland and roadside verges, even in the strongest of winds, hunting for mice and voles.

Similar in size and appearance but rarely seen is the **hobby** *(Falco subbuteo)* which appears in the summer months, often on the margins of woodlands.

The **green woodpecker** *(Picus viridis)* is not all green, sporting a bright red and black head. They are sometimes spotted clinging to a vertical tree trunk or feeding on the ground in open fields. The most common view, however, is as the bird flies away when disturbed. The undulating flight pattern is characterised by rapid wing beats as the bird rises followed by a pause when the bird slowly drops. This is accompanied by a loud laughing call that has earned the bird its old English name of 'yaffle'.

The **woodcock** *(Scolopax rusticola),* with its long straight beak and plump body, is common in damp woodland where it can lie hidden thanks to its leafy brown plumage. It is most easily sighted in spring at dusk and dawn. This is when the males perform their courtship flight, known as 'roding', which involves two distinct calls, one a low grunting noise, the other a sharp 'k-wik k-wik' call.

Using this guide

This route guide has been divided according to logical start and stop points. However, these are not intended to be strict daily stages since people walk at different speeds and have varying interests. The maps can be used to plan how far to walk each day but note that these are walking times only (see box below).

On pp32-4 are tables to help you plan an **itinerary**. To provide further help, **practical information** is presented clearly on the trail maps. This includes walking times for both directions, places to stay, camp and eat, as well as shops where you can buy supplies. Further service **details** are given in the text under the entry for each place. For an overview of this information see the **village and town facilities table** on pp30-1.

See also the **colour maps** (with **profile charts**) and the cumulative **distance chart** at the back of the book.

TRAIL MAPS   [see key map p208; symbols key p191]

Direction

(See p29 for a discussion of the pros and cons of walking direction.)

E If you're doing this walk in an **easterly direction** (E → ie towards Eastbourne having started in Winchester) follow the maps in an ascending order (from 1 to 42) and the text as below.

W If you're walking in a **westerly direction** (W ←, ie towards Winchester having started in Eastbourne), follow the maps in a descending order (from 42 to 1) and the route overviews in shaded text. Turn to p178 (or p182 for inland route) to start your walk in this direction.

Scale and walking times

The trail maps are to a scale of 1:20,000 (1cm = 200m; 3¹/₈ inches = one mile). Walking times are given along the side of each map and the

---

❑ **IMPORTANT NOTE – WALKING TIMES**

Unless otherwise specified, **all times in this book refer only to the time spent walking**. You should add 20-30% to allow for rests, photos, checking the map, drinking water etc, not to mention time simply to stop and stare. When planning the day's hike count on 5-7 hours' actual walking.

arrow shows the direction to which the time refers. Black triangles indicate the points between which the times have been taken. **See box overleaf for important note on walking times**. The time-bars are a tool and are not there to judge your walking ability. There are so many variables that affect walking speed, from the weather conditions to how many beers you drank the previous evening. After the first hour or two of walking you will see how your speed relates to the timings on the maps.

GPS waypoints
The numbered GPS waypoints refer to the list on pp188-91.

Up or down?
The trail is shown as a **dashed red line**. An arrow across the trail indicates the gradient; two arrows show that it's steep. Note that the *arrow points uphill*, the opposite of what OS maps use on steep roads. A good way to remember our style is: '**front-pointing** on crampons **up** a steep slope' and 'open arms – Julie Andrews-style – **spreading out** to unfold the view **down** below'. If, for example, you are walking from A (at 80m) to B (at 200m) and the trail between the two is short and steep it would be shown thus: A— — — >> — — – B. Reversed arrow heads indicate a downward gradient.

Other features
Features are marked on the map when pertinent to navigation. In order to avoid cluttering the maps and making them unusable not all features have been marked each time they occur.

ACCOMMODATION

Apart from in large towns where some selection of places has been necessary, almost every place to stay that is within easy reach of the trail is marked. Details of each place are given in the accompanying text.

The number of **rooms** of each type is stated, ie **S** = single bed, **T** = twin beds, **D** = double bed, **Tr** = triple room (for up to three people) and **Qd** = quad (for up to four). Note that most of the triple/quad rooms have a double bed and one/two single beds (or bunk beds); thus for a group of three or four, two people may have to share the double bed but it also means the room can be used as a double or twin.

Rates quoted for a double or twin in B&B-style accommodation are **per person (pp) based on two people sharing a room** for a one-night stay; rates are usually discounted for longer stays and also if three or more people are sharing a room. Where a **single room (sgl)** is available the rate for that is quoted if different from the rate per person. The rate for **single occupancy (sgl occ)** of a double/twin room may be higher. Unless specified, rates are for bed and breakfast; at some places the only option is a **room rate** – this will be the same whether one or two people (or more if permissible) use the room.

The accommodation will either have **en suite** (bath or shower) facilities in the room or **private,** or **shared, facilities** (in either case this is a separate room, with a bath and/or shower, often just outside the bedroom); in some places the facilities may be private if only one room is booked. The text also mentions whether the premises have: **wi-fi** (WI-FI); if a bath (◗) is available in/for at least one room, for those who prefer a relaxed soak at the end of the day; if **packed lunches** (Ⓛ) can be prepared subject to prior arrangement (though this has not been checked for cities or large towns where there are lots of options); and if **dogs** (🐾) are welcome in at least one room, or at campsites, subject to prior arrangement; see pp193.

If arranged in advance some B&B proprietors are happy to collect walkers from the nearest point on the trail and deliver them back again next morning; they may also be happy to transfer your **luggage** to your next accommodation place. Some may charge for this; check the details at the time of booking.

WINCHESTER   MAP 1, p76

Winchester is a city steeped in history. The area was settled as long ago as 450BC when the nearby **St Catherine's Hill** was inhabited by a Celtic tribe. After the Roman occupation came the Dark Ages of AD400-600 during which time it is believed that **King Arthur** reigned from here. Many romantics today believe the city to be the site of legendary Camelot.

Things brightened up after the Dark Ages when in 871 **King Alfred the Great** (849-899) made the city the capital of Saxon England. He has probably had the greatest influence on the city so it is not surprising that a **bronze statue** of him, constructed in 1901, stands on Broadway. **St Swithun** (see box below) is also inextricably linked with Winchester.

In 1066 **William the Conqueror** arrived in Hastings and made his way to Winchester where he duly took charge and ordered the building of the castle. Soon after, in 1079, work began on the cathedral.

Winchester has had a long and sometimes turbulent history but it is well worth spending an afternoon or the whole day exploring the compact city's many sights.

What to see and do

Winchester Cathedral (☎ 01962-857200, 💻 winchester-cathedral.org.uk; Mon-Sat 9am-5pm, Sun noon-3pm; £9.95) stands elegantly in parkland in the city centre. The spectacular nave is said to be the longest Gothic cathedral nave in the world. The best time to visit the cathedral is during the Sunday morning service when the choir can be heard. The cathedral has witnessed many an historic event: **Henry III** was baptised here in 1207 and it was also the scene of the marriage of **Mary Tudor** to **Philip of Spain** in 1554. In more recent history it became the final resting place in 1817 of **Jane Austen** (see box p74); her grave and memorial are in the north aisle of the cathedral. The ticket price includes a new exhibition, Kings and Scribes: The Birth of a Nation (Mon-Sat 11am-4pm, Sun 12.30-2.30pm), which includes a look at the 12th-century Winchester Bible. There's also a

---

Ⓛ THE LEGEND OF ST SWITHUN

St Swithun, once Bishop of Winchester, died in AD862. Before his death he asked to be buried outside the old Minster and was duly interred in accordance with his wishes. St Swithun, however, had not counted upon the wishes of Bishop Aethelwold who on 15 July 971 decided to extend the Minster. The expansion plans required the temporary opening of St Swithun's grave before he was carefully re-interred within the new Minster's walls. On the day of the re-interment it began to rain and did not stop for 40 days. To this day the legend says that if it rains on St Swithun's Day it will rain for the next 40 days. Some would say this is not unusual for England in July.

large *café* (Cathedral Refectory, see p77). Even though the cathedral is the centre-piece of the city there are other equally fas-cinating places such as the extensive **ruins of Wolvesey Castle** (Apr-Sep daily 10am-6pm; Oct to 4pm, Nov-Mar Sat, Sun and school hols 10am-4pm; free), the former palace (residence) for the bishops of Winchester, which in 1554 hosted Queen Mary's and Philip II of Spain's wedding breakfast, before being destroyed less than a century later by Roundheads in the English Civil War. At 8 College St, not far from Wolvesey Castle, is the house where **Jane Austen** died. However, this is a pri-vate residence so don't peer through the windows.

Nearby is one of Winchester's hidden gems: **St Swithun-upon-Kingsgate Church**, a tiny Church of England church, built on top of King's Gate, one of Winchester's two surviving city gates (the other being Westgate). Built during the Middle Ages, the church is unusual in that it actually formed part of the fabric of the old city walls.

Also near the cathedral is the **City of Winchester Museum** (☎ 01962-863064, 🖳 hampshireculturaltrust.org.uk/winches ter-city-museum; Apr-Dec Mon-Sat 10am-5pm, Sun 11am-5pm, Jan-Mar Mon-Sat 10am-4pm, Sun 11am-4pm; £5). The muse-um traces the history of the city from the Romans to the Victorians and most things in between.

Next to **Westgate**, one of the two sur-viving city gates, is the **Great Hall** (☎ 01962-846476, 🖳 hants.gov.uk/greathall; Thur-Tue 10am-4pm; £4), Castle Ave, the only surviving part of Winchester Castle. Here, on the west wall, hangs, so legend has it, *the* table around which King Arthur and

his Knights of the Round Table sat. Carbon dating has quashed that particular story, however, and the table is actually a few hundred years too young to have been used by Arthur, having been constructed around the end of the 13th century; but it's still a mightily impressive disc of oak, weighing over a ton and elaborately painted during the time of Henry VIII with a beautiful Tudor rose. The Great Hall is also famous for the trial of **Sir Walter Raleigh** for trea-son in 1603.

In the heart of the city is **City Mill** (☎ 01962-870057, 🖳 nationaltrust.org.uk/win chester-city-mill; **fb**; Wed-Mon 11am-4pm; admission free for all for 2022 but possibly a charge thereafter), sitting astride the River Itchen, and thought to be the country's old-est working water mill. Although there has been a mill on this site for centuries the present building dates from 1743. Check online or call for times if you're interested in the free-to-watch demonstrations of flour milling. City Mill is the official **'Gateway' to the South Downs National Park** and it doubles as an information centre for the park; it is now the official start (or end) of the walk too.

It is possible to visit **Winchester College** (☎ 01962-621209, 🖳 winchester college.org/guided-tours; one-hour tours, Mon-Sat 10.15am, 11.30am, 2.15pm & 3.30pm, Sun 2.15pm & 3.30pm; tour £9) which was founded in 1382 by William of Wykeham, then Bishop of Winchester; it is said to be the oldest continuously running school in the country. Originally it was home to 70 pupils but it now has over 700. Amongst the 80 listed buildings are the 14th-century chapel, the College Hall, the 17th-century schoolroom and the medieval cloister.

❏ **JANE AUSTEN**

Jane Austen, born near Basingstoke in Hampshire in 1775, is one of the most impor-tant English novelists, having written such classics as *Pride and Prejudice*, *Persuasion* and *Northanger Abbey*. In 1816 she began writing *Sanditon* but in the same year she contracted Addison's disease and the novel was never completed. As her condition worsened she moved to a house in Winchester where she spent the last few weeks of her life, dying at the age of 41 on 18 July 1817.

Services

The very helpful **visitor information centre** (☎ 01962-840500, ▭ visitwinchester.co .uk; May-Sep Mon-Sat 10am-4pm, Sun & bank holiday Mon to 3pm, Oct-Apr Mon-Sat 10am-4pm) is on the ground floor of the Guildhall on High St. For information on South Downs National Park see City Mill, p74.

On the pedestrianised High St there are countless **banks** and **ATMs** while the main **post office** (Mon-Sat 8.30am-6pm, Sun 10.30am-4.30pm) is inside WH Smith.

There are several **supermarkets**, including the biggest, Sainsbury's (Mon-Sat 7am-8pm, Sun 11am-5pm), adjoining **Brooks Shopping Centre** on Middle Brook St, and a handy Co-op (daily 7am-10pm) near the railway station. Last-minute hiking equipment (including blister kits) can be found in Mountain Warehouse **outdoor gear shop** (Mon-Sat 9am-5.30pm, Sun 10.30am-4.30pm), on the High St.

Lloyds **Pharmacy** (Mon, Wed-Fri 8.45am-5.30pm, Tue & Sat 9am-5.30pm) is near the visitor information centre at 155 High St. There's also a Boots and a Superdrug on the High St.

There's free **internet access** at the Bike Hub and also inside the Discovery Centre (Mon-Fri 9am-7pm, Sat to 5pm, Sun 11am-3pm), a small, modern **library** on Jewry St.

Public transport

Both South Western Railway and Cross Country Trains operate **train** services to Winchester (see box p44). The **railway station** is about five minutes' walk from the city centre.

A couple of National Express **coach** services (Nos 032 & 205; see box p45) call at the **bus station** opposite the visitor information centre. For Southampton you should take Bluestar's No 1 **bus** while for Petersfield and the villages in between take Stagecoach's No 67. Stagecoach's No 64 (from Alton) also calls here. For further details see p46.

Where to stay

Being a popular tourist destination, Winchester is blessed with plenty of hotels and guesthouses. However, the demand on accommodation throughout the year is such that **booking well in advance** is strongly recommended to avoid a night on a park bench by the cathedral.

The nearest **campsite** is the well-equipped *Morn Hill Caravan Club Campsite* (off Map 1; ☎ 01962-869877, ▭ caravanclub.co.uk; camping Mar-end Sep; limited WI-FI; dog if on a lead), 2¼ miles east of town. They charge from £6 per tent plus around £6 per adult. Stagecoach's bus No 64 (see p46) goes from the bus station to Winchester Science Centre, which is very close to the campsite, so it is possible to use it as a place to stay, but note they only have six tent pitches. The campsite is also two miles north-east of Chilcomb (Map 2) and 1½ miles north of Cheesefoot Head car park (Map 2).

The cheapest accommodation is probably that supplied by the local *Travelodge* (☎ 08719 846552, ▭ www.travelodge.co.uk; 62/D or Tr, all en suite; ☞; WI-FI; 🐾), on Market Lane. You may gripe at the lack of atmosphere and the complete absence of any personal touch, but you simply can't argue with the location. Rooms – if booked and paid in advance – start at £60 but can be double that. Wi-fi is free for 30 mins per 24hrs (£3/24hrs); dogs can stay (£20/week).

Cathedral Cottage (☎ 01962-878975, ▭ cathedralcottagebandb.co.uk; 1Tr en suite; WI-FI), at 19 Colebrook St, is just a stone's throw from the cathedral with a cosy room (from £47.50pp, sgl occ rate on request) overlooking a pretty cottage garden; your breakfast (full English or continental) can either be served in your room or other places in the house. Another room (1D separate bathroom; ☞; from £37.50pp, £65 sgl occ) is also sometimes available.

In a beautiful Grade II* Queen Anne house at the top of Blue Ball Hill is *St John's Croft* (☎ 01962-859976, ▭ st-johns-croft.co.uk; 2Tr, private bathrooms, 1Tr en suite bath but separate toilet; ☞; WI-FI) with B-&-'Aga-cooked'-B from £55pp (sgl occ £75). There are comfortable good-sized rooms with views over Winchester.

Winchester Royal (☎ 01962-840840, ▭ winchesterroyalhotel.com; 81/D or T

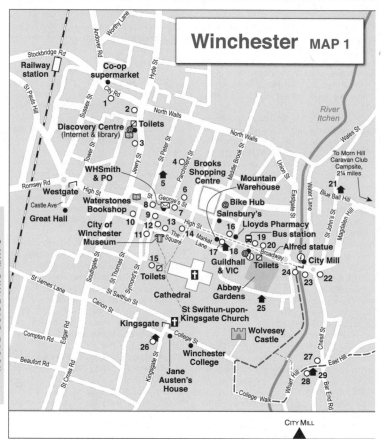

Winchester MAP 1

plus some suites, all en suite; ☞; WI-FI) is on St Peter St. This 16th-century town-house was once a bishop's residence then a convent but now offers luxurious hotel accommodation with four-poster beds in two rooms. Rates vary widely but expect to pay from £44.50pp (sgl occ rate) for room only, often less if booking more than a week in advance: check their website for special offers. If not included in the rate breakfast costs from £12pp.

At 75 Kingsgate St is **_The Wykeham Arms_** (☎ 01962-853834, 🖳 wykehamarms winchester.co.uk; 2S/10D/2T, all en suite;

☞; WI-FI), a cosy inn with quality rooms from £72 to £131.50pp (sgl/sgl occ £84-117); breakfast is not included in the rate. It's named after William of Wykeham who founded Winchester College (see p74).

Sounding as unattractive as its associated restaurant (The Black Rat; see Where to Eat), **_The Black Hole_** (☎ 01962-807010, 🖳 theblackholebb.co.uk; 10D, all en suite; ☞; WI-FI; 🐾) is in fact a quality, if somewhat quirky guesthouse with a small roof terrace overlooking the city. They charge £47.50-60pp (sgl occ room rate).

Where to stay
5 Winchester Royal
18 Travelodge
21 St John's Croft
25 Cathedral Cottage
26 The Wykeham Arms
29 The Black Hole

Where to eat and drink
1 Gurkha's Inn
2 Porterhouse Steakhouse
3 Brasserie Blanc
4 Piecaramba!
6 Caught – Fish & Chips
7 Forte Kitchen
8 ASK Italian
9 West Cornwall Pasty Co

Where to eat and drink *(cont'd)*
10 Café Winchester
11 The Old Vine
12 Cafémonde
13 The Eclipse Inn
14 Flat Whites
15 Cathedral Refectory
16 Chococo
17 Rick Stein Fish and Shellfish
19 Gandhi Restaurant
20 Crown and Anchor
22 Chesil Rectory
23 Bridge Patisserie
24 Bishop on the Bridge
26 The Wykeham Arms
27 The Black Rat
28 Black Boy

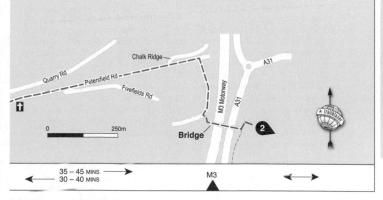

ROUTE GUIDE AND MAPS

Chalk Ridge
Quarry Rd
Petersfield Rd
Fivefields Rd
A31
M3 Motorway
A31
trailblazer
0   250m
Bridge

35 – 45 MINS
30 – 40 MINS
M3

Where to eat and drink
Cafés Just a few steps from City Mill, across the road, *Bridge Patisserie* (☎ 01962-890767, ⌨ thc-bridge-patisserie.co .uk; **fb**; WI-FI; 🐾; daily 9am-3pm) is very dog-friendly and does a good line in salads and tasty lunches.

The city centre is dotted with cafés. One of the most popular, and a great spot for breakfast, is *Cafémonde* (**fb**; Mon-Sat 8am-6pm, Sun 9am-5pm), a stone's throw from the cathedral and with a clutch of tables spilling out onto the pavement outside. At the other end of a nearby alleyway

is *Café Winchester* (⌨ www.cafe-winches ter.co.uk; Mon-Fri 7.30am-5.30pm, Sat 8am-6pm, Sun 9am-5.30pm) which does pastries, cakes and light lunches. The large, modern *Cathedral Refectory* (daily 10am-4pm) is another dependable option and also has plenty of outdoor seating for sunny afternoons. For something more quirky, try *Chococo* (⌨ chococo.co.uk; Sun-Fri 9.30am-5pm, Sat 9am-5.30pm) which, as the name suggests, specialises in all things chocolate, including hot-chocolate drinks. They also serve tea, coffee, cakes and soups. Serving arguably the best coffee of all, though, is *Flat Whites* (Mon-Thur 9am-2pm, Fri-Sun to 4pm), a coffee and snack van with a seemingly permanent position just off the High St. They do decent cakes here too, and there are tables and chairs scattered beside the van so you don't have to take away. For healthy breakfasts and brasserie-type lunches, *Forte Kitchen* (🖳 fortekitchen.co.uk; Mon-Fri & Sun 9am-4pm, Sat to 5pm) is an up-scale café at 78 Parchment St that's very popular.

Pubs There are numerous pubs to choose from. One of the most attractive and historic is *The Eclipse Inn* (☎ 01962-865676, 🖳 the-eclipse-winchester.co.uk; **fb**; food Mon-Wed noon-2.30pm, Wed-Fri 5.30-8pm, Sat noon-8pm, Sun to 4pm; WI-FI) at 25 The Square. It's a tiny whitewashed, timber-framed house which once served as a 16th-century rectory and is rumoured to be haunted. The food (standard pub food) is good value here.

Another good traditional pub is *Black Boy* (☎ 01962-861754, 🖳 theblackboy pub.com; bar Mon-Fri noon-2.30pm & 5-11pm, Sat noon-11pm, Sun to 10.30pm; WI-FI; 🐕 on lead), at 1 Wharf Hill, but note that at the time of research they were not serving food due to the COVID pandemic though they hope to again.

Opposite the cathedral, on Minster St, *The Old Vine* (☎ 01962-854616, 🖳 oldvine winchester.com; **fb**; WI-FI; 🐕 bar only) is another refurbished old pub that offers a traditional ploughman's lunch (£10.50) and sandwiches (from £6.50) as well as more substantial pub fare. At the time of research they were serving food daily all day (8am to 8.30/9pm) though it is not definite this will always continue.

The Wykeham Arms (see Where to stay; daily noon-8pm), south of the cathedral, is friendly, serves top-class fare (main

dishes around £15-19) and feels more like a country pub.

Another Fuller's pub, like The Wykeham Arms, and boasting a great location too, *Bishop on the Bridge* (🖳 www .bishoponthebridge.co.uk; food Mon-Sat noon-9pm, Sun to 8pm) is worth visiting for its sun terrace overlooking the River Itchen.

Crown and Anchor (☎ 01962-870074, 🖳 crownandanchorwinchester.co.uk; **fb**; food Mon-Thur noon-3pm & 5.30-8pm, Fri-Sun 11am-5pm; WI-FI; 🐕) is an unpretentious place, cheaper than most (mains from £10.50), friendly and, with a location on the High St just down from the bus station, central too. It also has vegan and gluten-free menus – a big and welcome surprise. The only drawback is that food isn't served in the evening at weekends (Fri-Sun) as, according to the barmaid, the place can get a bit rowdy then.

Restaurants & takeaways One of the most enjoyable places to eat is the café-cum-diner *Piecaramba!* (🖳 piecaramba.co .uk/winchester; Mon & Wed-Sat noon-8.30pm, Tue 5-8.30pm, Sun noon-4.30pm), 11 Parchment St; it's a pie-and-mash specialist with a soft spot for comic books. Superhero stories are plastered across the walls. The menu, meanwhile, is dominated by pies (including beef, chicken, lamb & veggie varieties), which go for just £9.95 as part of a pie-and-mash meal. Great value. Great fun.

There are numerous places to eat on nearby Jewry St too. At No 24, is *Porterhouse Steakhouse* (☎ 01962-810532, 🖳 porterhouserestaurant.co.uk; Sun-Thur noon-10pm, Fri & Sat to 10.30pm) with high-quality steaks (from £25.95) but a cheaper daytime menu.

A couple of TV chefs have opened branches of their restaurant chains in

---

Symbols used in text (see also pp72-3)
🐕 Dogs allowed; if for accommodation this is subject to prior arrangement (see p193)
🛆 Bathtub in, or for, at least one room   WI-FI means wi-fi is available
Ⓛ packed lunch available if requested in advance
fb signifies places that post their current opening hours on their Facebook page

Winchester, including the famous French chef Raymond Blanc's *Brasserie Blanc* (☎ 01962-810870, 🖥 brasserieblanc.com; daily noon-10pm), which is also on Jewry St. Mains start at £12.95 for the vegetarian jackfruit fritters and green papaya salad. While down on the High St, *Rick Stein Fish and Shellfish* (☎ 01962-587348, 🖥 rickstein.com; Mon-Fri 11.30am-10pm, Sat noon-10pm, Sun to 9pm) was Stein's first restaurant outside Cornwall. Mains cost from £14.95; the two/three-course set lunches (£20.95/25.95) are a good deal.

The Black Rat (☎ 01962-844465, 🖥 theblackrat.co.uk; Wed-Sun 7-9.15pm, plus Sat & Sun noon-2.15pm), 88 Chesil St, is one of two fancy restaurants at either end of Chesil St (it currently holds the only Michelin star in the city). Expect to spend around £40-50pp for a really memorable evening meal. The other, at 1 Chesil St, is *Chesil Rectory* (☎ 01962-851555, 🖥 chesil rectory.co.uk; food Wed Sat noon-2.30pm & 6-9.30pm, Sun noon-3pm & 6-9pm), housed in one of Winchester's best-preserved medieval buildings, which dates from around 1425, and was once owned by Henry VIII. Lunchtime set menus cost £19.95 for two courses or £24.95 for three.

For something more down to earth, grab some pizza or pasta at the Italian food chain, *ASK Italian* (☎ 01962-808986, 🖥 www.askitalian.co.uk; daily 11.30am-10pm), 101 High St, or go for a curry at *Gandhi Restaurant* (☎ 01962-863940, 🖥 gandhi restaurant.com; daily noon-2pm, Sun-Thur 5.30-10pm, Fri & Sat to 11pm) at 163 High St. For subcontinental fare with a Himalayan twist there's *Gurkha's Inn* (☎ 01962-842843, 🖥 gurkhasinnwinchester .com, daily noon-2pm, Mon-Sat 5.30-11pm, Sun to 10pm), a popular Nepalese restaurant and takeaway at 17 City Rd. Alternatively, *Caught – Fish & Chips* (Mon-Sat 11.30am-9pm) is a good chippy on St George's St, while *West Cornwall Pasty Co* (Mon-Fri 8.30am-5.30pm, Sat 9am-6pm, Sun to 5.30pm), on the High St, is your best bet for a pasty on the go.

The route guide

E➔ WINCHESTER TO EXTON   MAPS 1-6

These **12 miles (19.5km, 4¼-5¾hrs)** begin at the City Mill in the centre of Winchester and follow the River Itchen south before crossing it to leave the city and enter the rolling East Hampshire countryside.

Until May 2017 the route began at the cathedral in the centre of Winchester and went from the cathedral grounds, along the main shopping street, past the statue of King Alfred then down beside the River Itchen; it's a start that we think is superior. You may prefer to start the route this way.

On crossing the bridge spanning the noisy motorway (M3) spare a thought for the remains of Twyford Down. This once beautiful hill a few miles to the south was, despite vociferous demonstrations, ruthlessly sliced in two as part of a highly controversial road improvement scheme in the early 1990s.

Once away from the noise of the road the path crosses a field before arriving at **Chilcomb** (see p80). The church aside, there's little in the way of shops or services to keep you in Chilcomb so once you have admired the thatched cottages head on up the lane for the gradual but steady ascent to **Cheesefoot Head** (Map 2) where there are great views to the north over the Itchen Valley. The way then passes close to the pretty village of **Cheriton** (Map 4a; p82). The route continues from here along leafy country lanes and tracks through a typically English landscape of patchwork fields, hedgerows and pockets of woodland; and **Beacon Hill** (Map 6), a National Nature Reserve.

There have been plans to change the course of the South Downs Way across the Meon Valley for many years. For now the trail still goes through the pretty village of **Exton** (Map 6) – and all the better for it – though there is an alternative route for cyclists (clearly signposted) which skirts around the south of the village. It should also be noted that with no accommodation in Exton at the end of the stage, the only nearby B&B is in **Meonstoke** (see pp86-8).

CHILCOMB   MAP 2

Chilcomb is the first of several beautiful Hampshire villages. In fact Chilcomb is one of the older settlements, with a **church** (off the path to the south) that pre-dates Winchester Cathedral.

Campers will find tent pitches at *Morn Hill Caravan Club Campsite* (see p75), two miles north-east of here. To get there see Map 2 and at the A31/A272 roundabout turn right and follow this road as far as the big roundabout a mile further east. Keep to the left, over the roundabout, then go straight over a second, almost adjacent roundabout, and you'll see the campsite in front of you.

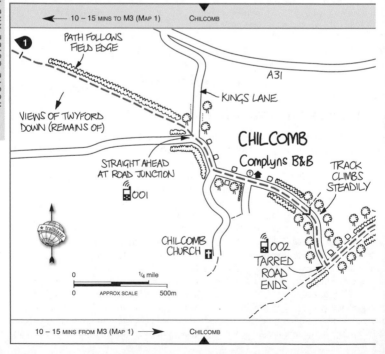

← 10 – 15 MINS TO M3 (MAP 1)   CHILCOMB

1

PATH FOLLOWS FIELD EDGE

A31

KINGS LANE

VIEWS OF TWYFORD DOWN (REMAINS OF)

STRAIGHT AHEAD AT ROAD JUNCTION

001

CHILCOMB

Complyns B&B

TRACK CLIMBS STEADILY

trailblazer

CHILCOMB CHURCH

002 TARRED ROAD ENDS

0   ¼ mile
0   APPROX SCALE   500m

10 – 15 MINS FROM M3 (MAP 1) →   CHILCOMB

There's also a charming **B&B** called *Complyns* (☎ 01962-861600 or ☎ 07890-447982, 🖳 complyns.co.uk; 1D/1T, shared bathroom; ☛; WI-FI; Ⓛ) in a 17th-century former farmhouse, which charges from £35pp (sgl occ £45). They have a boiler house where you can dry clothes. In the garden there is also a cosy **shepherd's hut** (from £25pp, sgl occ £30) with a double bed and access to toilet facilities; breakfast is also available.

CHERITON   MAP 4a, p82

If you're planning on visiting Cheriton (35-45 mins), take the path in the corner of the field (see Map 4, p83) rather than following the busy A272.

On hot sunny days the locals can be seen paddling in the clear waters of the tiny River Itchen, which bubbles out of the chalk about a mile south of Cheriton and runs straight through the village passing beautiful thatched houses and the village green.

The village is about 35-45 minutes from the Way so unfortunately, unless you are planning on staying the night here, you are likely to miss Cheriton's quaint charms.

Those who do visit should bear in mind that it was not always such a peaceful and charming spot. In 1644, during the English Civil War, the Battle of Cheriton took place just to the east of the village, off Lamborough Lane.

The clash between the Parliamentarians and the Royalists resulted in the deaths of 2000 men with the Parliamentarians coming out on top. To this day it is claimed that

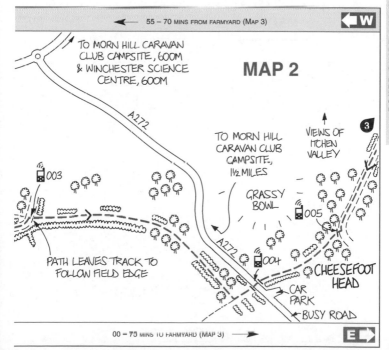

← 55 – 70 MINS FROM FARMYARD (MAP 3)   ◀W

TO MORN HILL CARAVAN CLUB CAMPSITE, 600M & WINCHESTER SCIENCE CENTRE, 600M

MAP 2

A272

TO MORN HILL CARAVAN CLUB CAMPSITE, 1½ MILES

VIEWS OF ITCHEN VALLEY

003

GRASSY BOWL

005

A272

PATH LEAVES TRACK TO FOLLOW FIELD EDGE

004

CHEESEFOOT HEAD

CAR PARK

BUSY ROAD

00 – 75 MINS TO FARMYARD (MAP 3) →   E▶

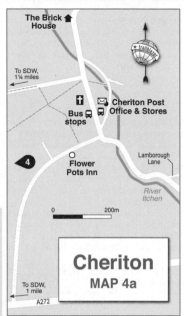

Cheriton

MAP 4a

'Lamborough Lane ran with the blood of the slain'.

In the village centre is the very useful *Cheriton Post Office & Stores* (☎ 01962-771251; Mon & Fri 7am-5.30pm, Tue, Wed & Sat to 2pm, Thur to 4pm, Sun 7.30am-12.30pm), a combined shop, newsagent, off-licence and **post office**. However, the post office opens only on Monday (1.30-4.30pm) and Thursday (9am-noon). Stagecoach's No 67 **bus** service (Winchester–Petersfield; see p46) stops near the church.

The charming *Flower Pots Inn* (☎ 01962-771735, 🖳 www.theflowerpots.co .uk; **fb**; food Tue noon-2pm, Wed-Fri noon-2pm & 6-8.30pm, Sat noon-3pm & 6-8.30pm, Sun noon-4pm; 🐾) is a great spot for a meal and a pint. It has its own **brewery**; their Flowerpots Bitter is definitely worth a taste. Note the pub is generally closed in the afternoon.

For **B&B**, there's *The Brick House* (☎ 01962-771334, 🖳 brickhousecheriton.co .uk; 2D both en suite; WI-FI; (Ⓛ)), just past the village centre. They charge from £57.50pp (sgl occ £105).

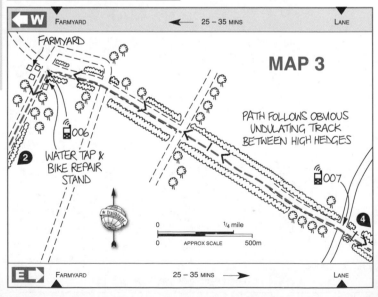

ROUTE GUIDE AND MAPS

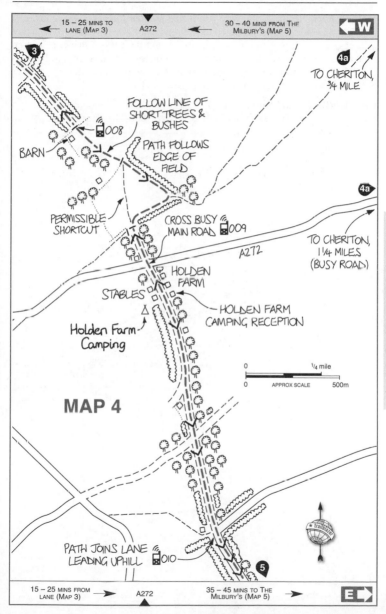

3

TO CHERITON, ¾ MILE

4a

FOLLOW LINE OF SHORT TREES & BUSHES

008

BARN

PATH FOLLOWS EDGE OF FIELD

PERMISSIBLE SHORTCUT

CROSS BUSY MAIN ROAD 009

4a

TO CHERITON, 1¼ MILES (BUSY ROAD)

A272

HOLDEN FARM

STABLES

HOLDEN FARM CAMPING RECEPTION

Holden Farm Camping

MAP 4

0   ¼ mile
0   APPROX SCALE   500m

PATH JOINS LANE LEADING UPHILL 010

5

ROUTE GUIDE AND MAPS

Holden Farm Right on the Way you'll find *Holden Farm Camping* (Map 4; ☎ 07599-553740, 🖳 holdenfarm.co.uk; 🐾 on lead; Easter to end Sep) with tent pitches (from £15pp, walk-in rate usually around the £10-12 mark) in a large field opposite the farmhouse. There are showers, toilets and washing-up facilities. They prefer to know people are coming but will always make space for SDW walkers; the charge can be paid in cash on arrival.

Beauworth *The Milbury's* (Map 5; ☎ 01962-771248, 🖳 themilburyspub.syn thasite.com; food Tue-Sat noon-2pm & 6-9pm, Sun-Mon noon-2pm; 🐾 on

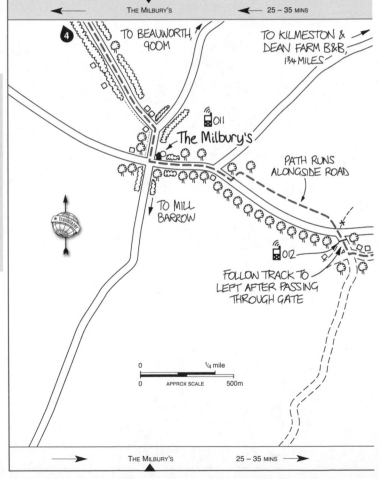

THE MILBURY'S ← — 25 – 35 MINS

4

TO BEAUWORTH, 900M

TO KILMESTON & DEAN FARM B&B, 1¾ MILES

011

The Milbury's

PATH RUNS ALONGSIDE ROAD

TO MILL BARROW

012

FOLLOW TRACK TO LEFT AFTER PASSING THROUGH GATE

0   ¼ mile

0   APPROX SCALE   500m

THE MILBURY'S   25 – 35 MINS →

ROUTE GUIDE AND MAPS

lead) is a pub full of character and an ideal lunch stop. A filled baguette and chips costs from £5.95; most mains are around £10. They also do **B&B** (1T/2D, all en suite; ●; Ⓛ) from £35pp (sgl occ £45). It's worth dropping in just for a drink (though the pub is always closed 3-6pm) and to admire the 250-year-old **indoor treadmill** and 300ft-deep (92m) **well** lit all the way to the bottom. They also have a traditional skittles alley.

If you're staying at *Dean Farm* (off Map 5; ☎ 01962-771286, 🖳 warrdean farm.co.uk; 1D private facilities, 1D/1T both en suite; ●; WI-FI; Ⓛ) take the

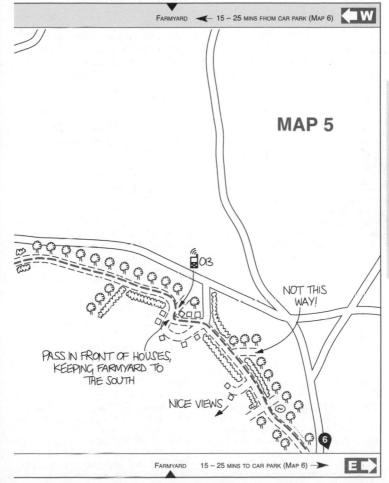

FARMYARD ◄── 15 – 25 MINS FROM CAR PARK (MAP 6) ◄W

MAP 5

013

NOT THIS WAY!

PASS IN FRONT OF HOUSES, KEEPING FARMYARD TO THE SOUTH

NICE VIEWS

6

FARMYARD   15 – 25 MINS TO CAR PARK (MAP 6) ──► E

ROUTE GUIDE AND MAPS

road north to Kilmeston. B&B, with a substantial continental breakfast, costs from £45pp (sgl occ room rate). Closed at time of research but reopening in 2022.

Beacon Hill The highlight of this stage appears rather unexpectedly at the top of Beacon Hill (Map 6), a National Nature Reserve and the first real taste of steep downland scenery. The view over the Meon Valley to Old Winchester Hill is a fine reward. Beacon Hill is one of a number of hills in southern England where beacons or bonfires were lit to warn of invasions, most notably in the 16th century because of the Spanish Armada. It was lit more recently, in June 2012, as part of the celebrations for the Queen's Diamond Jubilee.

W← EXTON TO WINCHESTER   MAPS 6-1

Though most walkers will probably be eager to get to the end by now, these final **12 miles (19.5km, 4¼-6hrs)** are not without their charms for those prepared to dally awhile. The initial climb out of **Exton** to **Beacon Hill** (Map 6), a National Nature Reserve, is perhaps the stiffest, though the kites and kestrels that follow your progress from above are a welcome distraction. Thereafter the route continues along a combination of hedge-lined paths and country lanes, via the turn-off to the village of **Cheriton** (Map 4a; p82) and straight through **Chilcomb** (Map 2) to the final 'bump' along the trail, **Cheesefoot Head** (Map 2), after which the South Downs Way admirably does its best to avoid schlepping through the suburbs on its way into **Winchester** (Map 1; see p76), the City Mill – and the end of your adventure.

EXTON   MAP 6

The Meon valley is known for its natural beauty and also for the Meon villages, all of which claim to be the prettiest in the area. Exton is the smallest of them, if you discount the adjoining hamlets of Meonstoke and Corhampton, and dates back to at least AD940 when it was first mentioned in official documents. It also merited an entry in the Domesday Book of 1086, described as a hamlet of one church and two mills.

Several readers have recommended comfortable, walker-friendly *Crossways B&B* (☎ 07904-047679, ☐ www.cross waysb.com; 1D or T or Tr en suite; WI-FI). They charge from £60pp for two in the room (reduction on full rate for sgl occ) for B&B in the self-contained annexe which

has its own kitchen. Cake on arrival and you make your own breakfast with everything provided – even for a full English!

The Shoe Inn (☎ 01489-877526, ☐ theshoeexton.co.uk; **fb**; 🐾; food Mon-Fri noon-2.15pm & 6-9pm, Sat/Sun noon-3pm & 6-9/8.30pm) is a friendly village pub with real ales and good food though it's closed 3.30-6pm during the week. It offers sandwiches (£8), pastries and soups at lunchtime, while the main menu includes slow-cooked belly of pork (£14.95) and haddock in beer batter (small/large £9/13); they always have a vegan option too. Booking is advised in the evenings. The pub's name derives from the building next door which used to be the village cobbler's. There's a nice beer garden across the road.

CORHAMPTON/MEONSTOKE MAP 6

A short distance south of Exton, Corhampton and nearby Meonstoke are useful for a village shop and a good place to stay. If you do stay down here note that there's a shortcut back to the South Downs Way following the disused railway track (see Map 7).

Meonstoke Village Store (☎ 01489-877374, ☐ www.meonstokepostoffice andvillagestores.co.uk; Mon-Sat 6am-5.30pm, Sun 7am-noon) incorporates the **post office** (Mon-Fri 9am-5.30pm, Sat to 12.30pm) and is 500m south of Exton. There's a good range of local produce here.

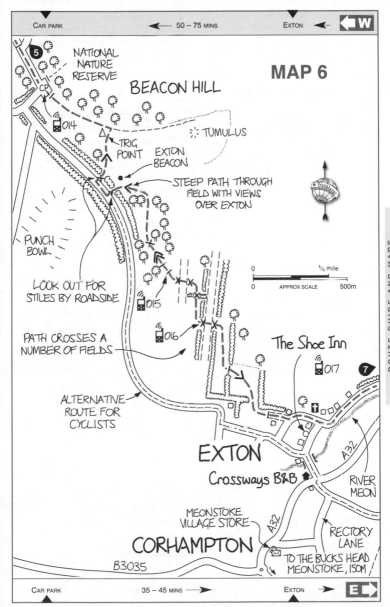

5

NATIONAL NATURE RESERVE

CP

014

BEACON HILL

MAP 6

☀ TUMULUS

△ TRIG POINT

EXTON BEACON

STEEP PATH THROUGH FIELD WITH VIEWS OVER EXTON

PUNCH BOWL

LOOK OUT FOR STILES BY ROADSIDE

015

016

0   ¼ mile
0   APPROX SCALE   500m

PATH CROSSES A NUMBER OF FIELDS

The Shoe Inn

017

7

ALTERNATIVE ROUTE FOR CYCLISTS

EXTON

Crossways B&B

MEONSTOKE VILLAGE STORE

CORHAMPTON

B3035

A32

RIVER MEON

RECTORY LANE

TO THE BUCKS HEAD MEONSTOKE, 150M

ROUTE GUIDE AND MAPS

The Bucks Head (☎ 01489-877313, ☐ www.thebucksheadmeonstoke.co.uk; **fb**; food Wed-Sun noon-3pm, Wed-Sat 6-9pm, Sun to 8.30pm; WI-FI; 🐾), on Bucks Head Hill, is another welcoming pub and they also offer **B&B** (2T/3D, all en suite;

🛏; Ⓛ) from £50pp (sgl occ £75). At the time of research they were closed on Monday and Tuesday (other than for B&B bookings) but they hope this will change post COVID. Follow the A32 south and turn first left onto Bucks Head Hill.

E→ EXTON TO BURITON   MAPS 6-10

This fine stretch of the Way covering **12½ miles (20km, 4½hrs-6hrs)** takes the walker beside **Old Winchester Hill** (Map 7) the top of which boasts one of the finest Iron Age hill-fort sites in the south. The path skirts around the southern side of the fort – you have to pass through a gate to enter the site itself – but there is a more direct trail (see Map 7) that goes straight to the heart of the fort from the path.

Following a flying visit to the friendly fly-fisherman of **Meon Springs** (Map 8), and after the turn off to the gorgeous village of **East Meon** (Map 8a)

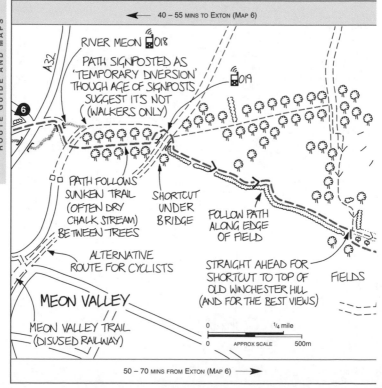

ROUTE GUIDE AND MAPS

← 40 – 55 MINS TO EXTON (MAP 6)

RIVER MEON 📶018

PATH SIGNPOSTED AS 'TEMPORARY DIVERSION' THOUGH AGE OF SIGNPOSTS SUGGEST IT'S NOT (WALKERS ONLY)

📶019

A32

6

PATH FOLLOWS SUNKEN TRAIL (OFTEN DRY CHALK STREAM) BETWEEN TREES

SHORTCUT UNDER BRIDGE

FOLLOW PATH ALONG EDGE OF FIELD

ALTERNATIVE ROUTE FOR CYCLISTS

STRAIGHT AHEAD FOR SHORTCUT TO TOP OF OLD WINCHESTER HILL (AND FOR THE BEST VIEWS)

FIELDS

MEON VALLEY

MEON VALLEY TRAIL (DISUSED RAILWAY)

0   ¼ mile
0   APPROX SCALE   500m

50 – 70 MINS FROM EXTON (MAP 6) →

there is a tough pull up the slope for about two miles to **The Sustainability Centre** (Map 9, p92). It is around here that the true line of the Downs begins, stretching east as a high-level ridge, interrupted only by a few river valleys, all the way to Beachy Head near Eastbourne.

The Way continues along the broad ridge with fine views over the Meon valley to the north culminating in the highest point of the South Downs at **Butser Hill** (270m), another National Nature Reserve. From the car park, which has toilets and a snack shop, the Way slopes down towards the less-than-attractive A3 dual carriageway that slices through the lower flanks.

Once past the din of racing traffic the path climbs steadily back to the top of the downland escarpment above Buriton, passing through **Queen Elizabeth Country Park** (Map 10; see box p96), a magnificent natural mixed woodland that covers the rolling Downs for miles around, just as it has done through the centuries. If the accommodation in **Buriton** is booked up you could head into **Petersfield** (Map 10a, p99), where there are several more places.

IRON AGE HILL FORT ← 50 – 70 MINS FROM WHITEWOOL FARM (MAP 8) ◄ W

MAP 7

020
IRON AGE
HILL FORT &
DISTANCE DIAL

023

GRASSY
BOWL

GO THROUGH GATE
AT FORK OF ROAD
AND DROP THROUGH
FIELDS

QUARRY

024

022

OLD
WINCHESTER
HILL

OLD
WINCHESTER
HILL NATURE
RESERVE

TURN LEFT AT
FARMYARD –
WHEN HEADING
WEST–EAST

025

021

PATH HAS BEEN
DIVIDED – WALKERS
KEEP TO UPPER
PATH

NO ENTRANCE
INTO FORT HERE

IRON AGE HILL FORT 40 – 50 MINS TO WHITEWOOL FARM (MAP 8) → E ►

Old Winchester Hill A typical downland hill of chalk grassland and steep ancient woodland and a National Nature Reserve. The top of the hill boasts one of the finest **Iron Age hill-fort** (Map 7) sites in the south. The old earthworks clearly mark the outline of the fort and a display board has an artist's impression of how it once would have looked when the earthy banks were lined with the wooden stakes that formed the walls of the fort. It is clear why it was positioned here since the views in all directions are spectacular, stretching as far as the Isle of Wight on a clear day. Presumably the soldiers of the time also appreciated the views for the strategic advantage it gave them.

Meon Springs Right on the SDW is the welcoming *Meon Springs* (Map 8; ☎ 01730-823134, 🖥 meonsprings.com), a fly-fishing base. Though the kitchen

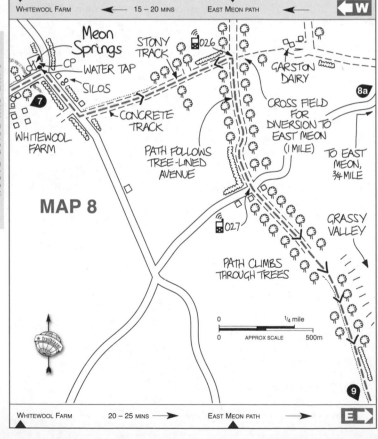

ROUTE GUIDE AND MAPS

WHITEWOOL FARM ◄— 15 – 20 MINS — EAST MEON PATH ◄— W

Meon Springs
CP
WATER TAP
SILOS
7
WHITEWOOL FARM

STONY TRACK
026

GARSTON DAIRY

8a

CONCRETE TRACK

CROSS FIELD FOR DIVERSION TO EAST MEON (1 MILE)

TO EAST MEON, ¾ MILE

PATH FOLLOWS TREE-LINED AVENUE

MAP 8

027

GRASSY VALLEY

PATH CLIMBS THROUGH TREES

0   ¼ mile
0   APPROX SCALE   500m

9

WHITEWOOL FARM   20 – 25 MINS —►   EAST MEON PATH —►   E

was being revamped at the time of research, you can still pick up a hot or cold drink and an ice-cream. When the kitchen's complete, they'll offer bacon rolls and sausage rolls. It opens at 8am and closes when the last fishermen go home (normally just before sunset), and there's an honesty box for payment if no one's around. There is now a **water tap** on the Way. You can **camp** (from £10pp; 🐴) here too if you have a tent. There's a toilet and washing facilities but no showers. Campers can just turn up but occasionally they are fully booked so it's worth checking the calendar on their website or phoning ahead. They have yurts and shepherd's huts too, but these can only be booked for multi-day stays.

EAST MEON   MAP 8a

East Meon is only a half-hour detour from the official path and is well worth the effort for a lunch stop or overnight stay. There are records of a settlement here as far back as AD400 and the whole area was once a royal estate belonging to King Alfred. If in the village, take a look at the 900-year-old **church** at the foot of the hill where you can also admire the 14th-century **courthouse**, once part of a monastery.

The **post office** (Mon-Fri 9am-5pm, Sat to noon) and **East Meon Stores** (Mon-Fri 7am-6pm, Sat to 5pm, Sun 8am-1pm) share premises on the High St. The Stores are surprisingly well stocked. Note, they accept cash only.

Stagecoach's No 67 **bus** service (Winchester–Petersfield) stops here; see p46.

Where to stay and eat

In the centre of the village, *Ye Olde George Inn* (☎ 01730 823481, 🖥 yeoldegeorge inn.net; WI-FI; 🐴) does upmarket pub **food** (Mon-Sat noon-2.30pm & 6-8.30pm, Sun noon-3pm & 6-8pm; book ahead at weekends); mains cost £16-26. They also offer **B&B** (4D/1D or T, all en suite; ▼; WI-FI; ⓛ; 🐴) for £45-65pp (sgl occ from £75). Note, the pub is closed 3-5.45pm Monday to Saturday but open all day on Sunday.

ROUTE GUIDE AND MAPS

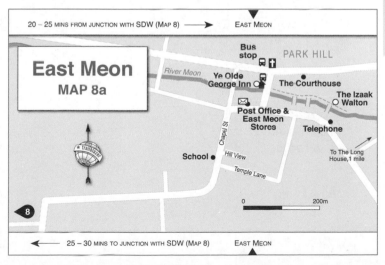

20 – 25 MINS FROM JUNCTION WITH SDW (MAP 8) ⟶   EAST MEON

East Meon
MAP 8a

River Meon

Bus stop

PARK HILL

Ye Olde George Inn

The Courthouse

Post Office & East Meon Stores

The Izaak Walton

Telephone

Chapel St

School ●

Hill View

Temple Lane

To The Long House, 1 mile

0   200m

8

⟵ 25 – 30 MINS TO JUNCTION WITH SDW (MAP 8)   EAST MEON

The Long House (off Map 8 & Map 8a; ☎ 07889 640353, ☎ 01730-823239, 🖳 thelonghouseeastmeon.co.uk; 1D/1T adjacent private bathroom; ☻; WI-FI; 🐾; Ⓛ) lies just round the corner from the end of Frogmore Lane, about a mile from the village on the Ramsdean road. B&B in this friendly place, with possibly the world's most powerful shower, costs from £45pp (sgl occ £55).

The Izaak Walton (☎ 01730-823252, 🖳 izaakwalton.biz; **fb**; food Tue-Sat noon-2pm & 6-8.30/9pm, Sun noon-6pm; WI-FI; 🐾) is a freehouse pub named after a famous local angler and it offers a cheaper pub-grub option (mains £10.25-15.25) to Ye Olde George Inn. It's closed every Monday, though, apart from bank holidays, and the pub closes 2.30-6pm Tuesday to Thursday.

The Sustainability Centre As you'd expect from the name, everything here is environmentally friendly and they use renewable energy. The rate for the hostel accommodation in *South Downs Eco Lodge* (☎ 01730-823549, 🖳 sustain ability-centre.org; 2T/10Tr/1 x 5-bed 'suite', shared facilities; WI-FI) is on a room basis (£48/52/68). Booking in general is recommended as the hostel is

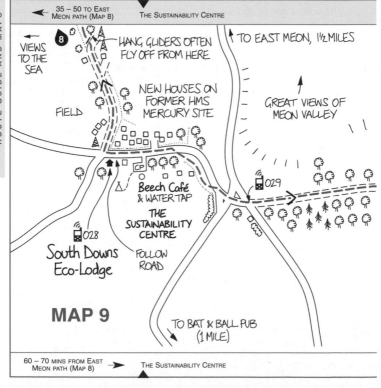

← 35 – 50 TO EAST MEON PATH (MAP 8)

THE SUSTAINABILITY CENTRE

8

VIEWS TO THE SEA

HANG GLIDERS OFTEN FLY OFF FROM HERE

↑ TO EAST MEON, 1½ MILES

FIELD

NEW HOUSES ON FORMER HMS MERCURY SITE

GREAT VIEWS OF MEON VALLEY

CP

Beech Café & WATER TAP

029

THE SUSTAINABILITY CENTRE

028

South Downs Eco-Lodge

FOLLOW ROAD

MAP 9

TO BAT & BALL PUB (1 MILE)

60 – 70 MINS FROM EAST MEON PATH (MAP 8) →

THE SUSTAINABILITY CENTRE

sometimes taken over by groups for sole occupancy use; online booking is available through their website. **Campers** (£15pp; 🐾 on lead) will appreciate the fact that they allow camp fires in designated areas (and they sell firewood). They also have **yurts** sleeping 2-4 people (Apr-Oct only, booking essential and two-night minimum stay for weekends); bedding is provided and the rate (£80-130) includes a batch of firewood for the heater. The (solar) shower block is open April to October; running water and compost toilets are available all year. They also now offer **B&B** (1S/4D/4T/2Qd, all en suite) in their eco lodge; rates (£75/S, £95/D or T, £125-130/Qd) are on a room basis and include a continental breakfast.

The hostel has self-catering facilities (though due to COVID these weren't available at the time of research) but there is also the on-site *Beech Café* (☎ 01730-823755, 🖥 thebeechcafe.co.uk; Wed-Sun & Bank Hol Mondays 8.30am-4pm, breakfast 8.30-10am, lunches from 11.30am; WI-FI; Ⓛ; 🐾 on lead), a vegetarian and vegan café which can also provide packed lunches if booked in advance. *(cont'd on p96)*

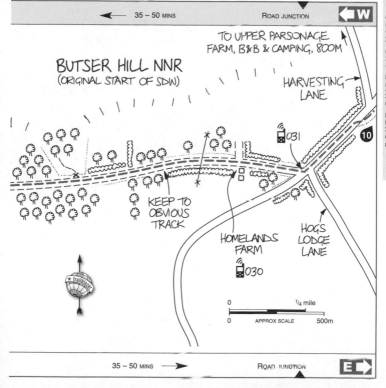

ROUTE GUIDE AND MAPS

← 35 – 50 MINS   ROAD JUNCTION   W

TO UPPER PARSONAGE FARM, B&B & CAMPING, 800M

BUTSER HILL NNR
(ORIGINAL START OF SDW)

HARVESTING LANE

031

10

KEEP TO OBVIOUS TRACK

HOMELANDS FARM

030

HOGS LODGE LANE

★ trailblazer

0   ¼ mile
0   APPROX SCALE   500M

35 – 50 MINS →   ROAD JUNCTION   E

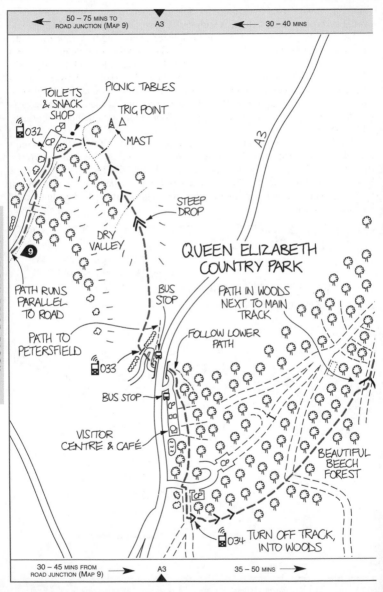

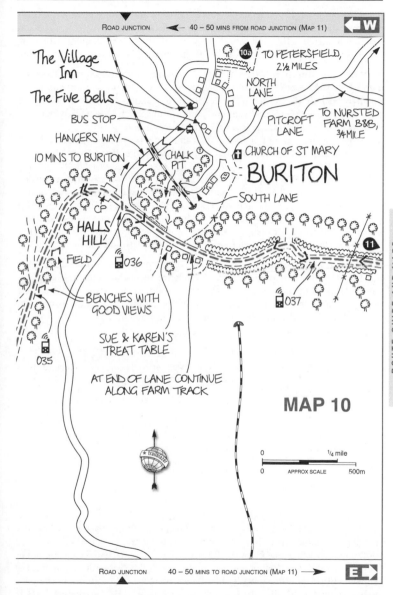

The Village Inn

The Five Bells

BUS STOP

HANGERS WAY

10 MINS TO BURITON

CHALK PIT

TO PETERSFIELD, 2½ MILES

NORTH LANE

PITCROFT LANE

TO NURSTED FARM B&B, ¾ MILE

CHURCH OF ST MARY

BURITON

SOUTH LANE

HALLS HILL

FIELD

036

11

BENCHES WITH GOOD VIEWS

035

037

SUE & KAREN'S TREAT TABLE

AT END OF LANE CONTINUE ALONG FARM TRACK

MAP 10

0   ¼ mile
0   APPROX SCALE   500m

ROUTE GUIDE AND MAPS

(cont'd from p93) If you're staying here and need an evening meal, the closest pub that does food is the excellent ***Bat & Ball*** (☎ 023-9263 2692, 🖳 batand ballclanfield.co.uk; **fb**; food Mon-Sat noon-8.30pm, Sun to 7.30pm; WI-FI; 🐾 bar only), about half an hour's walk away, just before the village of Hambledon.

Butser Hill Butser Hill (see Map 9) is another **National Nature Reserve**, earning its status for its fine chalk grassland. It is home to over 30 species of butterfly including the tiny, difficult-to-spot but exquisite chalkhill blue (see p65). It was also the original start/end point for the South Downs Way before it was decided to extend the path all the way to Winchester.

If you're walking east, before you reach the car park at the top of the hill, a signpost directs you north towards ***Upper Parsonage Farm*** (off Map 9; ☎ 01730-823490, 🖳 upperparsonagefarm.co.uk; 1D en suite; WI-FI; Ⓛ), about half a mile from the Way, on Harvesting Lane. This 1400-acre farm has **B&B** accommodation in either a large room (£47.50-55pp, sgl occ room rate), or in a cosy **shepherd's hut** in the garden (1D, toilet and shower facilities; £55-85 for the hut). Note that the breakfasts are no longer cooked, but various breakfast items are left for you to help yourself to in the morning. You can also **camp** (£10-20pp) in the garden. Each pitch has its own toilets and shower facilties.

Queen Elizabeth Country Park The South Downs Way cuts right through the heart of this vast protected area which includes the chalk downland of Butser Hill. To the east of the hill the park is dominated by one of the largest expanses of unbroken woodland cover in the South-East, comprising both ancient broadleaved wood and beech and conifer plantations.

❑ QUEEN ELIZABETH COUNTRY PARK   Map 10, p94

The park (open all the time) is popular with daytrippers and picnickers largely thanks to its proximity to the main A3 road. The **Visitor Centre** (☎ 023-9259 5040, 🖳 hants.gov.uk/qecp; **fb**; Mar-Oct Mon-Fri 10am-5pm, Sat & Sun from 9am, Nov-Feb 10am-4pm) can provide maps and guides to the park. The centre houses a **shop** and *café* offering cakes and snacks.

Stagecoach's No 37 **bus** (see p46; Havant–Petersfield) stops on the A3. The northbound stop lies just beyond the slip road under the A3 (the slip road needs to be used with care). Access to the park from the stop on the south side is no problem. Either way this is a **request stop** so make sure you let the driver know you want to stop here and also if you are waiting at the bus stop make sure you can be seen.

W ← BURITON TO EXTON   MAPS 10-6

This fine stretch of the Way covering **12½ miles (20km, 4¼-6hrs)** takes in a couple of notable hills. There's a lengthy perambulation around the perimeter of the **Queen Elizabeth Country Park** (QECP; Map 10) and a crossing of the A3 – a metaphorical low point immediately preceding a literal high point, for **Butser Hill** (Map 9) is actually the highest point on the entire trail. The path then meanders to the second major elevation, **Old Winchester Hill**

ROUTE GUIDE AND MAPS

(Map 7), lying just east of Exton and topped by a fine Iron Age hill-fort. Apparently it's one of the finest examples in the South according to experts, though I daresay the average walker will find the gentle bumps in the ground more curious than jaw-dropping. The official path, incidentally, actually skirts around the fort's southern side, and descends in a rather circuitous fashion, though there is a more direct and popular descent (see Map 7) that leaves from the centre of the fort.

Given these hills, it's hardly surprising that there a couple of fairly brutal ascents on this stage. But mercifully there are also several places to stop, rest and snack along the way, including cafés at: QECP; the top of Butser Hill (closed at the time of research but presumably it will reopen in a post-COVID world); **The Sustainability Centre** (Map 9); and at the friendly fishing centre of **Meon Springs** (Map 8).

It should also be noted that with no B&B in **Exton** (p86) at the end of the stage, the only option is in **Meonstoke** (p86).   [*Next route overview p86*]

BURITON   MAP 10, p95
Buriton is yet another pretty village commanding an enviable position at the foot of the wooded downland escarpment.

The **Church of St Mary**, by the duck pond, is of particular interest as the interior dates back to the 12th century.

Wheel Drive's No 94 **bus** operates between here and Petersfield (see p47).

Where to stay and eat
At the time of research *Nursted Farm* (✉ elaine.bray@btconnect.com), a 1½-mile walk up the lane, wasn't offering B&B but they may do in the future so email them to check.

The Five Bells (☎ 01730-263584, ✉ fivebells-buriton.co.uk; food Thur-Sat from 4pm, Sun noon-6pm; WI-FI; 🐾 bar only) is a great pub with friendly staff and excellent food (most mains cost around £9.95-12.95). At the time of research they were only open limited hours but hopefully will open more after COVID.

Nearby *The Village Inn* (☎ 01730-233440, ✉ villageinnburiton.co.uk), a more upscale pub, was closed at the time of research but they hope to open again and when they do they will provide **food** and **B&B**.

PETERSFIELD   MAP 10a, p99
This market town still retains pockets of charm, despite attempts to turn it into something bland and modern with supermarkets and a small shopping arcade.

An oasis of calm amongst the bustle is afforded by **Petersfield Physic Garden** (✉ petersfieldphysicgarden.org.uk; daily 9am-5pm, winter to 4pm; free), reached via an alley off the High St. It features many of the characteristics and plant varieties of a 17th-century town garden with herbs, topiary and an orchard and plenty of benches to relax on with your takeaway lunch.

Walkers on a day off might fancy a dip in Petersfield's newly renovated **heated** **open-air swimming pool** (☎ 01730-265143, ✉ petersfieldpool.org; Apr-Sep 6.30am-8pm; from £4.50/30 mins, £6.50/1hr) on Tor Way. See the website for more details. The other main tourist attraction in town, **Petersfield Museum** (☎ 01730-262601, ✉ petersfieldmuseum.co .uk; Wed-Sat 10am-5pm, Sun 11am-4pm; £8), has undergone a multi-million pound revamp which in effect has doubled the museum in size. The museum is largely housed in a Victorian police station, which before that was a court house, and exhibitions include a collection of 175 years of truncheons and handcuffs from the

Hampshire Constabulary – the oldest county police force in Britain; part of the revamp means the former police cells can now be visited and the court house has been restored. The Flora Twort Gallery now houses travelling exhibitions but also has some of the Petersfield-inspired watercolours and pastels of the late artist.

Services

The **Tourist Information Centre** (☎ 01730-264182, 🖥 www.visitpetersfield.com; Mon-Fri 9am-5pm) is now in the town hall on Heath Rd. They have information about accommodation but can't do any bookings.

The **library** (Tue, Wed & Fri 10am-5pm, Thur to 1.30pm, Sat to 4pm) has free wi-fi and **internet** access plus places where you can charge your laptop/phone.

On the High St there are various **banks** with ATMs, as well as a Boots **pharmacy** (Mon-Sat 8.30am-5.30pm, Sun 10am-4pm) and an M&S Foodstore (Mon-Fri 8am-8pm, Sat to 7pm, Sun 10.30am-4.30pm), while just off it to the north is a large Waitrose **supermarket** (Mon-Sat 7.30am-8pm, Sun 10am-4pm). There's a large Tesco south of the town centre (Mon-Fri 8am-10pm, Sat to 9pm, Sun 10am-4pm).

The **post office** (Mon, Wed, Thur & Fri 9am-5.30pm, Tue 9.30am-5.30pm, Sat 9am-12.30pm) is on the edge of The Square. There are two good bookshops: **Waterstones** (Mon-Sat 9am-5.30pm, Sun 10am-4pm) and **One Tree Books** (Mon-Sat 9am-5pm), which also has a nice *café* (see Where to eat).

Public transport

Petersfield is a stop on South Western Railway's London Waterloo to Portsmouth **train** service (see box p44).

Buses (see pp46-7) leave from the town centre. The most useful services are: Stagecoach's No 54 (to Chichester) and their Nos 91, 92 & 93 (to Midhurst); Stagecoach's No 67 (to Winchester), No 37 (to Havant), and No 38 (to Alton); and Wheel Drive's No 94 (to Buriton).

For a **taxi** or luggage transfer contact: **14U cars** (☎ 01730-300738, ☎ 07795-101895, 🖥 14ucarspetersfield.com).

Where to stay

Campers will have to trudge 1¼ miles (2km) out of town to reach the very basic *Ridge Farm Campsite* (off Map 10a; ☎ 07850-873055; 🐕), where a field and two portaloo toilets await those who wish to pitch their tent (£15pp). The turn-off for the campsite is about 200 metres past *The Cricketers Inn* (☎ 01730-261035, 🖥 www .cricketersinnsteep.co.uk; **fb**; WI-FI; 🐕; food daily noon-9pm). To get to the campsite, walk north-west along Station Rd, turn right at the roundabout up Bell Hill, and keep walking straight, over the A3 dual carriageway, and past The Cricketers Inn before taking the next left turn down a country track.

At 80 Rushes Rd, just west of the railway station, *Rushes Road B&B* (off Map 10a; ☎ 01730-261638, 🖥 rushes-road .co.uk; 1D or T private bathroom; ☛; WI-FI; Ⓛ) is run by a friendly former tour guide. B&B costs from £37.50pp (sgl occ £50); note that they do not accept card payment. From Swan St, walk under the railway bridge, turn left onto Rushes Rd then take the next right. *The Old Drum* (☎ 01730-300208, 🖥 theolddrum.com; 1S/4D/1Qd, all en suite; WI-FI) is a beautiful 18th-century inn, now classified as a 'boutique hotel bistro café' with friendly staff, good food (see opposite) and very smart rooms. B&B costs £47.50-62.50pp (sgl £75-85). At the time of research their single and quad rooms were being refurbished but they should be open in 2022.

Where to eat and drink

Petersfield is replete with eating places; some of them are excellent, particularly the town's numerous independent cafés.

Cafés Snug and rightly popular, *Natural Food Deli* (☎ 01730-858183, 🖥 thenatural fooddeli.co.uk; Mon-Sat 8.30am-4pm; WI-FI; 🐕 bar area) is a health-conscious café with rustic décor, wholesome food and great tea, coffee and cakes. Another fine choice, on the corner of Bakery Lane, is the bright and cheery *Bakery Lane Tea Room* (Mon-Fri 9am-3pm, Sat to 4pm, closed first Monday of the month), a traditional-style

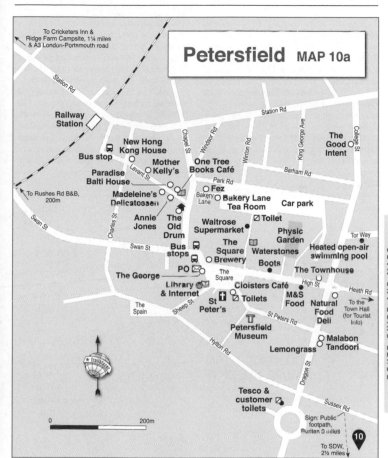

Petersfield MAP 10a

To Cricketers Inn &
Ridge Farm Campsite, 1¼ miles
& A3 London–Portsmouth road

Station Rd

Railway Station

Station Rd

Bus stop

New Hong Kong House

Mother Kelly's

Chapel St

Windsor Rd

One Tree Books Café

Winton Rd

King George Ave

College St

The Good Intent

Barham Rd

Paradise Balti House

Lavant St

Park Rd

Fez

Bakery Lane

Bakery Lane Tea Room

Car park

Madeleine's Delicatessen

To Rushes Rd B&B, 200m

Charles St

Annie Jones

The Old Drum

Waitrose Supermarket

Toilet

Physic Garden

Tor Way

Swan St

Swan St

Bus stops

The Square Brewery

Waterstones

Boots

Heated open-air swimming pool

The Townhouse

High St

Heath Rd

The George

PO

The Square

Library & Internet

Cloisters Café

Toilets

M&S Food

Natural Food Deli

To the Town Hall (for Tourist Info)

The Spain

Sheep St

St Peter's

St Peters Rd

Petersfield Museum

Hylton Rd

Lemongrass

Malabon Tandoori

Dragon St

Tesco & customer toilets

Sussex Rd

Sign: Public footpath, Buriton 0 miles

10

To SDW, 2½ miles

0   200m

trailblazer

English tearoom that's good for cream teas, jacket potatoes and the like.

Close to the railway station, *Madeleine's Delicatessen* (Mon-Sat 8.45am-5pm) is another great place for filled sandwiches and baguettes; you can eat in here too. Nearby, **One Tree Books** (see Services) has a *café* (Mon-Sat 8.45am-5pm) at the back of the shop. It's a friendly place that offers a good line of warm ciabatta rolls with various fillings (£7.75 each). Beside St Peter's Church, *Cloisters*

Café (☎ 07951 269419; fb; WI-FI; 🐾; daily 8am-5pm) is tiny but has extra seating outdoors, overlooking The Square. There's a good choice of breakfasts here.

Pubs *The Old Drum* (see Where to Stay; food daily 9am-3pm; WI-FI; 🐾) serves a range of breakfasts in the morning and then lunches; after 3pm they just serve drinks – there is a good selection of gins and ales – and bar snacks. This was once a favourite hangout of author HG Wells.

Round the corner, *The Square Brewery* (☎ 01730-264291, 🖥 www.square brewery.co.uk; food Wed-Sun noon-3pm; WI-FI; 🐾) is a welcoming locals-favourite Fuller's-owned pub. Pre-COVID it was a popular venue for live music and hopes to be so again. Also on The Square, *The George* (☎ 01730-265551, 🖥 www .grea tukpubs.co.uk/the-george-petersfield; food daily noon-8pm; WI-FI; 🐾) is a pub and restaurant which feels more like a city bar than a market-town pub, but is popular nonetheless.

The Good Intent (☎ 01730-263838, 🖥 good-intent-petersfield.co.uk; food Mon-Fri noon-3pm & 5-9pm, Sat & Sun noon-9pm; WI-FI; 🐾) serves standard pub grub such as gammon, egg & chips (£9.95). It is a short walk out of town, on College St.

Back on High St you'll find the award-winning *The Townhouse* (☎ 01730-265630, 🖥 townhousepetersfield.co.uk; **fb**; 🐾; food Wed-Thur noon-3pm & 5-9pm, Fri & Sat same but to 9.30pm, Sun noon-5pm) feels more like a restaurant than a pub. The quite pricey menu only adds to

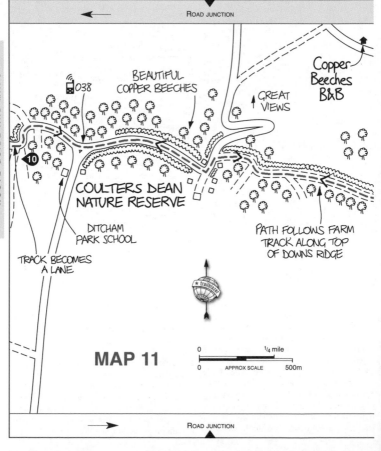

ROUTE GUIDE AND MAPS

ROAD JUNCTION

038

BEAUTIFUL
COPPER BEECHES

GREAT
VIEWS

Copper
Beeches
B&B

10

COULTERS DEAN
NATURE RESERVE

DITCHAM
PARK SCHOOL

TRACK BECOMES
A LANE

PATH FOLLOWS FARM
TRACK ALONG TOP
OF DOWNS RIDGE

MAP 11

0   ¼ mile
0   APPROX SCALE   500m

ROAD JUNCTION

this impression though there's no doubting the quality of the food, and if available the £12 chilli nachos sharing plate is delicious and filling.

Restaurants & takeaways One of the coolest places to eat is tucked away down the narrow alleyway known as Bakery Lane: *Fez* (☎ 01730-231266, 🖳 fezpeters field.com; daily 10am-9pm, food from 11.30am) is a Turkish restaurant, meze bar and café rolled into one and is a great place for lunch, an evening meal, or even just a

coffee (they have tables in the alleyway). Mains start at £11.95 for the Turkish equivalent of a pizza, *lahmacun*. Nearby, on Lavant St, *Annie Jones* (☎ 01730-262728, 🖳 anniejones.co.uk; **fb**; WI-FI; 🐾) is a long-established **tapas bar** (Tue-Thur noon-2pm & 6-9pm, Fri & Sat noon-2.30pm & 6-9.30pm) with good food and a pleasant atmosphere.

South-east of the centre, at 16-18 Dragon St, *Lemongrass* (☎ 01730-267077, 🖳 lemongrassgroup.co.uk/petersfield; daily noon-2.30pm & 5.30-11pm) is a good qual-

ROUTE GUIDE AND MAPS

ity yet inexpensive Thai restaurant with dishes such as green curry from £8.25. Next door *Malabon Tandoori* (☎ 01730-268352, 🖥 malabonrestaurant.co.uk; daily noon-2.30pm & 5-10pm) serves Indian & Bangladeshi meals to eat-in or takeaway. For a smarter Indian-food option, try *The Paradise Balti House* (☎ 01730-265162, 🖥 www.paradisebaltipetersfield.co.uk; daily

5-10pm) at 23 Lavant St. The best Chinese takeaway, meanwhile, is *New Hong Kong House* (☎ 01730-265256; Tue-Sun 5-10pm), also on Lavant St.

Also on Lavant St there's *Mother Kelly's Famous Fish & Chips* (☎ 01730-265702, 🖥 motherkellysfishandchips.co .uk; Mon 5-9pm, Tue-Sat 11.30am-2pm & 5-9pm) at No 29.

❑ **IMPORTANT NOTE – WALKING TIMES**

All times in this book refer only to the time spent walking. You will need to add 20-30% to allow for rests, photography, checking the map, drinking water etc.

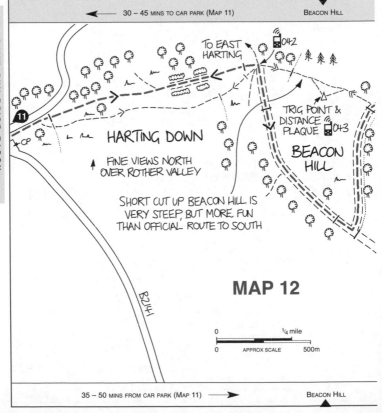

MAP 12

E→ BURITON TO COCKING

MAPS 10-14

The route from Buriton follows tracks and lanes along the top of the South Downs escarpment for **11¼ miles (18km, 3¾-4¾hrs)**. It is very wooded before reaching **South Harting** (Map 11) so although the views are limited there is plenty of beautiful shady woodland to enjoy. About 10 minutes south of the Way where it crosses the B2146 is **Uppark House** (see box p104).

After South Harting the trees begin to thin out as the Way passes over **Harting Down** (Map 12). The views open up over the patchwork fields below and the path climbs even higher onto **Beacon Hill**, one of two Beacon Hills on the Way. There then follows another wooded section, the **Monkton Estate** (Map 13), where it's worth listening out for peacocks, before the path continues through the pastureland of **Cocking Down**.

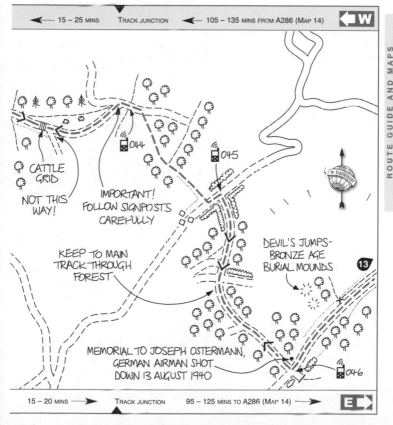

← 15 – 25 MINS   TRACK JUNCTION   ← 105 – 135 MINS FROM A286 (MAP 14)

ROUTE GUIDE AND MAPS

044

045

CATTLE GRID

NOT THIS WAY!

IMPORTANT! FOLLOW SIGNPOSTS CAREFULLY

KEEP TO MAIN TRACK THROUGH FOREST

DEVIL'S JUMPS- BRONZE AGE BURIAL MOUNDS

13

MEMORIAL TO JOSEPH OSTERMANN, GERMAN AIRMAN SHOT DOWN 13 AUGUST 1940

046

15 – 20 MINS →   TRACK JUNCTION   95 – 125 MINS TO A286 (MAP 14) →

The Way even takes you past a large **chalk boulder**, positioned there by the artist Andy Goldsworthy and then down to the main road leading to **Cocking** (Map 14). If the accommodation in Cocking is booked up you could head into **Midhurst** (p107, off Map 14), where there are other options.

❑ **UPPARK HOUSE**

Uppark House (off Map 11; ☎ 01730-825415, 🖳 www.nationaltrust.org .uk/uppark-house-and-garden; house Thur-Sun, garden and café daily; £8) is a magnificent 17th-century (Georgian) country home perched high on a hill with extensive views across the Downs and beyond. The house and gardens are now generally open but it is essential to check the website for details as they vary. Note, the café is only open to ticket holders. One of the most remarkable things about Uppark is the near-perfect restoration of the building after it was all but gutted by a rampant fire in 1989.

Stagecoach's No 54 **bus service** calls here (see p46).

SOUTH HARTING   MAP 11, p101

From the top of Harting Down the village of South Harting with its distinctive church steeple is clearly visible and looks very inviting. Note, the road down to the village from the Way doesn't have a footpath, so it's much safer, and more pleasant, to use the pathway running parallel to the road and immediately west of it. It's not a long walk but you do have to climb back up the hill through the woods on the return.

The **Church of St Mary & St Gabriel** is interesting and contains an impressive

ROUTE GUIDE AND MAPS

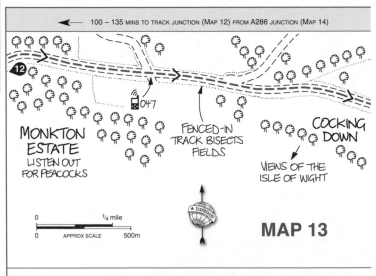

← 100 – 135 MINS TO TRACK JUNCTION (MAP 12) FROM A286 JUNCTION (MAP 14)

12

📱 047

MONKTON ESTATE
LISTEN OUT FOR PEACOCKS

FENCED-IN TRACK BISECTS FIELDS

COCKING DOWN

VIEWS OF THE ISLE OF WIGHT

0   ¼ mile
0   APPROX SCALE   500m

★ trailblazer

MAP 13

95 – 125 MINS TO A286 JUNCTION (MAP 14) FROM TRACK JUNCTION (MAP 12) →

Visit South Harting church to see Philip Jackson's statue of the Archangel Gabriel

statue of the Archangel Gabriel, by sculptor Philip Jackson, suspended from the ceiling. The **village stocks** are still by the path outside the church.

Services

Harting Stores (☎ 01730-825219, 🖳 hart ingstores.co.uk; **fb**; Mon-Fri 7am-6pm, Sat 8am-2pm, Sun to noon) is an excellent village shop, which sells a wide variety of provisions as well as various baked products, wine and beer. It also incorporates the local **post office** (Mon, Tue, Thur & Fri 9am-1pm & 2-5pm, Wed 9am-1pm, Sat 9am-noon). At the time of research the proprietor was hoping he would be allowed to have a sign at the viewpoint by the car park alerting walkers or whoever that they could call the shop saying what they want – such as water and/or food – and someone would bring it up to save the walk up and down.

Stagecoach's No 54 (Petersfield–Chichester) **bus** service calls here as does their No 91 (Midhurst–Petersfield); See pp46-8 for details.

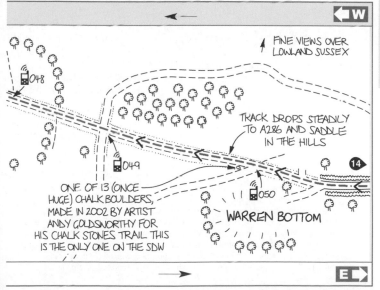

FINE VIEWS OVER LOWLAND SUSSEX

TRACK DROPS STEADILY TO A286 AND SADDLE IN THE HILLS

ONE OF 13 (ONCE HUGE) CHALK BOULDERS, MADE IN 2002 BY ARTIST ANDY GOLDSWORTHY FOR HIS CHALK STONES TRAIL THIS IS THE ONLY ONE ON THE SDW

WARREN BOTTOM

048
049
050

14

W

E

ROUTE GUIDE AND MAPS

Where to stay, eat and drink
The upmarket *White Hart* (☎ 01730-825124, 🖥 www.the-whitehart.co.uk; **fb**; 1T/4D/1Tr/1Qd, all en suite; ✍; WI-FI; 🐾) offers B&B from £35pp (sgl occ £65) though rates can be triple that so advance booking is recommended. The rate includes a continental breakfast but a cooked breakfast (£10) is also available. It also does excellent food (Mon-Fri noon-2.30pm & 5-8.30pm, Sat noon-8.30pm, Sun to 6pm).

Just over a mile west of South Harting along the Petersfield road (B2146) and directly accessible from the Way (see Map 12), is *Copper Beeches* (☎ 01730-826662, 🖥 copperbeeches.net; 1D/1Qd both en suite; ✍; WI-FI; Ⓛ; 🐾) with B&B from £45pp (sgl occ £60, £70 at weekends). The 'quad' has a double bed and bunk beds. During Goodwood events they accept bookings for a minimum of three nights.

W← COCKING TO BURITON   MAPS 14-10

If you've been walking in typically bright South Downs sunshine for the first part of your hike, it may come as a pleasant change to find yourself strolling in some welcome woods (and therefore shade) on this **11¼-mile (18km, 3¾-5hrs) stage**. Though the initial climb out of **Cocking** (Map 14) is on an exposed chalk path – and even takes you past a large **chalk boulder** (Map 13), positioned there by the artist Andy Goldsworthy – thereafter the path plunges into the woodland of the **Monkton Estate**. The first of two **Beacon Hills** on the trail provides some more familiar, open terrain, as does neighbouring **Harting Down** (Map 12), looming above **South Harting** (Map 11; p102), lying to the north of the trail, and **Uppark House** (see p104), a short distance to the south of the path. But it's not long before you're back traipsing between the trees of **Coulters Dean Nature Reserve** (Map 11) on the way to the **Buriton** (Map 10; p95) turn-off.

If accommodation in Buriton is unavailable you could head into **Petersfield** (p97), where there are several more places.   *[Next route overview p96]*

COCKING   **MAP 14, p108**
Cocking is pleasant enough but the busy main road that slices the village in two has rather taken the soul out of the place despite one or two pretty, old cottages. The consolation is that it is not too far from the Way. It is best reached by following the farm

track (by Manor Farm) down the hill to the village rather than walking along the busy main road.

Behind The Malthouse you'll find a bronze plinth known as **Cocking History Column**. Containing relief panels detailing

---

❑ **GLORIOUS GOODWOOD – NOT SO GLORIOUS FOR WALKERS**

Goodwood (🖥 goodwood.com), near Singleton, has long been associated with country pursuits such as horse-racing and shooting but is also host to sports such as flying and motor-racing. The Festival of Speed, held every July, celebrates the history of motor sport and is one of many events held here around the year. Whilst these are probably not of interest to walkers of the South Downs Way, the relevance is that accommodation in the area is often booked up months in advance so it is probably worth checking the dates for events (see the Goodwood website) before you set off.

Compass Travel's No 99 bus service calls here if prebooked (see p47).

ROUTE GUIDE AND MAPS

the town's history, it was sculpted by local resident Philip Jackson (see p105) and unveiled in 2005.

Services
The very small **Cocking Stores** (☎ 01730-817100, **fb**; Mon-Fri 7.30am-5.30pm, Sat 8am-4pm, Sun 10am-4pm), which also houses the **post office** (Mon-Fri 9am-5pm, Sat to noon), has takeaway sandwiches and pastries.

The **bus stop** is on the main road and Stagecoach's No 60 (see p46; Chichester–Midhurst) service passes through regularly.

Where to stay, eat and drink
The most convenient place to stay, particularly for campers, is on a busy working farm right beside the Way. In addition to rearing cattle, pigs and various crops, *Manor Farm* (☎ 01730-814156, 🖳 manor farmcocking.co.uk; Ⓛ) also offers accommodation in either a **shepherd's hut** (1D; WI-FI; well-behaved 🐾) or a **log 'hare' cabin** (1Qd). The cabin has a double bed with a bunk bed over the top and a separate sofa bed and both have private facilities. Rates include a continental breakfast and are from £80/130 for 2/4 people (£60 sgl occ). **Camping** (Mar/Apr to end Oct; 🐾 on lead) costs from £10pp for backpackers. If ordered in advance a simple breakfast (eg a bacon roll and a hot drink) is available from their farm shop (usually between 8 and 8.30am). The **farm shop** (Fri-Sun 11am-4pm) sells eggs and home-made sausages as well as sandwiches, drinks and ice-cream.

On Bell Lane there's *Downsfold* (☎ 01730-814376, 🖳 downsfold.co.uk; 1D/1T, share bathroom; 👄; WI-FI; Mar-Oct), with B&B from £45pp (sgl occ from £50). They

were closed at the time of research but plan to reopen.

There's a warm welcome for walkers at *Moonlight Cottage* (☎ 01730-815469, 🖳 moonlightcottage.co.uk; 1D en suite, 3D share bathroom; 👄; WI-FI; Ⓛ) from £47.50pp. Recently taken over, renovated and reopened with smart newly-decorated rooms and good continental breakfast. There was also a *café* here and it may yet reopen.

B&B at the community-owned *The Bluebell Inn* (☎ 01730-239669, 🖳 theblue bellatcocking.co.uk; 1D/2T, all en suite; WI-FI; Ⓛ) costs from £55pp (sgl occ room rate) but rates are double that over the Goodwood weekend. **Food** (Mon-Sat noon-9pm, Sun to 6pm) is served most of the day with breakfasts (Mon-Fri 8-10.30am, Sat & Sun guests only) starting at just £1.50 for two slices of toast and jam. Sandwiches cost from £6; the menu also includes your favourite pub classics (£10.50-18.50). Note that if staying here on a Sunday night and you want an evening meal you must arrive/order by 5.30pm. For cyclists they have a bike repair station including an air pump.

On the trail, *Flint Barn Café* (🖳 flint barncafe.co.uk; Apr-Sep Mon-Fri 10am-5pm, Sat & Sun 8.30am-5pm, Oct-Mar daily 10am-3pm) is an upmarket daytime eatery housed on an old dairy farm, with sophisticated versions of traditional lunches including slow-cooked mushrooms on toast with tomato & marrow relish, or smashed avocado, boiled hen's egg, hummous & burnt butter mayo (both £8.50).

If everywhere is booked take Stagecoach's No 60 (see p46) to **Midhurst**, about 2½ miles to the north, where there is a wider choice of accommodation.

MIDHURST   off MAP 14, p108
Midhurst has some accommodation options, a good range of eating places, a Tesco Express supermarket with an ATM outside it, and other services should you find yourself here.

Several (Stagecoach) **bus services** (see pp46-7) operate from here: to Worthing (No 1), to Chichester (No 60) and to Petersfield (Nos 91, 92 & 93).

The friendly *Pear Tree Cottage* (☎ 01730-817216, 🖳 peartreecottagebandb midhurst.co.uk; 1T/1D plus 4ft sofa bed, both en suite; WI-FI) is on Lamberts Lane. B&B costs from £45pp (sgl occ £60); during Goodwood events the rate is from £60pp but they are likely to be fully booked anyhow. The rooms are self-contained and have a fridge, microwave, toaster and kettle; the

❑ THE TWO COWDRAY GOLD CUPS

The Cowdray Estate is probably best known for the Polo Club and the polo matches (both national and international) held there during the year; the main event is the Gold Cup which is held in July.

The second 'Gold Cup' refers to the colour of the paint seen on the window frames and doors of cottages and buildings that are part of the estate, particularly around Midhurst. The 'cowardy custard' yellow, as some locals call it, was first used on the cottages by the 2nd Viscount Cowdray who was a Liberal MP (yellow being the colour particularly associated with the Liberal Party), thus it was a good way of promoting the Liberal Party. The paint was made specially for the Viscount and was originally called 'Cowdray Gold' but is now known as 'Gold Cup', though it is not exactly the same shade as the original colour.

ROUTE GUIDE AND MAPS

twin can sleep an additional child and the double can double-up to four people. The owner leaves the ingredients for a continental breakfast in the room the night before. They don't do packed lunches because there is often enough food in the breakfast for guests to make one but also they are behind a Tesco Express (daily 6am-10pm) supermarket.

Failing this have a look at 🖳 visitmidhurst.com for additional suggestions.

E➜ COCKING TO AMBERLEY   MAPS 14-18

It is **12 miles (19.5km, 3¾-5¼hrs)** from the Cocking turn off to the Amberley turn off. From the main road south of Cocking, the Way follows a chalk lane, climbing steadily through fields to rejoin the high escarpment.

There is a **water tap** (Map 14) by the farm buildings. Just after that you will notice that the window frames on the cottages here are painted yellow; this shows they are part of the Cowdray Estate (see p108). The track here used to be

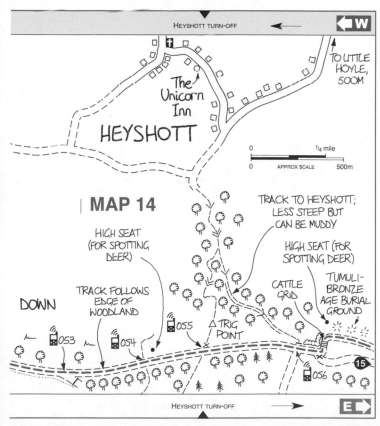

bordered on one side by dense woodland and on the other by a high hedge so the view was somewhat obscured in parts but the former South Downs Joint Committee and Graffham Down Trust created a wildlife corridor in order to link up two rich grassland sites: **Heyshott Down** (Map 14; see p109) and **Graffham Down** (Map 15).

The path passes a **Bronze Age burial ground** (Map 14) with **tumuli** clearly visible among the tussocks of grass; it continues on through a mixture of woodland and grassland, passing the turn-off for **Graffham** (Map 15a; see p112).

Climbing back up towards **Bignor Hill** (Map 17) the views open out spectacularly to the south. The rather outlandish-looking tent structure visible by the coast is the Butlins holiday complex at Bognor Regis. Of far greater interest is **Stane St**, the Roman road built around AD50 to connect Noviomagus

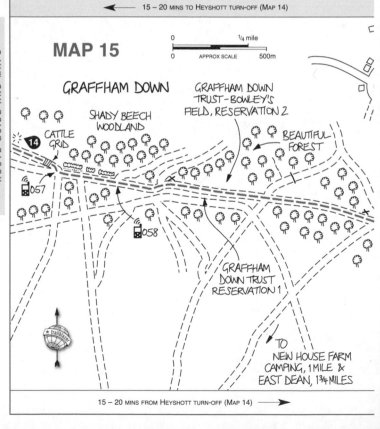

ROUTE GUIDE AND MAPS

← 15 – 20 MINS TO HEYSHOTT TURN-OFF (MAP 14)

MAP 15

0 ¼ mile
0 APPROX SCALE 500m

GRAFFHAM DOWN

GRAFFHAM DOWN TRUST-BOWLEY'S FIELD, RESERVATION 2

SHADY BEECH WOODLAND

14 CATTLE GRID

057

BEAUTIFUL FOREST

058

GRAFFHAM DOWN TRUST RESERVATION 1

TO NEW HOUSE FARM CAMPING, 1 MILE & EAST DEAN, 1¾ MILES

trailblazer

15 – 20 MINS FROM HEYSHOTT TURN-OFF (MAP 14) →

(Chichester) with Londinium (London). It's well worth going down to **Bignor** (Map 17a; see p116) from here to see the mosaics at **Bignor Roman Villa** (see box p116).

Continuing along the Way, there are sensational views to the east along the length of the Downs, as well as two possible routes north to the village of **Bury** (Map 18; see p119). Both follow pavement-less roads, although the country lane further west is more pleasant to walk along than the busier A29.

Follow the route down into the Arun valley for the villages of **Houghton Bridge** and **Amberley**, both on Map 18. If you have time it is well worth visiting **Arundel** (Map 18a; see p123), about five miles further south along the River Arun. You can reach it by following the riverside footpath but it's quicker to jump on the train (see p44).

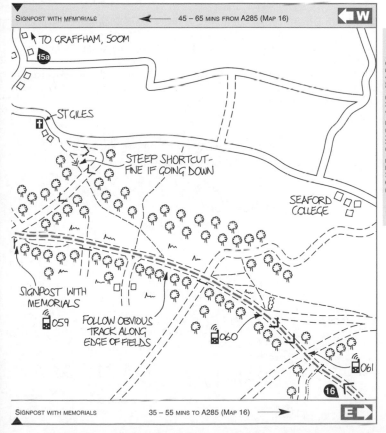

Heyshott Down Heyshott Down is one of the nature reserves in this area which is managed by the **Murray Downland Trust** (see p60) – making it easier for a lot of the flora and fauna here to survive. The best view is probably from the **trig point** (Map 14), about 50m off the path.

HEYSHOTT   MAP 14, p109

It's a steep and sometimes muddy descent from the Way, but Heyshott does have a nice pub. *The Unicorn Inn* (☎ 01730-813486, 🖥 unicorn-inn-heyshott.co.uk; **fb**; food Mon-Sat noon-2pm, Tue-Sat 6-9pm, Sun noon-2.30pm; WI-FI; 🐾 bar area & garden) is a smart country pub with excellent food. The menu changes regularly but usually includes some relatively unusual offerings such as spicy sweet & sour pork with rice & broccoli (£14.50), or chicken & chorizo pie with new potatoes and vegetables (£14). The views across the hay meadows to the Downs escarpment are lovely. Note, the pub is closed on Sunday and Monday evenings.

Graffham Down Turn south to *New House Farm Camping* (off Map 15; ☎ 01243-811685; 🐾 on lead; £5 per pitch and £5pp) 1¼ miles from the Way and on the edge of East Dean. It's a basic place with portaloos and a cold water tap but no showers.

After the Graffham turn off the Way eventually drops down across pasture to the A285 main road (Map 16). Compass's No 99 **bus** service calls here if booked in advance; see p47.

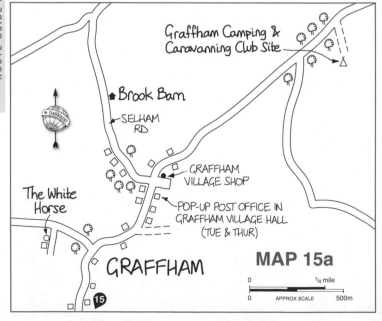

Graffham Camping & Caravanning Club Site

Brook Barn

SELHAM RD

GRAFFHAM VILLAGE SHOP

POP-UP POST OFFICE IN GRAFFHAM VILLAGE HALL (TUE & THUR)

The White Horse

GRAFFHAM

MAP 15a

0   ¼ mile
0   APPROX SCALE   500m

ROUTE GUIDE AND MAPS

GRAFFHAM   MAP 15a

There is little to see in Graffham but it has a lazy, peaceful air about it, being well away from any major roads, so makes for a pleasant overnight stay or lunch stop. The very well-stocked **Graffham Village Shop** (☎ 01798-867700, 🖥 graffhamvillageshop .co.uk; Mon-Sat 7am-7pm, Sun to 5pm) is more like a mini supermarket than a village store. It also sells hot drinks and baked goods and even has a small *café* area with a few seats and free wi-fi. There's a pop-up **post office** (Tue 8.30am-noon, Thur 2.30-4.30pm) in the village hall next door.

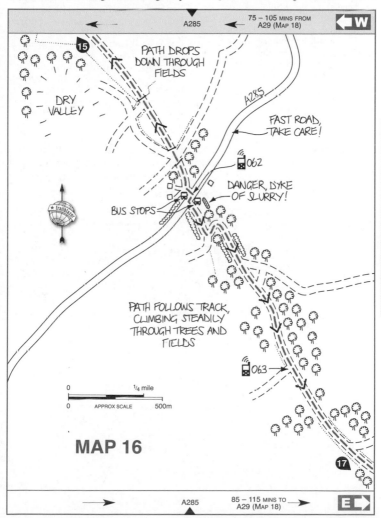

75 – 105 MINS FROM A29 (MAP 18)

◄▇W

A285

15

PATH DROPS DOWN THROUGH FIELDS

DRY VALLEY

A285

FAST ROAD, TAKE CARE!

📱062

DANGER, DYKE OF SLURRY!

BUS STOPS

PATH FOLLOWS TRACK, CLIMBING STEADILY THROUGH TREES AND FIELDS

📱063

0   ¼ mile
0   APPROX SCALE   500m

MAP 16

17

85 – 115 MINS TO A29 (MAP 18) ➤

A285

E▇►

Compass Travel's No 99 **bus service** calls here if booked in advance (see p47).

Campers can head up the road for about a mile to the well-run and welcoming *Graffham Camping & Caravanning Club Site* (☎ 01798-867476, 🖳 campingandcaravanningclub.co.uk; limited WI-FI; 🐾 on lead; end Mar to early Nov), set in a peaceful, forested location. The showers are decent and there are laundry facilities. The site has the usual unnecessarily complicated Camping & Caravanning Club prices, but to give you a quick example the price for one backpacker in early July is around £15 (£26 for two).

Brook Barn (☎ 01798-867356, 🖳 brookbarn-graffham.co.uk; 1D/1T shared bathroom but private if only one room booked; 🛋; WI-FI; 🐾), on Selham Rd, offers B&B for £35-45/55-65pp shared or private bathroom (sgl occ from £65). The rate includes a continental breakfast, a cooked one costs an extra £10pp (minimum two people).

The White Horse (☎ 01798-867331, 🖳 whitehorsegraffham.com; **fb**; **food** Wed-Fri noon-2pm, Sat & Sun to 2.30/3pm, Wed-Sat 6.30-9pm; WI-FI; 🐾 bar area only and on lead) itself is now a very upmarket restaurant, boasting a quiet garden and spectacular views onto the hills. The food's definitely a cut above your average trekker's grub, even if the menu itself is admirably straightforward and unpretentious, with mains for £14.50-19.50.

Bignor Hill The Way follows part of the old Roman road over Bignor Hill (Map 17). Look out for the signpost in Latin in the car park (not actually of Roman origin!) and look out, too, for any Roman coins that may be buried among the flint and chalk.

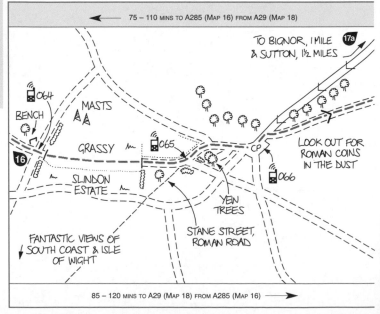

75 – 110 MINS TO A285 (MAP 16) FROM A29 (MAP 18)

TO BIGNOR, 1 MILE & SUTTON, 1½ MILES

17a

🔋064

BENCH

MASTS

GRASSY

🔋065

CP

LOOK OUT FOR ROMAN COINS IN THE DUST

16

🔋066

SLINDON ESTATE

YEW TREES

STANE STREET, ROMAN ROAD

FANTASTIC VIEWS OF SOUTH COAST & ISLE OF WIGHT

85 – 120 MINS TO A29 (MAP 18) FROM A285 (MAP 16) ⟶

❑ TUMULI

All along the crest of the Downs are numerous **burial mounds** known as tumuli. These are in the region of 4000 to 4500 years old. Some are overgrown or are not particularly distinct but many are surprisingly well preserved. A glance at an Ordnance Survey map of the area will indicate exactly where they are. Next time you stop for lunch on that nice grassy hump just remember you may be sitting on the grave of someone who has been dead for 4500 years.

SUTTON & BIGNOR   MAP 17a, p116

The main reason for dropping off the hills to these twin villages is to see the fabulous mosaics at **Bignor Roman Villa** but you can also stay comfortably in Bignor and eat well.

The **church** in Bignor dates from the 11th century; publisher John Murray (1909-95) is buried in the churchyard.

On a quiet corner of the Roman site is *Bignor Farms Camping* (☎ 01798-869259, 🖳 www.bignorromanvilla.co.uk/bignor-farms-camping; £15pp); it is a pop up campsite so the opening dates aren't certain and the number of pitches may vary. If it is open the owners can order local produce for you if given 24 hours' notice (order via website).

Very close to the Roman Villa is an excellent B&B, *Stane House* (☎ 01798-869454, 🖳 stanehouse.co.uk; 1D/1T both en suite, 1D private facilities; 🍴; WI-FI; ⓛ), with rooms from £45pp (£75 sgl occ).

There's a picnic area at Bignor Roman Villa and they've reopened the *teashop*

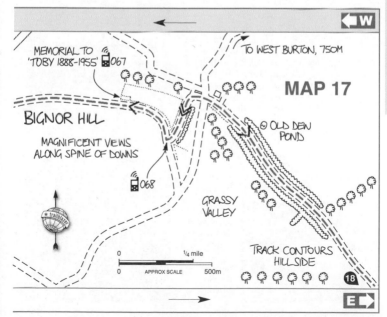

MEMORIAL TO 'TOBY 1888-1955' 📱067

TO WEST BURTON, 750M

MAP 17

BIGNOR HILL

MAGNIFICENT VIEWS ALONG SPINE OF DOWNS

◎ OLD DEW POND

📱068

★ trailblazer

GRASSY VALLEY

TRACK CONTOURS HILLSIDE

0 — ¼ mile
0 — APPROX SCALE — 500m

⑱

(Fri-Mon 10.30am-4pm, every day in August), though it serves only tea, coffee and cakes; no sandwiches or hot meals.

A mile further on, in **Sutton**, is *The White Horse Inn* (☎ 01798-869191, 🖥 whitehorseinn-sutton.co.uk; 7D/1D or T, all en suite; 🛏; WI-FI; 🐾), a magnificent isolated country pub with **B&B** for £60-90pp (sgl occ £90-150). In addition to the five rooms in the main building they also have three rooms in 'lodges' in the garden, one of which has a skylight above the bed, so you can fall asleep while gazing at the stars. They also have a large **restaurant** (food Mon-Sat noon-2pm & 6-9pm, Sun noon-4pm) and the food, much of it sourced locally, is exquisite. Non-residents can eat breakfast (daily 8-10am) here but prior booking is essential.

Compass's No 99 **bus service** calls at both Sutton and Bignor if pre-booked (see p47).

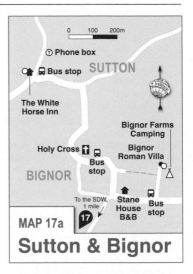

MAP 17a

Sutton & Bignor

❏ BIGNOR ROMAN VILLA   Map 17a

Just off the old Roman road of Stane Street are the remains of Bignor Roman Villa (☎ 01798-869259, 🖥 bignorromanvilla .co.uk; May, Jun, Jul, Sep & Oct Fri-Mon 10am-5pm, last entry 4pm, Aug open daily; £6.50). It was discovered by a farmer, George Tupper, who was ploughing his field in 1811.

Believed to date from the 3rd century AD, Bignor Villa was one of the biggest in England and probably home to a wealthy farmer considering its enviable position on fertile land close to the main road between Chichester and London. Bignor is most famous for the superb floor mosaics, said to be some of the world's best-preserved examples. Many are in near perfect condition, including a 24-metre length of the 70-metre corridor. It is the longest mosaic on display in Britain.

© BRYN THOMAS

BURY   MAP 18, p118

This unassuming village offers accommodation, food and a mobile **post office** (Fri 1.15-3.15pm). Compass's limited No 69 (Alfold–Worthing) and 71 (Storrington–Chichester) **bus** services call here; for details see p47

The Barn at Penfolds (☎ 01798-831496; 2D, both en suite; ✉; WI-FI; ⓛ), on Houghton Lane, offers **B&B** for £42.50-47.50pp (sgl occ from £50); they require a minimum stay of two nights at some times of the year. They also offer B&B in a cosy **shepherd's hut** (heated and insulated; 🐾) with its own shower and toilet and a deck area outside. *Harkaway* (☎ 01798-831843, ✉ harkaway.freeuk.com; 1D en suite,

1S/1T share facilties; WI-FI; ⓛ), also on Houghton Lane, offers B&B for £32.50-35pp (sgl £35-50, sgl occ from £50). Since there is no village shop here requests for a packed lunch must be made at least 24 hours in advance.

The Squire & Horse Inn (☎ 01798-831343, ✉ squireandhorsebury.co.uk; **food** Tue noon-2pm, Wed-Sat noon-2pm & 5.30-9pm, Sun noon-7pm; WI-FI; 🐾 bar area and garden), by the main road, is a freehouse with a busy restaurant. Main dishes include homemade steak & kidney pudding with roast potatoes (£13.95), and barbecued calves' liver with smoky bacon & mash (£14.95). Note, the pub is closed on a Monday.

HOUGHTON BRIDGE   MAP 18, p119

The village of Houghton Bridge, itself just a short walk from the village of Amberley, can easily be reached from the SDW as the trail almost passes through it.

Southern (see box p44) operates trains to London Victoria and south to Arundel and beyond, from the **railway station** (called Amberley Station). There are, however, no useful **bus** services other than school day services operated by Sussex Bus (✉ thesussexbus.com): their No 619 goes in the early morning to Amberley, Storrington and Steyning; their No 719 does the return route in the mid afternoon. One of Compass's No 74 services continues to Houghton mid afternoon on school days and their 69 (Tue, Fri) and 71 service (Wed) also drop in; see p46.

Right by the station you'll find the entrance to **Amberley Working Museum** (☎ 01798-831370, ✉ amberleymuseum.co.uk; mid Feb to end Oct Wed-Sun & Bank hols, daily during school holidays 10am-4.30pm, last entry 4pm; £14; tickets must be pre-booked online), situated in an old chalk pit. This extensive museum features a blacksmith's and foundry, as well as workshops producing traditional items such as brooms and walking sticks. There's a *café* here too. The quarry tunnel at Amberley was used as a film location in the James Bond film *A View To A Kill* in 1984.

Where to stay and eat

Foxleigh Barn (☎ 01798 839113, ✉ pete@foxleighbarn.co.uk; 🐾 on lead only and all mess must be cleared up; Easter to Oct) is conveniently located right on the SDW by the B2139. They offer **camping** (from £15pp) in a field with use of a camp kitchen, toilet and shower *for campers only*.

Just west of the river, the excellent *South Downs Bunkhouse* (☎ 01798-831100, ✉ southdownsbunkhouse.co.uk; 3 x 4-, 1 x 8-bed dorms, shared facilities; WI-FI; ⓛ; 🐾 in utility room) has bunk-bed dormitories and charges from £26pp if you bring your own sleeping bag, or you can rent a duvet, sheet and towel (from £5pp). Each bunk has its own power socket and USB charging port, and there's also a communal living room, self-catering and laundry facilities, and even a barbecue you can use in the courtyard outside. Continental breakfast (from £6pp) is also available if requested in advance.

Next door, and run by the same people, *Arun Valley B&B* (phone number as for the bunkhouse; ✉ arunvalleybandb.co.uk; 1D or T private bathroom, 1Tr en suite; ✉; WI-FI; ⓛ; 🐾 but can't sleep in the bedrooms) has very comfortable rooms from £60pp (sgl occ £75), including a full breakfast.

You can get breakfasts till noon but they also serve light lunches (hot food till

ROUTE GUIDE AND MAPS

3pm) and cakes at **Riverside** (☎ 01798-831066, 🖥 riversidesouthdowns.com; **fb**; Mon-Fri 10am-4pm, Sat & Sun 9am-4pm; WI-FI; 🐾); it's a café, bar and restaurant that's especially popular when the weather is good as they have a riverside garden.

Just across the road is **Bridge Inn** (☎ 01798-831619, 🖥 bridgeinnamberley.com; **fb**; food Wed-Fri noon-2.30pm & 6-

8.30pm, Sat noon-2.30pm & 5.30-8.30pm, Sun noon-4pm; WI-FI; 🐾 bar and garden only), a friendly, award-winning pub with real ales and very good food. At the time of research the pub was closed all day on Monday & Tuesday, and closing at 9.30pm (Wed-Sat) and at 5pm on Sunday but they hope the hours will be more normal by/in 2022.

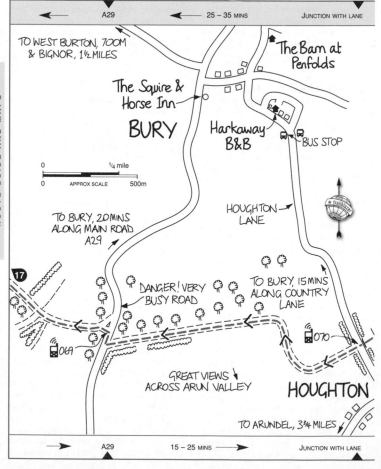

W← AMBERLEY TO COCKING   MAPS 18-14

This scenic **12 mile (19.5km, 3¾-5¼hrs)** stage is perhaps the trail at its most typical: a wide chalky track leading up and along the escarpment, with distant views to the sea away to the south and cosy little villages skirting the folds of the downs below to the north. So far, so familiar. But later on in the day there are also several patches of woodland, most notably at Graffham Down, that give those who started their adventure in Eastbourne a taste of things to come, with woodland becoming more prevalent as the trail continues west. All of which makes for a lovely day's walking if the sun's out.

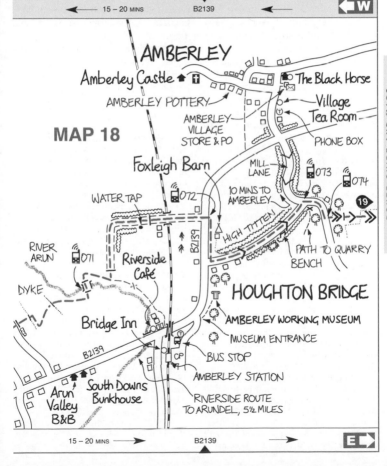

Though the walking may be 'typical' for the South Downs, there are some unique attractions on this stage. To the north of the trail, the mosaics at **Bignor Roman Villa** (see box p116) are really great and always manage to make you feel that the lengthy and steep trudge down from the top of **Bignor Hill** (Map 17) to it was worth doing. It's not surprising the villa was built here, with **Stane Street**, the Roman road built around AD50 to connect Noviomagus (Chichester) with Londinium (London), passing nearby.

The Way continues on through a mixture of woodland and grassland. The track here used to be bordered on one side by dense woodland and on the other by a high hedge so the view was somewhat obscured in parts but the former South Downs Joint Committee and Graffham Down Trust created a wildlife corridor in order to link up two rich grassland sites – **Graffham Down** (Map 15) and **Heyshott Down** (Map 14). The path passes a **Bronze Age burial ground** with **tumuli** clearly visible among the tussocks of grass.

There is a **water tap** by Manor Farm's farm buildings and a track from here leads down to **Cocking** (p106). Just after that you will notice that the window frames on the cottages here are painted yellow; this shows they are part of the Cowdray Estate. [Next route overview p106]

AMBERLEY   MAP 18, p119

Perched on a sandstone ridge below the chalk Downs with the wild marshland of **Amberley Brooks** stretching to the north, Amberley claims to be the prettiest village on the Downs and it would be hard to argue otherwise. The quiet lane leading to the church and castle is lined with thatched cottages; hollyhocks and foxgloves bloom in the small front gardens in the summer months. Unlike other downland villages, where local flint is prominent in the architecture, many of Amberley's cottages were built using local sandstone, making the village distinctive. There are records referring to Amberley dating back to AD680.

The pretty **church** was built by Bishop Luffa between 1091 and 1125. Next to the church is the **castle** (now a hotel, see Where to stay) which used to be the bishop's residence until it was recognised as a castle upon completion of the walls in 1377.

More information on the history of the village and the local area can be found at Amberley Working Museum (see p117). **Amberley Village Pottery** (☎ 01798-831876, 🖳 amberleypottery.co.uk; Thur-Tue 11am-3pm), housed in an 1867 former chapel on Church St, is open to visitors.

Amberley Village Store (☎ 01798-831171, 🖳 avsshop.co.uk; **fb**; Mon & Wed 9am-2pm, Tue-Thur & Fri to 5pm, Sat to 3pm, Sun 11am-3pm) stocks a good range of groceries and also houses the **post office** (Mon, Thur & Fri 9am-1pm, Tue to noon).

Amberley **railway station** is about a mile away in Houghton Bridge; see p46 for details of Compass Travel's 74A bus service that calls in Amberley and continues to the railway station on school days.

Where to stay and eat

If you fancy a splurge, there's every luxury at *Amberley Castle* (☎ 01798-831992, 🖳 amberleycastle.co.uk; 15D/4D or T, all en suite; ✎; WI-FI). Gorgeous rooms cost from £137.50pp (sgl occ room rate), though it is always worth enquiring about special offers; there's a minimum two-night stay at weekends. There's a grand **restaurant** (Wed-Sun 12.30-9pm; smart casual) serving a three-course meal for £75pp in the evening. Afternoon tea (12.30-4pm) costs £40pp. Booking is recommended.

The local pub, the very smart *Black Horse* (☎ 01798-831183, 🖳 www.amberley blackhorse.co.uk; **fb**; WI-FI; 🐾; Mon-Sat noon-2pm & 6-9pm, Sun noon-6pm) serves top-notch food in the bar, or in their Garden Room which boasts excellent views over the South Downs. They also have some charming bedrooms (8D/3D or T, all en suite; ☞; WI-FI; 🐾) with **B&B** rates from £60pp (sgl occ £105).

Amberley Village Tea Room (☎ 01798-839196; **fb**; 🐾; Apr-Sep Thur-Tue 10.30am-4pm, Sat & Sun only in Feb-Mar & Oct-Nov) prides itself on sourcing locally produced food and their cream teas (from £6) are very popular. Cheese scones (£2.20) and fennel & carrot bread are some of their savoury options and there are plenty of sweet items including toasted teacakes, crumpets, tea breads and mouth-watering slices of home-made chocolate cake.

East of the village, about a mile down the lane, is *The Sportsman* (Map 19; ☎ 01798-831787, ☐ thesportsmansussex .co.uk; **fb**), a very pleasant pub with sweeping sunset views across Amberley Brooks from both its beer garden and conservatory. As well as good **food** (Tue-Sat noon-2.30pm & 5-7.30pm, Sun noon-2.30pm) and some fine real ales, they offer **B&B** (3D/2T, all en suite; ☞; WI-FI; 🐾) from £47.50pp (sgl occ £85).

Next door to the pub is *Woody Banks Cottage* (Map 19; ☎ 01798-831295, ☐ woodybanks.co.uk; 1T, private shower room; WI-FI) with B&B from £47.50pp (sgl occ £60); the sitting room for guests now has a 'tea station' so tea can be made and there are biscuits. Another bedroom is available for family and friends.

About 90 metres further along is *Two Farm Cottages B&B* (Map 19; ☎ 01798-831266, ☐ twofarmcottages.co.uk; 1D/1T private bathroom; ☞; WI-FI). However, at the time of research they were closed and weren't certain if they would re-open in 2022 so check in advance.

☐ INTERNATIONAL DARK SKY RESERVE (IDSR)

In May 2016 the South Downs National Park became an IDSR, with 66% of the park being recognised as having Bronze Level Skies. Not only are such dark skies great for star-gazing, they also help nocturnal wildlife such as moths and bats thrive.

Areas with the darkest skies on the South Downs include Old Winchester Hill, Butser Hill, Devil's Dyke, Ditchling Beacon and Birling Gap.

ARUNDEL   MAP 18a, p123

The town of Arundel is about 1½ hours from the South Downs Way via the riverside path from Houghton Bridge or a 5-minute train ride from Amberley Station. Those who are walking the entire South Downs Way in one trip will find that a visit to this historic town makes an ideal rest day.

Arundel boasts a fine cathedral but it is the perfectly preserved castle with its grand turreted walls that really catches the eye. **Arundel Festival** (☐ arundelfestival.co .uk) is held in the castle in August.

What to see and do

The **castle** (☎ 01903-882173, ☐ arundel castle.org; Easter to early Nov Tue-Sun 10am-5pm, plus Mon in Aug & on bank holidays; £20 for castle & gardens, £12 for gardens only) is the centrepiece of this historical town. Rising grandly from the trees it looms over the Arun Valley and is everything you imagine an English castle to be, complete with imposing walls, turrets and winding stone staircases. Of Norman origin it is now home to the Duke of Norfolk but is open to the public most of the year. At the time of research the chapel was closed due to COVID but normally entry was included as part of the castle and garden ticket.

Arundel's gothic-style **cathedral** (☐ arundelcathedral.uk; check the website for opening hours) is somewhat upstaged by the immense castle down the road but is still a fine building in its own right. Founded by Henry, the 15th Duke of Norfolk, the cathedral is relatively new, dating back to 1873. A good time to visit is during the Corpus Christi festivities in early June when the main aisle of the cathedral is covered in a spectacular carpet of flowers.

Arundel Museum (☎ 01903-885866, 🖳 arundelmuseum.org; daily 10am-4pm; £4) is down by the river, opposite the entrance to the castle. The museum's exhibits focus on local history with interesting displays on the castle, the Catholic dukes of Norfolk and their association with the town. The old photographs portraying local life through the years are also rather wonderful.

Arundel Wetland Centre (☎ 01903-883355, 🖳 www.wwt.org.uk/wetland-cen tres/arundel; daily 10am-4.30pm; £14, free for WWT members, see p59) is a natural wetland site bordered by ancient woodland and is a perfect diversion for anyone interested in birds. The hides provide opportunities for viewing a variety of warblers and waders as well as the odd buzzard circling above the oak trees.

Swimmers might fancy a dip in **Arundel Lido** (☎ 01903-884772, 🖳 arun del-lido.com; mid/late Apr to early/mid Sep daily 6am-8.30pm; £5.50 for an hour), a heated open-air pool with views of the castle.

Services
There is no tourist information centre here but for online **information** visit 🖳 www.visitarundel.co.uk or 🖳 sussexbythe sea.com. For **internet** access, the **library** (Mon-Wed 1-5pm, Thur-Sat 9am-1pm) is at the western end of Tarrant St.

If you're looking for the ingredients of a good picnic, **Pallant of Arundel** (☎ 01903-882288, 🖳 pallantofarundel.co.uk; Mon-Sat 9am-6pm, Sun 10am-5pm) is the town's excellent **deli** and specialist grocery store. Food supplies can also be found at the small **shop**, McColl's (Mon-Sat 6am-7pm, Sun 7am-7pm), near the bridge at the bottom of the High St, while across the bridge is a Co-op **supermarket** (daily 7am-10pm).

The **post office** (Mon-Sat 9am-5.30pm, Sat to 1pm) lies just across the road from McColl's.

Some pharmaceutical items are available in the Co-op but the nearest **pharma**cy is now inconveniently located in the local NHS health surgery on Green Lane Close, off Canada Rd, beyond the round-about at the western end of Maltravers St.

There's an **ATM** outside the museum, and another outside the Co-op.

Chocoholics will be pleased to know that Arundel is home to **Castle Chocolates** (☎ 01903-884419, 🖳 castlechocolates .com; Thur-Sun 10am-6pm), 11 Tarrant St, who claim to produce what is 'probably the finest confectionery, chocolate and fudge in the South of England'.

Public transport
The **railway station** is a 10-minute walk from the town centre; services (see box p44) are operated by Southern.

Compass Travel's No 85/85A (see p47) is the only choice for travel by **bus** to Chichester, though their No 69 service (Tue & Fri only) calls in on its way between Alford and Worthing; the bus stop is near the bridge.

For a **taxi** call Castle Cars (☎ 01903-884444 or ☎ 01903-889988, 🖳 castlecars ltd.co.uk).

Where to stay
Arundel is a popular tourist centre so you must book well in advance. Over some weekends (eg during local events) there may be a two-night minimum stay for some places.

On the road leading from the town centre to the railway station is *Arundel Park Hotel* (☎ 01903-882588, 🖳 arundel parkhotel.co.uk; 1S/9D/3T/1Tr/1Qd, all en suite; ☛; WI-FI; mid Jan to mid Dec); it has plenty of rooms and an unpretentious style. B&B costs from £47.50pp (sgl/sgl occ from £65/65-85).

Nearby is *Portreeves B&B* (☎ 01903-885392, 🖳 portreeves.co.uk; 2D or T, both en suite; ☛; WI-FI; 🐾). It's a well-run, friendly place offering B&B from £55pp (sgl occ £105) in their two apartments. However, the apartments are often let on a self-catering basis for a week or more, particularly in the summer months, so it is essential to book in advance. Both apart-ments have a sofa bed so they can sleep three

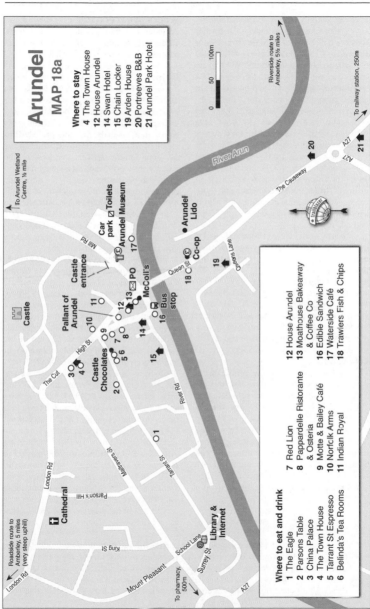

Arundel
MAP 18a

Where to stay
4 The Town House
12 House Arundel
14 Swan Hotel
15 Chain Locker
19 Arden House
20 Portreeves B&B
21 Arundel Park Hotel

Where to eat and drink
1 The Eagle
2 Parsons Table
3 China Palace
5 Tarrant St Espresso
6 Belinda's Tea Rooms
7 Red Lion
8 Pappardelle Ristorante & Osteria
9 Motte & Bailey Café
10 Norfolk Arms
11 Indian Royal
12 House Arundel
13 Moathouse Bakeaway & Coffee Co
16 Edible Sandwich
17 Waterside Café
18 Trawlers Fish & Chips

To Arundel Wetland Centre, ½ mile

River Arun

Riverside route to Amberley, 5½ miles

To railway station, 250m

The Causeway

A27

20

21

Castle

Castle entrance

Car park

Toilets

Arundel Museum

PO

McColl's

Bus stop

Queen St

Co-op

Chichester Lane

Mill Rd

Pallant of Arundel

High St

The Cut

Castle Chocolates

River Rd

Tarrant St

Maltravers St

Parson's Hill

Cathedral

London Rd

Roadside route to Amberley, 5 miles (very steep uphill)

King St

Surrey St

School Lane

Mount Pleasant

To pharmacy, 500m

Library & Internet

Arundel Lido

A27

0 50 100m

adults or a family with up to two children.

In the centre of Arundel in a former fisherman's cottage at 14 River Rd is *Chain Locker* (☎ 01903-882661, ☎ 07540 552810, 💻 chainlocker.org.uk; 1D private bathroom; ✒; WI-FI). Being a cottage it is a small place and the room and bathroom are on the ground floor. They don't do breakfast but it's wonderful value (£22.50pp, sgl occ room rate), though do note that between April and September they accept bookings for a minimum of two nights only.

House Arundel (☎ 07745 526945, 💻 housearundel.co.uk; 4D, all en suite; WI-FI; 🐾), near the post office at 11 High St, is an intimate little boutique restaurant with rooms. It's in a good location and a gorgeous place to stay. B&B costs from £50pp (sgl occ room rate).

Nearby is the elegant *Swan Hotel* (☎ 01903-882314, 💻 www.swanarundel.co .uk; 4T/7D/3Tr, all en suite; ✒; WI-FI; 🐾) with B&B from £55pp but it can cost around £100pp (sgl occ from £95).

The Town House (☎ 01903-883847, 💻 www.thetownhouse.co.uk; 4D/1D or T, all en suite; ✒; WI-FI), opposite the castle at the top of the High St (No 65), is a very attractive place with immaculate and stylish rooms. Expect to pay £55-155pp (sgl occ from £110).

On Queen's Lane, a few minutes from the centre, is *Arden House* (☎ 01903-884184, 💻 www.ardenhousearundel.com; 1D/2D or T all en suite, 2D/1T shared facilities; WI-FI; ⓛ). B&B costs £47.50-49.50pp (sgl occ £85-89) but during Goodwood and other major events the rate rises; phone bookings are preferred. They offer a packed breakfast option for those wanting to leave early but also have room only rates. They also have a lockable garage for up to four bicycles.

Where to eat and drink
Arundel is bursting with excellent pubs, cafés and restaurants, most of which are centred on or around the High St.

Cafés Starting down by the river, *Waterside Café* (☎ 07779-930236; **fb**; 🐾; daily 9.30am-6pm) is a no-frills café with good-value food including breakfasts, jacket spuds, sandwiches, cream teas and more substantial 'specials' focusing on fish dishes, all of which can be enjoyed while sitting on their simple terrace overlooking the river; a wonderful spot on a sunny day.

Also beside the river, on the other side of the bridge, *Edible Sandwich* (☎ 01903-885969, 💻 ediblesandwich.co.uk; Mon-Fri 7am-4pm, Sat 8am-4pm, Sun 8.30am-4pm; 🐾) doesn't have such good riverside seating, but it's friendly, opens early, and does good pastries, cakes and coffee.

Nearby, at 9 High St, is the hugely popular *Moathouse Bakeaway and Coffee Co* (☎ 01903-883297, 💻 moathousecafe arundel.co.uk; Mon-Sat 7.45am-5.30pm, Sun 8.30am-5.30pm, may close a bit earlier in winter; WI-FI; small 🐾), with an excellent range of breakfasts, toasties, filled baguettes and hot drinks. Up towards the top of the High St, and also very popular, is the bright and modern *Motte & Bailey Café* (☎ 01903-883813, 💻 www.motteandbaileycafe.com; **fb**; 🐾 during the day only; daily 8.30am-5pm, kitchen closes at 4pm), which as well as being arguably the best café in town also opens up some evenings (Wed-Thur 6-9pm, Fri-Sat till 9.30pm) for tapas.

Sidling off down Tarrant St will bring you to two more fine cafés: *Belinda's Tea Rooms* (☎ 01903-882977, 💻 www.belin dastearooms.com; **fb**; daily 9am-5pm; well-behaved 🐾), housed in a charming 16th-century building, has been serving teas and light lunches amongst the wooden

ROUTE GUIDE AND MAPS

Symbols used in text (see also pp72-3)
🐾 Dogs allowed; if for accommodation this is subject to prior arrangement (see p193)
✒ Bathtub in, or for, at least one room   WI-FI means wi-fi is available
ⓛ packed lunch available if requested in advance
fb signifies places that post their current opening hours on their Facebook page

beams for several decades now. But for the best coffee beans in town, head next door to the pocket-sized *Tarrant St Espresso* (Tue-Sat 8.30am-4pm, Sun 10am-2pm; WI-FI; 🐾); they also do filled rolls and salads.

In their 'living room' *House Arundel* (see Where to stay; Wed-Fri 3-9/10pm, Sat & Sun 11am-9/10pm) serves drinks and platters (from £7.50) of locally sourced cheeses/cured meats; at the weekend they also serve coffees, teas and pastries during the day. By 2022 they plan to open a deli.

Pubs One of the best pubs in town is *The Eagle* (☎ 01903-882304; **fb**; bar Mon-Fri 5-11pm, Sat & Sun 11am-11pm; WI-FI; 🐾), on Tarrant St. They serve an impressive array of beers (including Harvey's) and sometimes have live music at weekends. It's a popular place; locals spill out onto the pavement on warm summer evenings. They do bar snacks but no food.

On the High St, *The Red Lion* (☎ 01903-882214, 🖳 redlionarundel.com; **fb**; food daily noon-9pm; WI-FI; 🐾 on a lead) is a large no-nonsense pub (with a rear garden) serving cheap and filling dishes. There's a choice of real ales, and it opens for breakfast on Saturdays (10am-noon).

Opposite, *Norfolk Arms* (☎ 01903-882101, 🖳 norfolkarmsarundel.com; food daily noon-3pm & 5.30-8.30pm; WI-FI; 🐾 bar only) has a traditional restaurant serving English dishes as well as a pub-grub menu in its rather quiet bar.

Restaurants & takeaways The very highly regarded *Parsons Table* (☎ 01903-883477, 🖳 theparsonstable.co.uk; Tue-Sat noon-2pm & 6-9pm) is run by husband-and-wife team Lee and Liz Parsons and prides itself on dishes made from locally sourced seasonal ingredients. The results are excellent. A set two-/three-course lunch will set you back £25/30; evening mains start at around £16.50 rising to £34. Booking is recommended.

Although there are better-known Italian-food chain restaurants in town, it's worth seeking out the Italian-run *Pappardelle Ristorante & Osteria* (☎ 01903 882025, 🖳 pappardelle.co.uk). The informal **Osteria** (Tue 9am-4pm, Wed-Sat to 9pm, Sun to 5pm) downstairs serves drinks and light meals with antipasto plates (£7.50) as well as wraps and bruschettas (£7.50-8.50). Booking is recommended for the traditional **Ristorante** (Wed-Sat 5.30-9.30pm). The pizzas are excellent and they also have a vegan and gluten-free menu.

For decent Indian food, head to *Indian Royal* (☎ 01903-884224; daily noon-2.30pm & 5.30-11.30pm) at 3 Mill Lane just off the High St. At 67 High St, *China Palace* (☎ 01903-883702, 🖳 chinapalacearundel.com; daily 6pm-midnight) is a smarter than average Chinese restaurant.

The best chippy in town is *Trawlers Fish & Chips* (Mon-Wed 11.45am-2pm & 4-8pm, Thur-Sat same but to 9pm, Sun 3-7pm) on Queen St.

❏ DEW PONDS

The permeability of the chalk on the Downs means there is rarely any standing or free-flowing water available for livestock. To combat the problem farmers have, since prehistoric times, constructed dew ponds. These small, circular ponds are designed to collect and retain water for the sheep and cattle that graze the dry hilltops. Despite their name, dew accounts for very little of the moisture that collects in these man-made bowls; most of it is rainwater. The water is prevented from filtering through the chalk thanks to a base layer of straw and clay, although modern-day dew ponds usually have a layer of concrete instead.

Many dew ponds are hundreds of years old and in a state of disrepair, being overgrown and barely recognisable as ponds. However, in recent years many have been restored, either because of their historic interest or simply to be used again for their original purpose. Good examples of dew ponds can be seen near Chanctonbury Ring and also between Southease and Alfriston.

E→ AMBERLEY TO STEYNING   MAPS 18-22

The first half of this **10-mile (16km, 3¼-4¾hrs)** stretch is an easy stroll along the high crest of the Downs with great views over the swamp-like **Amberley Wild Brooks** nature reserve and the Low Weald. The quickest way to **Storrington** (Map 20a) is along the path leading off the Way at GPS Waypoint 079. Alternatively take the road leading off from Rackham Hill car park.

For **Washington** (Map 21; p132) there is an **alternative South Downs Way path** (Maps 20 & 21) which is longer but, in our opinion, superior to the main trail as it both leads the walker directly into this pleasant village *and* allows the walker to pass above the A24 on a bridge, rather than taking your life in your hands trying to cross it as you do on the 'normal' route.

The A24 dual carriageway (Map 21) is something of a blot on the landscape but it is soon forgotten once the steep climb up Chanctonbury Hill (Map 21) begins. At the top there are the somewhat storm-ravaged remains of **Chanctonbury Ring** (see box p129).

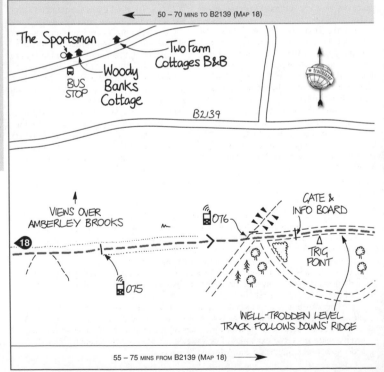

ROUTE GUIDE AND MAPS

←— 50 – 70 MINS TO B2139 (MAP 18)

The Sportsman

Two Farm Cottages B&B

BUS STOP

Woody Banks Cottage

B2139

VIEWS OVER AMBERLEY BROOKS

🔋076

GATE & INFO BOARD

18

🔋075

TRIG POINT

WELL-TRODDEN LEVEL TRACK FOLLOWS DOWNS' RIDGE

55 – 75 MINS FROM B2139 (MAP 18) —→

Acting almost as suburbs of **Steyning** (Maps 22 & 22a), the twin villages of **Bramber** & **Upper Beeding** (Map 22a; see p137) lie either side of the River Adur. They're easily accessed from Steyning, but can also be reached directly from the Way (Maps 22 & 23).

STORRINGTON   MAP 20a, p128

In comparison to many of the other towns and villages along the Downs the busy little town of Storrington is functional rather than attractive. It is a convenient place for topping up on supplies, getting a bite to eat or a bed for the night but apart from that there is little reason to make the detour.

There's a small **museum** (🖥 www .storringtonmuseum.org; Wed & Sat 10am-4pm, Sun to 1pm; free) covering the local history of the area. Near the museum

is a wonderfully ornate **Indian doorway**, set into the wall on Browns Lane.

Services

Storrington has everything you would expect in a small but prosperous town.

Waitrose **supermarket** (Mon-Sat 8am-8pm, Sun 10am-4pm) is in a small shopping arcade just off the High St. For more local supplies there's the *Village Deli* (☎ 01903-744644, 🖥 thevillagedelistorrington.co.uk;

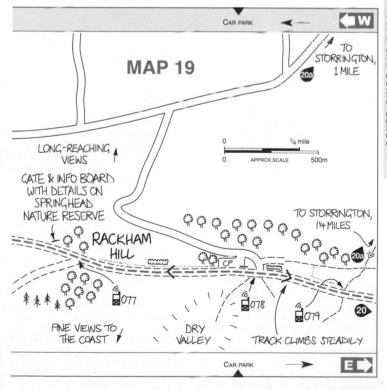

ROUTE GUIDE AND MAPS

MAP 19

CAR PARK ◀ ◀W

TO STORRINGTON, 1 MILE

20a

LONG-REACHING VIEWS ↑

GATE & INFO BOARD WITH DETAILS ON SPRINGHEAD NATURE RESERVE

0   ¼ mile
0   APPROX SCALE   500m

RACKHAM HILL

TO STORRINGTON, 1¼ MILES

20a

CP

077

078

079

20

FINE VIEWS TO THE COAST ▼

DRY VALLEY

TRACK CLIMBS STEADILY

CAR PARK ➡ E▶

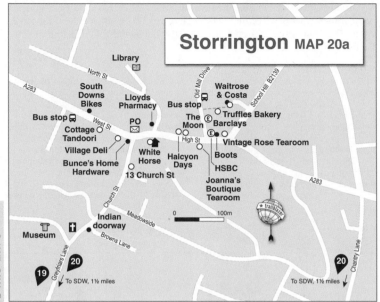

Storrington MAP 20a

Library

North St

A283

South
Downs
Bikes

Lloyds
Pharmacy

Old Mill Drive

School Hill B2139

Waitrose
& Costa

Bus stop

Bus stop

West St

PO

The
Moon

Truffles Bakery

Barclays

Cottage
Tandoori

Village Deli

White
Horse

High St

Halcyon
Days

Vintage Rose Tearoom

Boots

Bunce's Home
Hardware

13 Church St

HSBC

Church St

Meadowside

Joanna's
Boutique
Tearoom

A283

Indian
doorway

0   100m

trailblazer

Museum

Browns Lane

Greyfriars Lane

19

20

To SDW, 1½ miles

Chantry Lane

20

To SDW, 1½ miles

fb; Mon-Sat 9am-4pm), a great place for picnic ingredients as well as offering take-away hot drinks and sandwiches.

The **post office** (Mon-Fri 9am-5.30pm, Sat to 4pm) is on West St. Just round the corner at 1 North St is Lloyds **pharmacy** (Mon, Wed & Fri 9am-6.30pm, Tue & Fri to 5.30pm, Sat to 5pm) and there's a branch of Boots (Mon, Wed & Fri 9am-5.30pm, Tue & Thur to 6.30pm, Sat to 5pm) on the High St.

For **ATMs** there's an HSBC and a Barclays Bank next to each other where Old Mill Drive meets the High St.

If you need bike parts or repairs, head to **South Downs Bikes** (🖥 southdowns bikes.com; Mon-Fri 9am-6pm, Sat to 5pm, Sun 10am-4pm).

Stagecoach's No 1 (Midhurst–Worthing) **bus** service calls here as do Compass's No 100 (Burgess Hill–Pulborough) and their No 74/74A/74B (to Horsham); see p46.

Where to stay

There is a much wider choice of places to stay in Arundel and Steyning. In fact the only accommodation here is at the 400-year-old *White Horse* (☎ 01903-745760, 🖥 whitehorsestorrington .co.uk; 9D/1T/1Tr, all en suite; WI-FI; ✶) which offers rooms from £42.50pp (sgl occ room rate). Breakfast costs an additional £7.95pp.

Where to eat and drink

There are several cafés and tearooms including the bright and cheery *Joanna's Boutique Tearoom* (☎ 01903-742226, 🖥 joannasboutiquetearoom.com; Tue-Fri 10am-4pm, Sat & Sun to 6pm), with cream teas and cakes, all-white décor, and a friendly welcome. Booking is advised.

Also very popular, *Vintage Rose Tearoom* (☎ 01903-744100, 🖥 vintage rosetearoom.co.uk; fb; WI-FI; Mon-Sat 9am-4.30pm) is housed in a Grade II-listed building and serves teas and coffees – on interestingly mismatched china – as well as light lunches.

For cheaper fare (now takeaway only), including tea, coffee, pastries and breakfasts, there's *Truffles Bakery* (☎ 01903-742459; Mon-Sat 7.30am-4pm; WI-FI), near Waitrose.

Two doors down from Waitrose, meanwhile, is a branch of *Costa Coffee* (Mon-Sat 7am-6.30pm, Sun 8am-5pm).

In the middle of the High St, *Halcyon Days Café* (☎ 01903-746076, ☐ halcyondayscafe.co.uk; fb; Tue-Sat 10am-5pm, Sun to 4pm; 🐾 courtyard garden) has different themes for each room and a pleasant little courtyard garden. The menu is not particularly original but the people seem friendly and it's more down-to-earth than some of the other eateries on the Way.

Pubs include *The Moon* (☎ 01903-744773, ☐ themoonpub.co.uk; fb; food

Mon-Fri noon-2.30pm & 6-9pm, Sat noon-3pm & 6-9pm, Sun noon-3pm; WI-FI; 🐾); they also do breakfasts (Mon-Sat 10-11am) and have a takeaway menu when the kitchen is open.

The White Horse (see Where to stay; Tue-Sat noon-2.30pm & 6-9pm, Sun noon-4pm & 5-9pm) is also very reasonably priced, with most mains around the £10 mark.

For something a bit fancier, *13 Church Street* (☎ 01903-746964, ☐ thirteenchurchstreet.co.uk; fb; Tue-Sat noon-3pm & 6-10.30pm) serves high-quality, freshly prepared Thai specialities. Mains cost from £17

Storrington also has a popular Indian restaurant: *Cottage Tandoori* (☎ 01903-743605; daily noon-2.30pm & 6-11pm).

WASHINGTON   MAP 21, p132

Despite the proximity of the busy A24 dual carriageway this village is a peaceful place with most of the traffic noise being absorbed by the trees.

Stagecoach's **bus** No 1 stops here en route between Midhurst and Worthing.

Compass's No 100 (Burgess Hill–Horsham) also calls here as does Metrobus' No 23 (Crawley–Worthing) service. See p47 for details.

For **camping**, walk a few hundred metres north of the village, on London Rd,

❑ CHANCTONBURY RING   Map 21, p133

This exposed hilltop is one of the great viewpoints of the South Downs but more significantly it is the **site of an Iron Age hill-fort** believed to date back to the 6th century BC. Today it is equally famous for the copse of beech trees that were planted on the site of the fort by Charles Goring in 1760 and which grew to become one of the
most famous landmarks in Sussex. Sadly, the copse was badly damaged by the storm of October 1987 and despite a replanting programme the skyline has not yet recovered its distinctive crown of trees.

Chanctonbury Ring is also known for its folklore, tales of witchcraft, fairies and other mysterious goings-on. Perhaps the most famous story goes that while Satan was digging the nearby Devil's Dyke valley, spadefuls of earth landed here creating the hill you see today. The ring is also said to be haunted. It may be a beauty spot by day but it takes a brave person to spend the night there.

to the very welcoming *Washington Park* (☎ 01903-892869, 🖥 washcamp.com; WI-FI; 🐾 on lead; open all year) which charges from £8 per tent for backpackers plus £6pp. The rate includes showers and they also have laundry facilities (coin operated).

There's **B&B** for £40-42.50pp (sgl occ £45-60) at friendly *Holt House* (☎ 07796-936444, ☎ 01903-893542, or 🖥 annesim

monds_holthouse@yahoo.co.uk; 1D en suite, 1D/1T shared bathroom; 🛥; WI-FI; Ⓛ; 🐾); it is at the end of the road that runs off The Holt.

You can get pub **food** at *Frankland Arms* (☎ 01903-891405, 🖥 thefrankland arms.com; **fb**; WI-FI; 🐾 on lead; food Mon-Sat noon-2pm & 6-8.30pm, Sun noon-5pm).

To Steyning The town of Steyning (see p134), 1½ miles north of the path, is well worth the minor detour and not just to replenish supplies and energy. A couple of possible pathways lead down to the village; the best is the more westerly option, between the trig point and the small memorial to a local farmer (Map 22). The descent is a leisurely one with fine views over Steyning Bowl and down to the coastal towns of Worthing and Lancing.

ROUTE GUIDE AND MAPS

← 20 – 35 MINS TO CAR PARK (MAP 19)   CHANTRY POST   ← 5 – 10 MINS

TO STORRINGTON (1 MILE)   20a   SMALL WATERFALL

GREYFRIARS LANE   TO STORRINGTON (1 MILE)

CHANTRY LANE   POND

MAP 20

19   KITHURST HILL

DEW POND

0   ¼ mile
0   APPROX SCALE   500m

CAR PARK

CHANTRY POST

VIEWS TO ARUNDEL CASTLE FROM HERE

25 – 40 MINS FROM CAR PARK (MAP 19) →   CHANTRY POST   5 – 10 MINS →

W ← STEYNING TO AMBERLEY   MAPS 22-18

The highlight today occurs fairly early on in this **10-mile (16km, 3¼hrs-4¾hrs)** stage as you tackle the gentle ascent of Chanctonbury Hill to **Chanctonbury Ring** (see p129); it's still a magical place despite the devastation caused by a storm more than 30 years ago. The **A24** dual carriageway (Map 21) afterwards is both a metaphorical and literal come-down, but a rather hairy crossing of it can be avoided by a short-but-sweet **alternative trail** via the village of **Washington**. Alternatively, off the trail is **Storrington** (Map 20a; see p128) reached by turning off the trail at Chantry Post car park. As a reward for your exertions the remainder of the stage is an uncomplicated, untaxing stroll along the high crest of the Downs overlooking the **Amberley Wild Brooks** and the Low Weald.

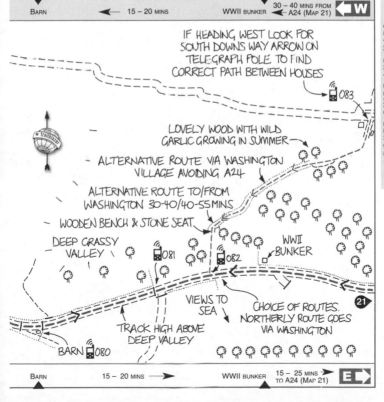

ROUTE GUIDE AND MAPS

The obvious choice of destination at the end of this stage is either **Amberley** or **Houghton Bridge** (both Map 18); both are beautiful, conveniently situated close to the trail and have some good pubs, cafés and accommodation. But if you

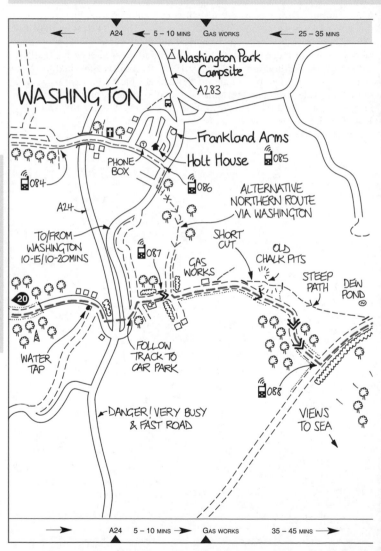

can't find what you're looking for in these villages, the even more lovely town of **Arundel** (p121) is just a short train ride away.

[*Next route overview p119*]

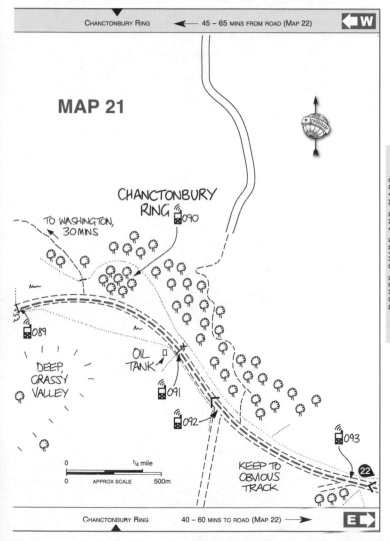

STEYNING   MAP 22a, p137

This small town has retained all the charm of a downland village and it is worth taking an afternoon off to wander around and maybe visit one or two of the sights. There are some beautiful old buildings, particularly along Church St where the **Grammar School (Brotherhood Hall)**, dating from 1614, really catches the eye with its black timber framing. Next to the library is the small **Steyning Museum** (☎ 01903-813333, 🖥 steyningmuseum.org.uk; Wed-Sun 10am-4pm) with displays on local history. Entrance is free.

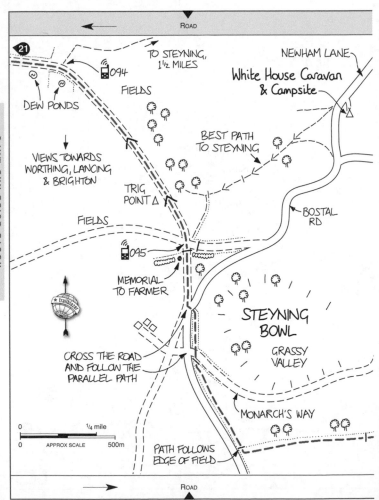

ROUTE GUIDE AND MAPS

ROAD

21

DEW PONDS

📱094

TO STEYNING, 1½ MILES

NEWHAM LANE

White House Caravan & Campsite

FIELDS

VIEWS TOWARDS WORTHING, LANCING & BRIGHTON

BEST PATH TO STEYNING

TRIG POINT △

FIELDS

📱045

MEMORIAL TO FARMER

BOSTAL RD

STEYNING BOWL

GRASSY VALLEY

CROSS THE ROAD AND FOLLOW THE PARALLEL PATH

trailblazer

MONARCH'S WAY

0   ¼ mile

0   APPROX SCALE   500m

PATH FOLLOWS EDGE OF FIELD

ROAD

Services

The High St has plenty of **banks** and **ATMs** and there's a **post office** (Mon-Fri 9am-5pm, Sat 10am-4pm) too.

The main **supermarket**, Co-op (daily 7am-10pm) is also on the High St; there's also the more expensive Budgens (The Sussex Grocer). Steyning also has a good

bookshop (Mon-Sat 9.30am-5.30pm) that sells maps.

There is **internet access** (free for library card holders, £2/hr otherwise; free WI-FI) in the **library** (Mon-Fri 10am-5pm, Sat to 2pm).

Bus services (see pp46-8) calling here are Brighton & Hove Buses' No 2 (to

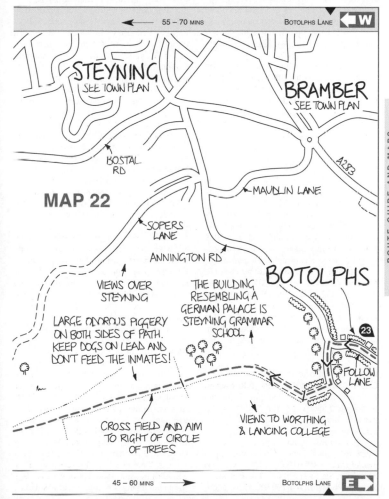

← 55 – 70 MINS   BOTOLPHS LANE ◄W

STEYNING
SEE TOWN PLAN

BRAMBER
SEE TOWN PLAN

A283

BOSTAL RD

MAUDLIN LANE

MAP 22

SOPERS LANE

ANNINGTON RD

BOTOLPHS

VIEWS OVER STEYNING

THE BUILDING RESEMBLING A GERMAN PALACE IS STEYNING GRAMMAR SCHOOL

LARGE ODOROUS PIGGERY ON BOTH SIDES OF PATH. KEEP DOGS ON LEAD AND DON'T FEED THE INMATES!

23

FOLLOW LANE

CROSS FIELD AND AIM TO RIGHT OF CIRCLE OF TREES

VIEWS TO WORTHING & LANCING COLLEGE

45 – 60 MINS →   BOTOLPHS LANE E►

Brighton) and Compass's No 100 (Burgess Hill to Horsham & Pulborough; see box p44 for details of rail services from Pulborough).

Where to stay

Campers should head to Newham Lane, where they'll find *White House Caravan and Campsite* (☎ 01903-813737; 🐾; Mar-end Oct) which charges £15 for a pitch and up to two people. They kept busy over lockdown and have installed a new shower block. The walk into town takes about eight minutes; see also Map 22.

Walker-friendly *Uppingham B&B* (☎ 07990-532030, ☎ 01903-812099; 1T/1D private bathrooms; ☞; WI-FI; ⒧; 🐾) is on Kings Barn Villas. B&B costs from £40pp (sgl occ £50). *Springwells House B&B* (☎ 01903-812446, 🖳 springwells.co.uk; 4D/1Qd, all en suite; ☞; WI-FI; ⒧; 🐾), 9 High St, offers some very smart accommodation. One of the rooms has a four-poster bed and a Z-bed can be put in some rooms (£25 per bed inc breakfast). One of the other delights of this lovely place is the heated swimming pool in the old walled garden. The prices reflect the quality of the place; they vary throughout the year but in August on a weekday you can expect to pay from £84.50pp (sgl occ £150); weekends are more expensive and there's a two-night minimum stay.

Though the bar can sometimes be noisy, *Chequer Inn* (☎ 01903-814437, 🖳 chequer inn.co.uk; 1T/1D/1Qd, all en suite; limited WI-FI), at 41 High St, offers comfortable B&B from £50pp (sgl occ £60). Note that they cannot offer breakfast before 7.30am but if requested in advance they may be able to provide a takeaway breakfast.

Where to eat and drink
Cafés, restaurants and takeaways
Baked goods, breakfasts, tea and coffee can be bought at the bakery, *Truffles* (☎ 01903-816140; fb; WI-FI; Mon-Sat 7.30am-5pm, café 8am-4pm).

For takeaway lunch packs there are filled rolls, buns, cakes and savouries at *Model Bakery* (☎ 01903-813785; Mon-Fri 8am-2pm, Sat to 1pm), on Church St, with a second branch (☎ 01903-813126; Mon-

Sat 8am-2pm) at the northern end of the High St.

A classier place is *The Steyning Tea Rooms* (☎ 01903-810103; fb; Mon-Fri 10.30am-3.30pm, Sat & Sun to 4pm, winter hours variable; 🐾); it does very good breakfasts – including traditional bacon sandwiches or scrambled eggs with smoked salmon – as well as light lunches and cream teas.

For something more intriguing, turn off the High St down Cobblestone Walk, a part-covered alleyway where, amongst a curious collection of boutique shops and gift stalls, you'll find the ever-so charming *Cobblestone Tea House* (☎ 01903-366171; fb; daily 9am-5pm; WI-FI; 🐾), housed in a 16th-century timber-framed cottage.

Down the hill a bit further, *Victoria's Sponge* (☎ 01903-814517; fb; Wed-Sun 9am-4pm; WI-FI; 🐾) is a relatively new place but is proving to be very popular, possibly in part because it allows dogs. The food's good too, with hearty breakfasts, sandwiches, light lunches – and, of course, a good selection of delicious cakes.

Finally, at the other end of town, *Big Fish* (Mon-Thur & Sat 5-9pm, Fri noon-2pm & 5-9pm) is the town's chippy.

Pubs *The White Horse* (☎ 01903-814084, 🖳 www.thewhitehorsesteyning.com; food Mon-Sat noon-9.30pm, Sun to 9pm; limited WI-FI; 🐾 on a lead), has recently rebranded itself as a 'smokehouse and grill'. It sits at the crossroads on the High St and the food is decent value, especially some of the lunchtime deals.

Chequer Inn (see Where to stay; limited WI-FI; 🐾 in parts of the pub only; food Mon-Tue noon-2.30pm, Wed-Thur noon-2.30pm & 6-8.30pm, Sun noon-5pm) is a more traditional pub with local ales, good food, and an antique three-quarter-sized snooker table that's still in use. Pre COVID they sometimes had live music on weekend evenings and they may do again.

At the bottom end of the High St there is another traditional pub, *The Star Inn* (☎ 01903-813078; fb; food Mon-Tue & Thur noon-2.30pm & 6-9pm, Fri & Sat same but till 9.30pm, Sun noon-2.30pm; WI-FI; 🐾); the menu changes regularly but is standard

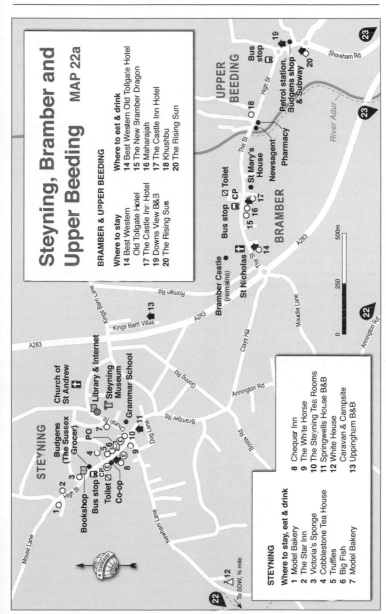

Steyning, Bramber and Upper Beeding MAP 22a

BRAMBER & UPPER BEEDING

Where to stay
14 Best Western Old Tollgate Hotel
17 The Castle Inn Hotel
19 Downs View B&B
20 The Rising Sun

Where to eat & drink
14 Best Western Old Tollgate Hotel
15 The New Bramber Dragon
16 Maharajah
17 The Castle Inn Hotel
18 Khushbu
20 The Rising Sun

STEYNING

Where to stay, eat & drink
1 Model Bakery
2 The Star Inn
3 Victoria's Sponge
4 Cobblestone Tea House
5 Truffles
6 Big Fish
7 Model Bakery
8 Chequer Inn
9 The White Horse
10 The Steyning Tea Rooms
11 Springwells House B&B
12 White House Caravan & Campsite
13 Uppingham B&B

pub-type food (mains around £14). Food is not served in the pub on Wednesdays and the pub itself only opens at 4pm but a pizza van is in the car park from 5.30pm and stays till it sells out.

BRAMBER & UPPER BEEDING
MAP 22a, p137

The main attraction is **Bramber Castle** (free, dawn to dusk). It was built by William de Broase in 1073 on a prominent knoll behind the village. In truth there is not much left of it, save for a few old ramparts and some collapsed sections of wall but the old moat, despite now having no water and having been taken over by trees, is still clearly visible. The only surviving part of the castle that's still in use is the **Church of St Nicholas** which was built around the same time.

St Mary's House (☎ 01903-816205, 🖳 stmarysbramber.co.uk; May-Sep Thur, Sun & bank holidays 2-6pm; £10, garden only £6) is a magnificent place which claims to be the finest example of a 15th-century timber-framed house in Sussex. The perfectly manicured front garden, with its topiary and fish ponds, only adds to the charm. Despite the house being a private residence the owners do allow visitors in to admire the antiques, an Elizabethan *trompe l'oeil* painted room, four-poster beds, a 'mysterious, ivy-clad monks' walk' and octagonal dining-room. It is a popular location for TV dramas, most notably *Dr Who*.

Services

On the main street in Upper Beeding there is a **newsagent** (Mon-Fri 5.30am-5pm, Sat to 1pm, Sun to noon) as well as a **pharmacy** (Mon-Fri 9am-1pm & 2-5.30pm, Sat 9am-12.30pm).

There's a small Budgens **shop** (Sun-Fri 7am-11pm, Sat to noon) that sells hot drinks and snacks; it is in a petrol station on the way out of town.

Brighton & Hove Buses' No 2 **bus** service (Steyning–Rottingdean) passes through both Bramber and Upper Beeding. Compass Bus No 100 also calls at both on its way between Horsham and Burgess Hill via Pulborough; see pp46-8.

Where to stay

In **Upper Beeding** you'll find *Downs View B&B* (☎ 01903-816125, 🖳 upperbeeding .com; 1D/4D or T/2Qd, all en suite; ☛; WI-FI; Ⓛ), which featured on the Channel 5 TV series *To B&B the Best*. It gets great reviews from visitors and is a friendly place to stay. B&B in their comfortable rooms costs from £47.50pp (sgl occ £75-85). The breakfasts include home-made bread, and when COVID restrictions are lifted they hope to make muffins and jams and other things again.

The Rising Sun (☎ 01903-814424, 🖳 risingsunupperbeeding.com; **fb**; 1D/1T, both en suite; WI-FI; Ⓛ) is a friendly pub with clean rooms and B&B from £40pp (sgl occ £60). They may have an additional twin room in 2022.

In **Bramber**, there are two smart options: *The Castle Inn Hotel* (☎ 01903-812102, 🖳 castleinnhotel.co.uk; 12D or T/4Tr, one room sleeping up to 5, all en suite; ☛; WI-FI; Ⓛ; 🐾) is an old-worlde pub with B&B in a variety of rooms for around £36.25-47.50pp (sgl occ from £47.50). Note there's a minimum two-night stay at weekends.

If you have cleaned the mud from your boots you could splash out on a four-poster bed room at the *Best Western Old Tollgate Hotel* (☎ 01903-879494, 🖳 oldtollgateho tel.com; 28D, two with four posters/6D or T/4T, all en suite; ☛; WI-FI; Ⓛ, 🐾) which incorporates a smart restaurant (see Where to eat) and lots of pristine rooms and charges from around £41pp (sgl occ room rate). However, their rates vary by the day and are generally better if you book in advance; also at times they have some special offers, so it is worth checking online.

Where to eat and drink

In **Bramber** there is a surprising number of food outlets for such a small village. One of the best places is *The Castle Inn Hotel* (see

Where to stay; food daily noon-3pm & 6-9pm; WI-FI; 🐾), which is also open for breakfast (daily 7-9am) for non-residents. They also serve real ale;. They also have Bramber Ale which is brewed nearby at Downlands Brewery (🖳 www.downlands brewery.com).

Eating at *Best Western Old Tollgate Hotel* (see Where to stay; food Mon-Sat noon-2pm & 6-9pm, Sun noon-9pm; WI-FI) is a classy experience with a three-course dinner (inc dessert and a cheese) for £26.50 (Mon-Sat); on Sunday they serve an all-day roast (£25 for three courses).

For a cheaper night out try *The New Bramber Dragon* (☎ 01903-812408, 🖳 bramberdragon.com; Sun & Tue-Thur 5-10.30pm, Fri & Sat to 11pm), a Chinese restaurant that also serves Thai food.

Maharajah (☎ 01903-812123, 🖳 maharajahofbramber.co.uk; daily noon-2.30pm & 5-11.30pm) claims to be the 'largest and most famous Indian restaurant in Sussex'.

Moving into **Upper Beeding** there is more Indian food at *Khushbu* (☎ 01903-816646; daily 5.30-11pm). There is also pub food at *The Rising Sun* (see Where to stay; WI-FI; 🐾; food Tue-Sat noon-2.30pm, Tue-Thur 5.30-8.30pm, Fri & Sat to 9pm, Sun noon-4pm) at the far end of the village. The bar opens at 4pm on a Monday but they don't serve food then.

Finally, a branch of the international chain *Subway* (Mon-Fri 8am-7pm, Sat from 9am, Sun 10am-3pm) has opened by Budgens in the petrol station.

E➜ STEYNING TO PYECOMBE MAPS 22-26

The going is easy for most of this **10¼-mile (16.5km, 4-5½hrs, plus 20-30 mins from Steyning to the South Downs Way) section** with a good track leading the way along the level escarpment of the Downs. There are, once again, great views in all directions once you climb out of the Adur Valley to **Truleigh Hill** (Map 23; see p141), particularly to the north across the Weald, with the villages of **Fulking** (Map 24; see p142) and **Poynings** (p143) lying hidden at the foot of the Downs below.

Despite the ugly pub and car park at the top of the hill the highlight of this stretch has to be **Devil's Dyke** (Map 24, p143), a spectacular dry valley, 100 metres deep. During Victorian times Devil's Dyke became something of a tourist attraction and even had its own railway station.

After leaving the Dyke the Way drops down to Saddlescombe Farm and then over the flanks of **Newtimber Hill** (Map 25, p144), owned by the National Trust and an oasis of calm after the crowds that flock to the Dyke. **Pyecombe** (Map 26; see p146) is perhaps one of the more disappointing villages on the trail, blighted as it is by the constant roar of traffic, but there are accommodation and services here, and buses to Brighton and Crawley, for those unwilling or unable to push on.

ROUTE GUIDE AND MAPS

❏ IMPORTANT NOTE – WALKING TIMES

All times in this book refer only to the time spent walking. You will need to add 20-30% to allow for rests, photography, checking the map, drinking water etc.

TRULEIGH HILL   MAP 23

At the foot of Truleigh Hill, on the busy A283, mention must be made of the *South Downs Way Fodder Box* (☎ 07557 853541; **fb**; Tue-Sun 7am, shutting at 3.30/4pm if trade is slow and to 3pm in the winter months), a small but thoroughly pleasant snack van (a converted horse box) in the car park that serves hot drinks and cakes. They have a licence to extend their hours to 6pm and hope to do this in/by 2022.

Right on the Way, *YHA Truleigh Hill* (reservations ☎ 0345-371 9047, or ☎ 01903-813419, 🖳 yha.org.uk/hostel/truleigh-hill; 6 x 2-, 1 x 4-, 6 x 6-bed rooms; shared facilities; WI-FI communal area; ⓛ;

Mar-Oct) is a tree-shaded, purpose-built hostel with all the usual useful facilities including a day room and a drying room. Private rooms cost £29-100 for 2-6 sharing; two of the 6-bed rooms have a double bed and one of the 4-bed rooms so technically they can sleep 7/5. At the time of research (due to COVID) dorm beds were not available and the self-catering facilities were closed. However, the *café* (daily 8am-10pm, winter usually weekends only) serves meals (to 8.30/9pm), hot drinks, cold beer and ice-creams and is open to the public too, though at the time of research for takeaway only. There's also a small **shop**.

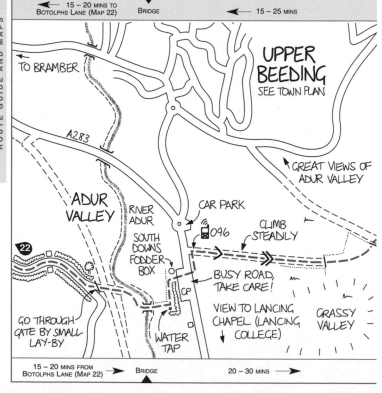

ROUTE GUIDE AND MAPS

15 – 20 MINS TO BOTOLPHS LANE (MAP 22)   BRIDGE   15 – 25 MINS

TO BRAMBER

UPPER BEEDING
SEE TOWN PLAN

A283

GREAT VIEWS OF ADUR VALLEY

ADUR VALLEY

RIVER ADUR

CAR PARK

096

CLIMB STEADILY

SOUTH DOWNS FODDER BOX

22

CP

BUSY ROAD, TAKE CARE!

VIEW TO LANCING CHAPEL (LANCING COLLEGE)

GRASSY VALLEY

GO THROUGH GATE BY SMALL LAY-BY

WATER TAP

15 – 20 MINS FROM BOTOLPHS LANE (MAP 22)   BRIDGE   20 – 30 MINS

Camping (Mar-Oct; £8-14pp) is also available in the field opposite. There's a 24hr 'campers' washroom' with toilet, shower and changing room beside the **water tap** outside the entrance to the hostel. They also have two **bell tents** (£50-100 for up to five sharing); each has a double bed, two single beds and a fold-out bed; as well as some **land pods** (a cross between a room and a tent, sleeping four people in a double bunk bed, with bedding and electricity sockets too), with rates as low as £39 for the pod, though they can be over £100 in high season and at weekends. Dogs on lead are welcome for all camping type accommodation.

FULKING   MAP 24, p143

This tiny village has little of specific interest to the walker except for the delightful *Shepherd & Dog Inn* (☎ 01273-857382, 🖥 shepherdanddogpub.co.uk; **fb**; food Wed-Sat noon-4pm & 6-8.30pm, Sun noon-6pm; limited WI-FI; 🐕 on lead). It's everything a proper country pub should be with plenty of real ales, good **food** (mains from £13.50) and a beer garden with views of the Downs. On Sundays they serve a roast (sittings are at: noon, 2pm, 4pm & 6pm). At the time of research the pub is closed on Mondays and

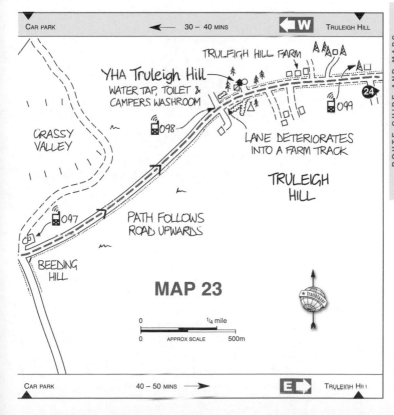

CAR PARK   ← 30 – 40 MINS   ◀W TRULEIGH HILL

TRULEIGH HILL FARM

YHA Truleigh Hill
WATER TAP, TOILET &
CAMPERS WASHROOM

📱099

📱098

GRASSY
VALLEY

LANE DETERIORATES
INTO A FARM TRACK

TRULEIGH
HILL

📱097

PATH FOLLOWS
ROAD UPWARDS

BEEDING
HILL

MAP 23

0   ¼ mile
0   APPROX SCALE   500m

CAR PARK   40 – 50 MINS →   E▶ TRULEIGH HILL

ROUTE GUIDE AND MAPS

Tuesdays but they hope to open daily when fully staffed. The pub gets its name from Fulking's reputation for having a rather large population of sheep: in the early 19th century the village was home to ten times as many sheep as people and the pub was the place where the shepherds would meet after a hard day's shearing to spend their earnings on the local brew.

Next to the pub car park is the locally famous **Victorian fountain**, placed there in memory of John Ruskin, the man responsible for installing the village's water supply.

Devil's Dyke Devil's Dyke (Map 24) is a spectacular dry valley said to have been carved out by Satan himself in order to let the sea flood over the lowland Weald and destroy all the churches. Geologists have blown this theory out of the water by proving that it is in fact a result of folding of the chalk strata due to pressure building between the African and Eurasian plates.

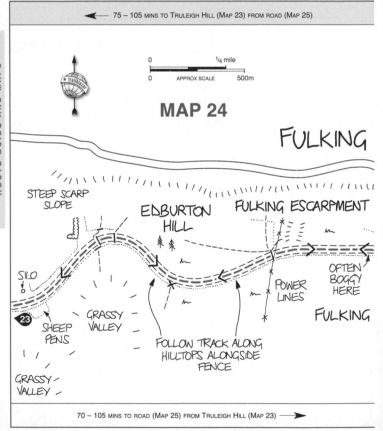

ROUTE GUIDE AND MAPS

75 – 105 MINS TO TRULEIGH HILL (MAP 23) FROM ROAD (MAP 25)

0   ¼ mile
0   APPROX SCALE   500m

MAP 24

FULKING

STEEP SCARP SLOPE

EDBURTON HILL

FULKING ESCARPMENT

SILO

OFTEN BOGGY HERE

POWER LINES

FULKING

23

SHEEP PENS

GRASSY VALLEY

FOLLOW TRACK ALONG HILLTOPS ALONGSIDE FENCE

GRASSY VALLEY

70 – 105 MINS TO ROAD (MAP 25) FROM TRULEIGH HILL (MAP 23)

POYNINGS
MAP 24

The hidden leafy village of Poynings sits at the foot of the escarpment away from the hustle and bustle high above at the beauty spot of Devil's Dyke. Poynings is a scenic two-mile walk from the Dyke.

Dyke Lane Cottage (☎ 01273-857335, ⌨ amberric27@gmail.com; 2D en suite/1T private bathroom; ▰; wi-fi; Ⓛ; 🐾) is both walker- and cyclist-friendly. B&B here costs from £45pp (sgl occ £50). Note that the bathroom for the twin is downstairs.

Set in the heart of the village, the *Royal Oak* (☎ 01273-857389, ⌨ royaloak poynings.pub; **fb**; food Mon-Fri noon-3pm & 6-8pm, Sat noon-8pm, Sun to 7pm; wi-fi; 🐾) serves all the pub-grub classics (mains £14-15.50).

If descending to the Royal Oak does not appeal, the only other choice is the somewhat characterless *Devil's Dyke* (☎ 01273-857256, ⌨ vintageinn.co.uk/restau rants/south-east/thedevilsdykebrighton; **fb**; food Mon-Sat noon-10pm, Sun to 9pm; wi-fi; 🐾), whose most eye-catching feature is the fabulous views from its benches outside. Main dishes cost £11.25-19.50 and sandwiches from £7.75.

ROUTE GUIDE AND MAPS

NEWTIMBER HILL   MAP 25

There used to be a basic campsite at **Saddlescombe Farm** but it is unlikely to reopen. What is open, however, is the marvellous *WildFlour Café* (🖳 wildflourcafe .co.uk; **fb**; Mar-Oct Tue-Fri noon-3pm, Sat & Sun 11am-4pm, check for their winter hours; cash only) serving cream teas, cakes and hot food, such as dhals, in a courtyard. Nearby is one of the last examples of a **donkey wheel** used to pump water from the well.

W← PYECOMBE TO STEYNING   MAPS 26-22

It's with little regret that westbound Way walkers finally leave the cacophony of traffic at Pyecombe behind to climb out of the valley and back onto the serenity of the Downs. It's a lovely, straightforward **10¼-mile (16.5km, 4¼-5¾hrs, plus 25-35 mins to Steyning)** walk too, as you follow a good track along the level escarpment of the Downs.

Wonderful views once again stretch out on either side, blighted only slightly by the crowds swarming over the trail along here on high days and holidays. Many have made the journey from Brighton, which lies just a few miles to the south, but what brings them here is the scenery surrounding the dry valley of **Devil's Dyke** (Map 24; see p143), a deep, distinctive crumple in the land

ROAD ← 65 – 80 MINS FROM PYECOMBE (MAP 26)

MAP 25

ROAD 50 – 65 MINS TO PYECOMBE (MAP 26) →

caused by tectonic pressure. If the weather's on your side a pleasant day can be had meandering along the crest of the Downs, enjoying a lunch at Wildflour Café at **Newtimber Hill** (Map 25; p144) – possibly our favourite eatery on the entire trail – and then perhaps dropping off the trail to visit the twin villages of **Poynings** (p143) or **Fulking** (p142), or remaining on it to eat or stay at the YHA on **Truleigh Hill** (Map 23; p141). While the YHA is in a lovely location and right on the trail, for many the villages of **Upper Beeding** (Map 23 & Map 22a; see p138), and its neighbours **Bramber** (see p138) and **Steyning** (see p138; both on Map 22 & Map 22a), all just off the trail, provide a natural, logical end to the day.   [*Next route overview p131*]

PYECOMBE   MAP 26, p146

Pyecombe, like many a downland village, has some very pretty ivy-clad flint houses but the peace and tranquillity that it evidently once had has been somewhat spoilt by the constant hum of traffic from the A23 which converges with the A273 just below the village. The trees hide the roads from view but struggle to do the same with the constant drone. Nevertheless, it's a convenient place to stay being right on the Way and with a campsite, B&B and a pub.

The Norman **church** (daily 9am-6pm, to 4pm in winter) is very welcoming, allowing you to make yourself a cup of coffee or tea in their kitchen, or use the **toilet**. The former **forge** in the house opposite was once the source of some of the best shepherds' crooks in southern England.

If you're looking for a picnic lunch, the BP petrol station just south of the village has a 24hr **M&S food outlet** stocked with treats, as well as a **Wild Bean Café**.

Metrobus's No 270 (East Grinstead–Brighton) **bus** stops here as do their 271 and 273 (both Crawley–Brighton); see pp46-8.

Where to stay and eat

Camping is available at *Chantry Farm Campsite* (off Map 26; ☎ 07540-350384, ⌨ chantry farm.org; ⚑ but on a lead at certain times of the year); it must be booked at least 24hrs in advance but flexibility is shown to walkers. It's a small eco-friendly place (hot-water tap-and-bucket 'showers'; compost toilets; phone-charging) with room for up to 30 tents (from £18pp) and a couple of cosy shepherd's huts (see the website for details).

Tallai House (☎ 01273-845848, ⌨ grahamsmudge@talk21.com; 2D or T, shared facilities; WI-FI) charges from £55pp (sgl occ room rate) for **B&B** and is very welcoming.

The Plough (☎ 01273-842796, ⌨ the ploughpyecombe.co.uk; **fb**; **food** daily noon-8.30pm) commands unenviable views of the traffic hurtling down the A23 to and from Brighton. Despite this it is a good pub with tasty food; they also do takeaways.

ROUTE GUIDE AND MAPS

E➔ PYECOMBE TO SOUTHEASE   MAPS 26-31

This reasonably long stretch, **15 miles (24km, 5-7hrs)** provides sweeping views north. The high ground in the distance is the High Weald, a large area of sandstone incorporating Ashdown Forest, the home of Winnie the Pooh, while to the south is Brighton and the English Channel.

The high point of this section is **Ditchling Beacon** (Map 27) with its namesake **Ditchling** village (Map 27a; see p150) within walking distance of the trail. After leaving the hustle and bustle of the Beacon the route continues towards **Black Cap** (Map 28, p152) where the track takes a sharp right-hand turn and the first turn-off point for those wanting to visit **Lewes** (p153).

After the Lewes turn-off the path heads to, and then across, the **A27 dual carriageway** (Map 29), then returns to the ridge of the Downs before crossing the Greenwich Meridian to reach the villages of **Kingston-near Lewes** (Map 30; see p159), **Rodmell** (see p160) and **Southease** (both Map 31, p163) where the smell of the sea will probably be prevalent and the chalk cliffs of Seaford Head can be seen in the distance. There are a few accommodation and food options on the way.

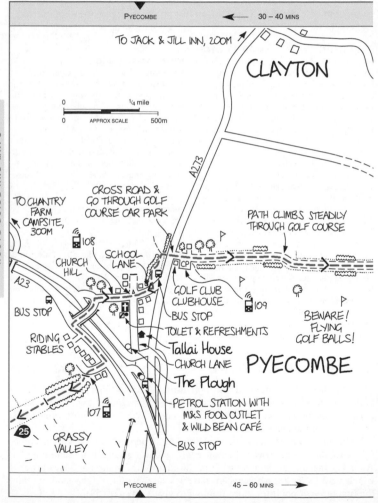

CLAYTON   MAP 26

The main attraction of Clayton is not the small village at the foot of the hill but the two **windmills** (see box p148) just two minutes from the path.

There's no B&B in the village itself but out on the bend on the main road, about five minutes' walk away, is *Jack & Jill Inn*

(☎ 01273-843595, 🖥 thejackandjillinn.co.uk; **fb**; 3T/1D, all en suite; WI-FI; (L); 🐾 bar only), a family-run pub with good-value **food** (Mon-Fri noon-2pm & 5.30-8.30pm, Sat noon-9pm, Sun to 8pm), real ale (see box p22) and four rooms. **B&B** costs £37.50-57.50pp (sgl occ from £55); room-only about £10pp less.

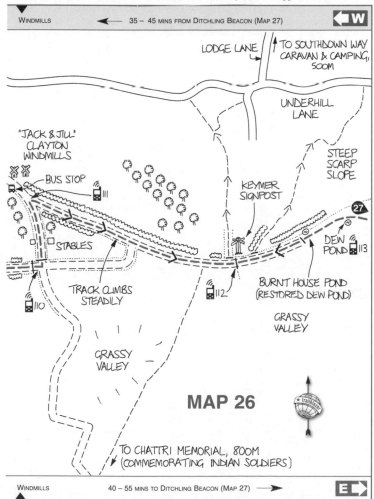

WINDMILLS   ◄— 35 – 45 MINS FROM DITCHLING BEACON (MAP 27)   ◄ W

TO SOUTHDOWN WAY CARAVAN & CAMPING, 500M

LODGE LANE

UNDERHILL LANE

"JACK & JILL" CLAYTON WINDMILLS

BUS STOP

KEYMER SIGNPOST

STEEP SCARP SLOPE

STABLES

TRACK CLIMBS STEADILY

DEW POND

BURNT HOUSE POND (RESTORED DEW POND)

GRASSY VALLEY

GRASSY VALLEY

MAP 26

TO CHATTRI MEMORIAL, 800M (COMMEMORATING INDIAN SOLDIERS)

WINDMILLS   40 – 55 MINS TO DITCHLING BEACON (MAP 27) —►   E ►

ROUTE GUIDE AND MAPS

❑ JACK AND JILL WINDMILLS

Map 26, p147

The twin windmills above Clayton, known as Jack and Jill, are famous local landmarks that can be seen for miles around. There is evidence that suggests the first windmill was erected way back in 1765. The names of the windmills are said to originate from the 1920s when tourists first came to visit.

The post mill Jill, the white windmill, has been fully restored and occasionally grinds out some wholemeal flour. It is the only one of the two that is open to the public (🖳 jillwindmill.org.uk; May-Sep, most Sun & bank hols 2-5pm; free). Pre-COVID there was a *tea shop* that was open when the windmill was, though at the time of writing it was uncertain whether it would continue.

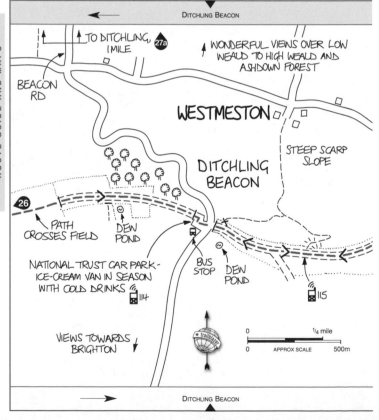

ROUTE GUIDE AND MAPS

Ditchling Beacon Ditchling Beacon (Map 27) is a National Nature Reserve and a popular tourist spot. The name refers to the pyres that were burnt here and at other sites along the Downs such as the Beacon Hill (see p87) in Hampshire. The beacons were lit to warn of impending attack, most notably during the time of the Spanish Armada. More recently they were used for celebrating the Queen's Diamond Jubilee in 2012. Access is made easy by the road that winds in hairpins up the escarpment from Ditchling village. Brighton & Hove Buses operate a seasonal and weekend only **bus** service (No 79; see p46) between the car park at the beacon and Brighton.

DITCHLING **MAP 27a, p150**

It is about a mile from the Downs to this village but if you are trying to decide on a place to spend the night this is a good choice and worth the short detour. Ditchling is among the prettiest of the pretty, perhaps bettered only by Alfriston and Amberley. There is a multitude of historic buildings centred

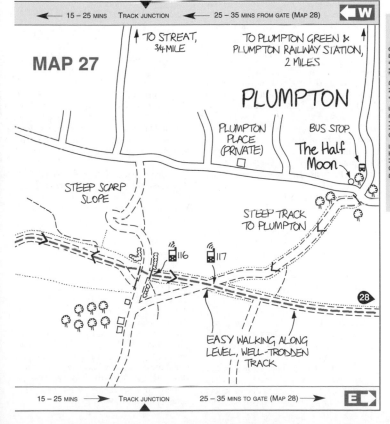

ROUTE GUIDE AND MAPS

around the crossroads but the oldest of all is the fine 13th-century Norman **St Margaret's Church**. Opposite the church you can see the house, **Wings Place**, bought by Henry VIII for his fourth wife, Anne of Cleves (see Plumpton p151 and Lewes p153), as part of a 'pay off' at the end of their marriage.

Not far from the church, in the old Victorian village school, is **Ditchling Museum of Art + Craft** (☎ 01273-844744, 🖥 ditchlingmuseumartcraft.org.uk; mid Jan to mid Dec Thur-Sun 10.30am-1pm & 2-5pm; £8.75). It's well worth visiting, with impressive collections by famous local artists and craftspeople such as the sculptor and engraver Eric Gill, the printer Hilary Pepler, the weaver Ethel Mairet and the painters David Jones and Sir Frank Brangwyn.

Services

There are two small **village shops** with limited provisions. One, called **Parkers of Ditchling** (daily 8-11am) is a short way up the High St next to Church Lane while the other, incorporating the **post office** (☎ 01273-842736; shop & PO daily 8am-1pm), is at the crossroads in the centre of the village. Close by is **Ditchling Pharmacy** (Mon-Thur 9am-1pm & 2-5.30pm, Fri 9am-1pm & 2-6.30pm).

For further information look at: 🖥 www.visitditchling.co.uk.

Where to stay and eat

Campers should head about a mile west along Clayton Rd to find *Southdown Way Caravan & Camping Park* (off Maps 26 & 27a; ☎ 01273-841877 or ☎ 07483 251792, 🖥 www.southdown-caravancamping.org .uk; **fb**; 🐾 on lead), which is exceptionally welcoming for a big caravan park. They charge from £9pp for backpackers, the shower block is spotlessly clean and there's a laundry room and a small shop in reception (daily 9am-6pm). The campsite can also be reached from the Way, via a footpath from Keymer Signpost (Map 26); at the bottom of the path turn right onto Underhill Lane, left along Lodge Lane and the campsite is opposite the end of the road.

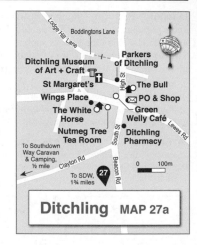

Ditchling MAP 27a

The Bull (☎ 01273-843147, 🖥 the bullditchling.com; 4D/2T, all en suite; WI-FI; 🐾 in bar area only) is a wonderful old pub on the High St. There's very comfortable **B&B** from £67.50pp (sgl occ room rate); at weekends they have a minimum two-night stay. It's a good place to eat (**food** Mon-Sat 8am-9pm, Sun noon-8pm), though you may have to book a table at weekends.

There's also *The White Horse* (☎ 01273-842006, 🖥 whitehorseditchling .com; **fb**; 3D all en suite, 2D/2D or T private bathroom; 🚿; WI-FI; (L); 🐾 bar only), which charges from £47.50pp (sgl occ from £75) for room only. **Food** (Mon-Fri 9am-3pm & 5-8.30pm, Sat noon-8.30pm, Sun noon-6pm) is available in the pub or in their restaurant. Note that they also have a **shop-cum-café** (daily 9am-4pm).

For breakfast, lunch or an afternoon tea try the *Green Welly Café* (☎ 01273-841010, 🖥 www.thegreenwellycafe.co.uk; **fb**; Tue-Sun 9am-3pm; WI-FI; 🐾) and either sit indoors or in their pleasant courtyard garden. The menu includes delicious breakfast ciabattas. The alternative is just round the corner at *Nutmeg Tree Tea Room* (☎ 01273-842708; **fb**; Mon & Wed-Fri 8.30am-4pm, Sat & Sun 8am-4.30pm; temperamental WI-FI; 🐾).

PLUMPTON   **MAP 27, p149**

Famous for its agricultural college, Plumpton is also the location for the privately owned **Plumpton Place**, a 16th-century mansion complete with moat, once owned by Anne of Cleves after it was given to her by Henry VIII. The best view of the mansion is from the Way on the top of the hill, so the only real reason for walkers to come down off the trail here is to visit The Half Moon pub.

The Half Moon (☎ 01273-890253, 🖥 www.thehalfmoonplumpton.co.uk; **fb**; **food** Mon-Fri noon-2.30pm & 6-9pm, Sat noon-9pm, Sun to 4pm; WI-FI; 🐾) is an excellent local pub with a wide selection of interesting dishes and real ales on tap. For lunch you can choose from one of their delicious mains (£13-18) or, less expensive, hot paninis (£6.50-8).

Plumpton **railway station** (see box p44) is actually in Plumpton Green, 2½ miles due north of Plumpton; it's a stop on Southern's London to Eastbourne/Hastings/Ore line. Compass's **bus** No 166 (see p47) will take you to Lewes.

To Lewes Those wishing to visit Lewes can either walk or catch public transport. The turn-off from the trail for those walking is at **Black Cap** (Map 28), but note it's at least an hour's walk from here. For those looking to use public transport, there are frequent buses running between Brighton and Lewes along the A27 that stop in front of Housedean Farm (see Map 29 and p158). Also note, it is possible to take a side trip from Lewes to the isolated hill of **Mount Caburn** (see p156-8), the only part of the South Downs that is not covered by the South Downs Way.

❏ **THE LEWES POUND**

In 2008, Lewes town took the unusual step of issuing its own currency, to be used alongside sterling. The idea behind the 'Lewes Pound' (🖥 thelewespound.org) is to encourage demand for local goods and services, and the logic behind it is simple: money spent in shops in the town that are merely another branch of a national chain does not stay in the local economy; but money spent in shops owned by locals or on local services does. So while the Lewes Pound would not be accepted in, for example, the local outlet of a nationwide superstore, of which there are several in Lewes, it would be accepted by a local trader – who would then spend it locally with another local trader, and so on and so on. Thus, by ensuring that money is spent locally and so stays within the community, the wealth of the locals is safeguarded.

People buy Lewes Pounds (with sterling) at one of the issuing points (including Lewes Town Hall, Mays General Store on Cliffe High St, and Richards & Son, Butchers, on Western Rd) – or from the website (see above) – then spend them with participating traders.

Whilst the establishing of a new currency may seem like a highly bizarre step to take, it isn't without precedent; indeed, Lewes itself had its own currency for over a century between 1789 and 1895. The issuers of the latest Lewes Pound, however, admit that their currency is not actually legal tender, in that there is no obligation on the part of retailers to accept the pound. Some residents, though, see the Lewes Pound as an unnecessary complication. They argue that they can support local traders by buying from them using good old-fashioned sterling. And it's true that the Lewes Pound doesn't seem to be quite as much in evidence as it was in the past.

ROUTE GUIDE AND MAPS

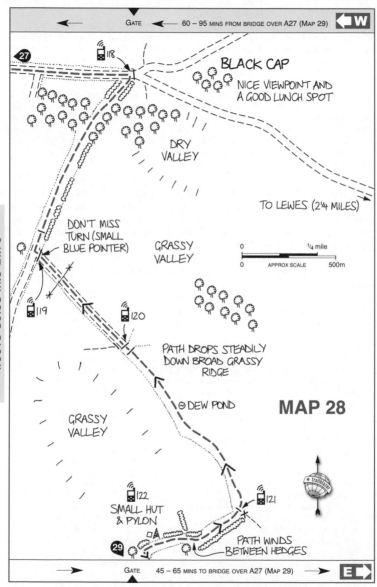

27

118

BLACK CAP

NICE VIEWPOINT AND A GOOD LUNCH SPOT

DRY VALLEY

TO LEWES (2¼ MILES)

DON'T MISS TURN (SMALL BLUE POINTER)

GRASSY VALLEY

0   ¼ mile

0   APPROX SCALE   500m

119

120

PATH DROPS STEADILY DOWN BROAD GRASSY RIDGE

⊙ DEW POND

MAP 28

GRASSY VALLEY

122

121

SMALL HUT & PYLON

PATH WINDS BETWEEN HEDGES

29

ROUTE GUIDE AND MAPS

LEWES   MAP 28a, p155

'Lewes ... lying like a box of toys under a great amphitheatre of chalky hills ... on the whole it is set down better than any town I have seen in England' **William Morris**

Lewes, the county town of East Sussex, is still an attractive place to visit and one of the most desirable places to live in the South-East. Like Totnes in Devon, it's a Transition Town (⌨ transitionnetwork.org) populated by a vibrant community of people, some of whom are dedicated to following this movement based on permaculture and sustainability. They've even issued their own currency (see box p151). For the visitor it's interesting to see somewhere that's paying more than lip service to being green. It also means there's a profusion of places to buy and eat good healthy food; it's well worth spending the night here.

Lewes lies in a strategic position by the River Ouse with Mount Caburn (see p156) rising steeply to the west. This did not go unnoticed by William the Conqueror who had William de Warenne fortify the town soon after the Battle of Hastings in 1066.

The town's focal point is **Lewes Castle** (☎ 01273-486290, ⌨ sussexpast.co .uk; Mar-Oct daily 10am-5.30pm, Nov-Feb to 3.30/4pm; £8), which sits proudly at the very highest point on a grassy bluff. This Norman castle was built by Lieutenant William de Warenne shortly after the Battle of Hastings in 1066. The well-preserved castle gate and walls can be explored and the ticket also gives access to the **Museum of Sussex Archaeology (Barbican House)** opposite, which has artefacts from the castle, a scale model of 1880s Lewes and a 12-minute video on the history of the town.

Prior to COVID you could buy a joint ticket for both Lewes Castle and the **Anne of Cleves House**, down the hill from the castle. Unfortunately, the house was closed at the time of research but if it has reopened by the time of your visit to Lewes, it's well worth dropping in to see the beautiful interior with timber beams and oak furnishings; see ⌨ sussexpast.co.uk for details.

Lewes still has some excellent bookshops, the oldest of which, **The Fifteenth Century Bookshop** (Sat & Sun 11am-5pm), can be found at the top of the High St near the castle entrance. The timber-framed building that houses the shop is worth a visit in itself.

At the same end of the High St is **Bull House** where Thomas Paine, the founder of American Independence, lived between 1768 and 1774. During his time in Lewes he acted as the local tobacconist and exciseman. A commemorative plaque can be seen on the outside wall, but the building isn't open to the public.

Priory Park and the ruins of the 11th-century **Priory of St Pancras** are worth visiting and the ruins are well labelled with interesting panels. There's also a little garden of medicinal herbs once grown by the monks. The park and there's no entry charge. Between here and the castle are the flower-filled **Southover Grange Gardens**, with a scattering of art sculptures, a 350-year-old mulberry tree and a tulip tree planted in 1951 by Princess Elizabeth before she became Queen Elizabeth II.

Real-ale drinkers cannot go to Lewes without visiting **Harvey's Brewery** (⌨ harveys.org.uk) though with a waiting list of more than a year for guided tours most fans will get no further than the shop. Harvey's is the oldest brewery in Sussex and has been producing real ales (see box p22) for well over 200 years using hops from Sussex and Kent and water from their own spring. The company is still run by the same family that founded it seven generations ago. The **shop** (☎ 01273-480217; Tue-Sat 10am-5pm) sells a vast array of Harvey's products and paraphernalia.

Services

The **tourist information centre** (☎ 01273-483448, ⌨ visitlewes.co.uk; all year Mon-Fri 9.30am-4.30pm, Apr-Sep Sat 9.30am-4pm, Sun & bank hols 10am-2pm, Oct-Mar Sat 10am-2pm) is at No 187 High St, on the corner with Fisher St. They can help find local accommodation (although they can't book it for you) and also sell maps, books and guides.

The **post office** (Mon-Sat 8.30am-5.30pm) is at the lower end of the High St. There is also a **chemist** and several **banks** with **ATMs**. Waitrose **supermarket** (Mon-Sat 7.30am-9pm, Sun 10am-4pm) is on Eastgate St while **walking equipment and camping gear** (including fuel for camping stoves) can be found at The Outdoor Shop (☎ 01273-487840; Mon-Fri 9.30am-5.30pm, Sat 9am-5.30pm) just past the river. In the same area there's a Waterstones **bookshop** (Mon-Sat 9am-5.30pm, Sun 10am-4pm) and *café* (Mon-Sat 9am-5pm, Sun 10am-3.30pm).

Public transport

Lewes is a stop on several of Southern's **train** services (see box p44); the **railway station** is on the southern side of town.

The **bus station** is on Eastgate St and there are several useful **bus** services (see pp46-8): Brighton and Hove Buses' No 28 (Brighton to Tunbridge Wells) and No 29 (Brighton to Tunbridge Wells/Uckfield). For Rodmell, Southease or Kingston-near-Lewes take Compass's No 123 (to Newhaven); for Eastbourne take Compass's No 125, or it's their No 166 (to Haywards Heath) for Plumpton and their 143 for Hailsham.

For a **taxi** try Lewes Town Taxis (☎ 01273-474747, 🖳 lewestowntaxis.co.uk) or GM Taxis (☎ 01273-477567 or 01273-473737, 🖳 gmtaxislewes.co.uk).

Where to stay

As with any other popular tourist town booking in advance is advised in Lewes.

Aleberry (☎ 01273-480865, 🖳 aleberry .co.uk; 1S/1D or T shared bathroom; 🛏; WI-FI) charges from £45pp (sgl/sgl occ £45/65) for B&B with a healthy breakfast of fruit, yoghurt, cereal and toast. There is a minimum two-night booking for bank holiday weekends and the bonfire festival (see box p14).

The Dorset (☎ 01273-474823, 🖳 the dorsetlewes.co.uk; 5D/1D or T, all en suite; 🛏; WI-FI) is a Harvey's Brewery pub which has rooms for £25-50pp (sgl occ room rate). The rate includes a continental breakfast.

Climbing the hill from the river towards the castle, you'll soon reach *Montys* (☎ 01273-476750, 🖳 montys accommodation.co.uk; 1D, all en suite; 🛏; WI-FI), Broughton House, 16 High St, which charges from £50pp (sgl occ room rate). It's a lovely room, with a kitchenette (but no cooking facilities), a four-poster bed and free-standing bath. The rate includes a continental breakfast with home-made muesli or granola. Note, however, that a two-night minimum stay is preferred.

See pp46-8 for additional options between Lewes and Kingston-near-Lewes.

Where to eat and drink

Cafés At the bottom end of town, on the eastern side of the river, *Café du Jardin* (☎ 01273-480777, 🖳 cafedujardin.co.uk; **fb**; Tue-Sat 9am-4pm, Sun 10am-3pm; WI-FI; 🐾) is a quirky little courtyard café serving lunches and teas. Set amongst an antique shop and a studio it's right at home here in Lewes.

Overlooking the river, **Riverside** (🖳 riverside-lewes.co.uk) is a small, market-like food hall with a *café* (☎ 01273-487888; daily 8am-7pm; WI-FI; 🐾), a deli-catessen, an ice-cream parlour and various other stalls on the ground floor, and a good-value *brasserie* (☎ 01273-472247; Mon-Fri 9am-4pm, Sat to 5pm, Sun 10.30am-3.30pm; WI-FI; 🐾) upstairs.

Next door, *Bake Out* (Mon-Fri 7.30am-4pm, Sat 7.30am-4.30pm, Sun 9am-4pm) is a small bakery with some seating for coffee drinkers.

Further up the hill, *Flint Owl Bakery* (🖳 flintowlbakery.com/pages/lewes; Mon-Fri 8.30am-5pm, Sat 9am-5pm, Sun to 4pm) is a lovely bakery-cum-café, with more comfortable seating including some in a small back garden.

Across the road, *Robson's of Lewes* (☎ 01273-480654; Mon-Sat 9am-5pm, Sun 10am-5pm; WI-FI; 🐾 garden only) is a coffee shop and takeaway that serves breakfasts, light lunches, teas and ice-cream.

For sandwiches, try *Castle Sandwich Bar* (☎ 01273-478080; Mon-Fri 9am-3pm)

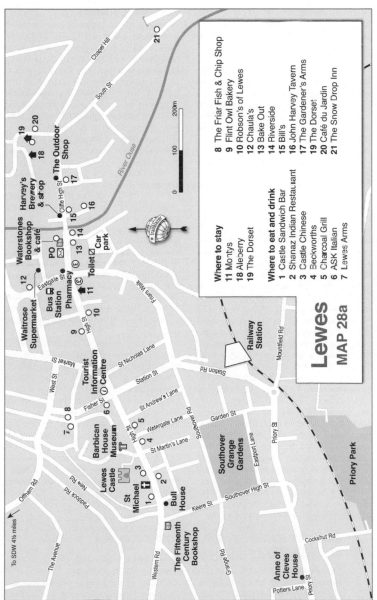

Where to stay
11 Morty's
18 Aleberry
19 The Dorset

Where to eat and drink
1 Castle Sandwich Bar
2 Shanaz Indian Restaurant
3 Castle Chinese
4 Beckworths
5 Charcoal Grill
6 ASK Italian
7 Lewes Arms
8 The Friar Fish & Chip Shop
9 Flint Owl Bakery
10 Robson's of Lewes
12 Chaula's
13 Bake Out
14 Riverside
15 Bill's
16 John Harvey Tavern
17 The Gardener's Arms
19 The Dorset
20 Café du Jardin
21 The Snow Drop Inn

Lewes
MAP 28a

or nearby **Beckworths** (☎ 01273-474502; Mon-Sat 9am-4pm) which is set in a tiny timber-framed house at 67 High St and is also a deli serving a variety of cold meats.

Pubs With a brewery in town it's not surprising that there's a wide choice of pubs with a cracking selection of real ales.

Harvey's (see p153) owns and serves its ales in several pubs in town. Pubs include **The Dorset** (see Where to Stay; food Mon-Thur noon-3pm & 5-9pm, Fri & Sat noon-9pm, Sun to 4pm; WI-FI; 🐾 bar only), on Mailing St, and **John Harvey Tavern** (☎ 01273-479880, 🖥 johnharvey tavern.co.uk; **fb**; food Mon-Sat noon-8pm, Sun to 4pm; WI-FI; 🐾), opposite the brewery. Both serve food. Another good spot for a pint of the local brew, and many others since it's a real ale pub is **The Gardener's Arms** (☎ 01273-474808; bar Mon-Sat 11am-10.30pm, Sun noon-10pm; WI-FI; 🐾) which is conveniently situated a short way down the High St; it is a popular place with locals wanting a quiet drink.

Tucked away in the side streets behind the castle, **Lewes Arms** (☎ 01273-473152, 🖥 lewesarms.co.uk; food Mon-Fri noon-8.30pm, Sat to 9pm, Sun to 8pm; WI-FI; 🐾) is a lovely traditional pub with snugs and quiet corners where you can enjoy a beer; they offer good pub fare too.

Perhaps best of the lot, though, is **The Snow Drop Inn** (☎ 01273-471018; **fb**; food Thur-Sat noon-9pm, Sun to 6pm; WI-FI; 🐾); it's situated under the chalk cliffs that tower above the quiet end of South St, and named to commemorate the eight people who were killed here in the 1836 avalanche; the deadliest avalanche in British history. The community ties are strong, and it's a very friendly place with good food, fine ale, some courtyard seating and a menu of pub classics. When COVID is not an issue they hope to open daily again.

Restaurants & takeaways

There are several decent restaurants down by the river. **Bill's** (☎ 020-8054 5395, 🖥 bills-website.co.uk/restaurants/lewes; Mon-Tue 8am-9.30pm, Wed-Thur to 10pm, Fri & Sat to 11pm, Sun 9am-10pm) is a popular place with tables outside on the cobbled street. It's become a nationwide chain, but the original was here in Lewes (albeit at different premises before they were destroyed in a flood). Wholesome offerings range from shepherd's pie and hamburgers to halloumi salad and Thai green curry.

For Italian food you could try **ASK Italian** (☎ 01273-019090, 🖥 www.askital ian.co.uk/italian/restaurants/lewes; daily 11.30am-10pm), a reliable chain serving the usual pizza and pasta dishes.

There are several Indian restaurants, of which **Chaula's** (☎ 01273-476707, 🖥 chaulas.co.uk; Tue-Thur 5-10pm, Fri & Sat to 10.30pm, Sun to 9.30pm), at 6 Eastgate St near the bus station, is amongst the best, with **Shanaz Indian Restaurant** (☎ 01273-488028, 🖥 shanazlewes.co.uk; Sun-Wed 5.30-9pm, Fri & Sat 5.15-9.15pm) up at the top end of the High St, proving a worthy rival.

For the flavours of the Orient there's **Castle Chinese** (☎ 01273-473235, 🖥 www.castlechinese.co.uk; **fb**; Sun-Thur 5-10pm, Fri & Sat to 10.30pm, Sun to 9.30pm) near the castle, which is a takeaway and a sit-down restaurant, while for takeaway only there's **Charcoal Grill** (☎ 01273-471126; Sun-Thur noon-midnight, Fri & Sat to 1am), with kebabs and burgers, and **The Friar Fish and Chip Shop** (☎ 01273-472016, 🖥 www.thefriarlewes.co .uk; Tue-Thur noon-1.45pm & 5-9.30pm, Fri-Sat noon-2pm & 5-9.30pm) on the aptly named Fisher St.

SIDE TRIP (FROM LEWES) TO MOUNT CABURN

The only part of the South Downs not covered by the South Downs Way is the isolated hill near Lewes, known rather grandly as Mount Caburn. It is something of an anomaly, being the only part of the Downs separated from the main spine of chalk hills. The hill's unique position makes it an excellent

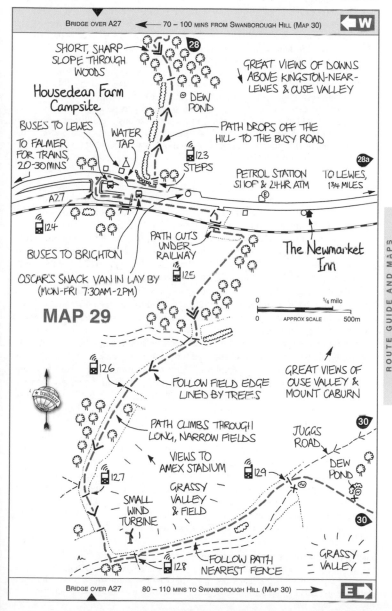

28

SHORT, SHARP SLOPE THROUGH WOODS

GREAT VIEWS OF DOWNS ABOVE KINGSTON-NEAR-LEWES & OUSE VALLEY

Housedean Farm Campsite

⊖ DEW POND

BUSES TO LEWES

WATER TAP

PATH DROPS OFF THE HILL TO THE BUSY ROAD

TO FALMER FOR TRAINS, 20-30 MINS

123 STEPS

28a

PETROL STATION SHOP & 24 HR ATM

TO LEWES, 1¾ MILES

A27

124

PATH CUTS UNDER RAILWAY

The Newmarket Inn

BUSES TO BRIGHTON

125

OSCAR'S SNACK VAN IN LAY BY (MON-FRI 7:30AM-2PM)

MAP 29

0   ¼ mile
0   APPROX SCALE   500m

GREAT VIEWS OF OUSE VALLEY & MOUNT CABURN

126

FOLLOW FIELD EDGE LINED BY TREES

PATH CLIMBS THROUGH LONG, NARROW FIELDS

JUGGS ROAD

30

VIEWS TO AMEX STADIUM

129

DEW POND

127

GRASSY VALLEY & FIELD

SMALL WIND TURBINE

30

128

FOLLOW PATH NEAREST FENCE

GRASSY VALLEY

★ trailblazer

ROUTE GUIDE AND MAPS

vantage point for admiring the rest of the Downs stretched out to the south, as well as the Ouse Valley and the county town of Lewes. The top of the hill is a National Nature Reserve renowned for its butterflies as well as its paragliders.

The hill is best approached from the village of **Glynde** where there is a railway station (trains leave hourly from Lewes; 5 mins). From Glynde station, Mount Caburn (152m/498ft) looms above. Head towards the hill by walking up the road for five minutes. Just past the old village smithy (blacksmith), which is still being used, is a junction that marks the centre of Glynde village. Turn left and look for the stile in the hedgerow opposite the village shop. The path to the top of Mount Caburn follows the obvious route through the fields from the stile and takes about 30-45 minutes. The return is by the same route or via a path further to the north which drops through a small copse to emerge on the lane north of Glynde village.

Around the A27 There are both accommodation and possible food options between Lewes and Kingston-near-Lewes. For accommodation right on the trail there's *Housedean Farm Campsite* (Map 29; ☎ 07919-668816, 🖳 housedean.co .uk; **fb**; 🐾; Easter-early Oct). In addition to its 25 **pitches** (£15pp) they also have three **camping pods**, two of which sleep two people (£55), and one which sleeps four (£70); bedding is not provided. There's also a fully furnished **shepherd's hut** (sleeps two; £160 for two nights) and a **Pig Ark** (1Qd; £90) set in its own private area of the field and with its own cooking shelter and electricity supply and outdoor bath. Note that the double bed has a duvet and pillows but you'll have to supply bedding for the two single beds. For all pitches, pods and pig arks there is sometimes a 2-night minimum stay at weekends, during June to August. There are toilets, showers and a fire pit at each pitch.

From outside the farm, on the A27, is the bus stop for **buses to Lewes**. The stop for buses to Brighton is on the southern side of the road.

For accommodation (and food too), half a mile up the A27 from here and also convenient for the SDW (though being right by the road it's hardly the most beautiful location), *The Newmarket Inn* (☎ 01273-470021, 🖳 www.relax-innz.co.uk/ashcombe; 2S/7D/5T/1Tr, all en suite; 🛁; WI-FI; Ⓛ) has **B&B** from £35pp (sgl/sgl occ from £50/52.25), although rates can be a lot higher when there are events in the area. At the time of research they weren't serving food (other than breakfast for guests) but hope to when life is back to normal so check their website. However, for those in need of sustenance there's no need to divert from the trail this far, at least for those walkers who pass through this way before 2pm, as there is always the excellent *Oscar's* **snack van** (Mon-Fri 7.30am-2pm) that parks very nearby in a layby on the A27 on weekdays. It does huge cooked breakfasts as well as jacket potatoes, bacon baps and hot drinks, and has some tables and chairs on the grass verge beside it.

KINGSTON-NEAR-LEWES   MAP 30

This is one of the larger downland villages. From the top of the hill the rather out-of-place housing estate is all too obvious but once you're down in the village it is well hidden. The main street, lined with pretty cottages, comes as a pleasant surprise.

SWANBOROUGH HILL ◄ 65 – 80 MINS FROM SOUTHEASE (Map 31) E W

TO LEWES, 2 MILES
ASHCOMBE LANE
THE AVENUE
The Juggs
WELLGREEN LANE
KINGSTON RIDGE
BUS STOP
KINGSTON-NEAR-LEWES
OLD POND
THE STREET
29 📱 130
VERY STEEP & DANGEROUS IN WET WEATHER. DO NOT ATTEMPT ON BIKE!
CATTLE GRID
TO/FROM KINGSTON-NEAR-LEWES 10-15/15-25 MINS
MAP 30
STEEP GRASSY VALLEY
0   ¼ mile
0   APPROX SCALE   500m
SWANBOROUGH HILL
📱 131
VIEWS OF MOUNT CABURN & FIRLE BEACON →
GO THROUGH GATE IN CORNER OF FIELD
IFORD HILL
CONCRETE TRACK
VIEWS OF LEWES
GRASSY VALLEY
FINE VIEWS TO THE COAST
LONG CONCRETE TRACK FOLLOWS HIGH BROAD RIDGE
31

ROUTE GUIDE AND MAPS

Compass Travel's No 123 **bus** service (Lewes–Newhaven) calls here; see pp46-8.

The Juggs (☎ 01273-472523, 🖳 the juggs.co.uk; WI-FI; 🐾; food Mon-Sat noon-8pm, Sun to 6pm) is an excellent pub with a pretty front garden. The unusual name refers to the baskets once used for carrying fish from Brighton to the market in Lewes.

RODMELL   MAP 31

Rodmell is famous for having been home to Virginia Woolf (see box p162) and her husband Leonard. **Monk's House** (☎ 01273-474760, 🖳 nationaltrust.org.uk/monks-house; £5.75, free to NT members), where they once lived, is open to the public. At the time of research opening days/hours were limited and booking was essential; check their website for details.

For general information about Rodmell visit 🖳 rodmell.net.

Compass Travel's No 123 **bus** service also calls here; see p47.

Where to stay, eat and drink

Opposite the pub is the friendly ***Sunnyside Cottage B&B*** (☎ 01273-476876; 1T en suite but see note re sitting room; Ⓛ; 🐾) with B&B from £45pp (sgl occ also £45) including a good cooked breakfast. The accommodation is like a separate flat though the entrance is through the main house. The sit-

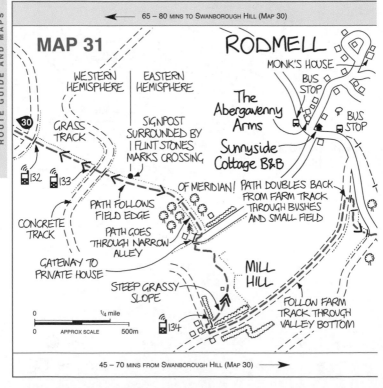

← 65 – 80 MINS TO SWANBOROUGH HILL (MAP 30)

MAP 31 RODMELL

MONK'S HOUSE

WESTERN HEMISPHERE   EASTERN HEMISPHERE

30 GRASS TRACK

📱132 📱133

SIGNPOST SURROUNDED BY 1 FLINT STONES MARKS CROSSING

The Abergavenny Arms

BUS STOP

BUS STOP

Sunnyside Cottage B&B

OF MERIDIAN!

PATH DOUBLES BACK FROM FARM TRACK THROUGH BUSHES AND SMALL FIELD

PATH FOLLOWS FIELD EDGE

CONCRETE TRACK

PATH GOES THROUGH NARROW ALLEY

GATEWAY TO PRIVATE HOUSE

MILL HILL

STEEP GRASSY SLOPE

0   ¼ mile
0   APPROX SCALE   500m

📱134

FOLLOW FARM TRACK THROUGH VALLEY BOTTOM

45 – 70 MINS FROM SWANBOROUGH HILL (MAP 30) →

ting room has a single sofa bed so three can sleep here but with access to the shower and toilet is through the main bedroom. Note they accept cash or cheques only.

The Abergavenny Arms (☎ 01273-472416, 🖳 abergavennyarms.com; food Tue-Fri noon-2.30pm & 6-8.45pm, Sat

noon-8.45pm, Sun to 3.30pm; WI-FI; 🐾) is a great place to take a break and sit by the log fire if it's cold. The sandwiches (from £7.50) make a perfect light lunch. The well inside the pub was once the main source of water for the entire village. Note the pub is closed on Mondays except bank holidays.

W← SOUTHEASE TO PYECOMBE   MAPS 31-26

This stage is long at **15 miles (24km, 5-7hrs)** but with plenty of compensations including views north all the way to the High Weald and Ashdown Forest, the home of Winnie the Pooh. By way of contrast, to the south is Brighton and, glinting beyond, the English Channel, now decorated with military rows of wind turbines. It's because the trail is sandwiched between bustling Brighton and lively **Lewes** (Map 28a; p155; about an hour off the trail via Kingston-near Lewes), that this stage is, perhaps, the busiest of them all. It's possible to

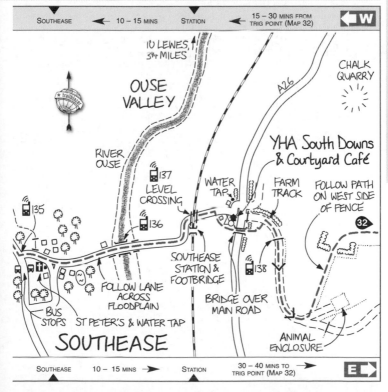

ROUTE GUIDE AND MAPS

take a side trip from Lewes to the isolated hill of **Mount Caburn** (see p156), the only part of the South Downs that is not covered by the South Downs Way. In addition to these large urban centres there are plenty of smaller places on or just off the trail, too.

❏ VIRGINIA WOOLF AND THE BLOOMSBURY GROUP

Born in 1882 in London, Virginia Woolf was a highly accomplished novelist, writing such titles as *The Voyage Out*, *Night and Day*, and *Jacob's Room*. In 1912 she married Leonard Woolf. Their links with Sussex began in 1919 when they moved to the 18th-century **Monk's House** in Rodmell. Their friends included a number of famous artists and writers of the time, not least Virginia's sister the artist Vanessa Bell. Along with the poet TS Eliot and the artists Duncan Grant, Roger Fry and Clive Bell they were known collectively as the Bloomsbury Group.

Many of the paintings from the Bloomsbury Group can be seen in the gallery at the former home of Vanessa Bell and Duncan Grant, **Charleston** (see p165), and also in the small church of St Michael and All Angels at **Berwick** (see p166).

Woolf's life was beset by frequent and sometimes enduring spells of mental breakdown. She tried to kill herself through defenestration (ie throwing herself from a window) before finally, on 18 March 1941, filling her pockets with stones and drowning herself in the nearby River Ouse. Her husband was left with a suicide note in which she spelt out the depths of her love for him: 'If anybody could have saved me it would have been you. Everything has gone from me but the certainty of your goodness'.

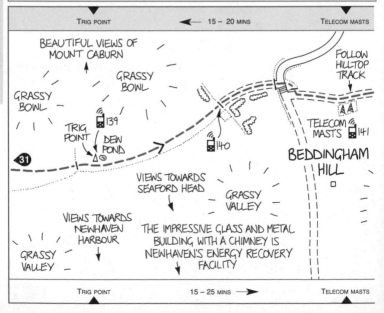

The highest point, **Ditchling Beacon** (Map 27) is a National Nature Reserve and magnet for dog-walkers, cyclists and horse riders. Those who want to break up this stage will find food and accommodation at **Ditchling** (Map 27a) and **Clayton** (Map 26) and a shop and café at **Pyecombe** (p145), which lies right on the trail. *[Next route overview p144]*

SOUTHEASE   MAP 31, p161

Pretty little Southease is tucked away from any main roads, with a tiny Saxon church, **St Peter's**, incorporating an unusual Norman round tower. This round tower is one of three in Sussex, all in the Ouse Valley and all built in the first half of the 12th century. Inside the church are the remains of some 13th-century wall paintings which once covered the whole church; they were revealed again in the 1930s. There is a **water tap** at the church.

Because Southease is a stop on Southern's **train** service (see box p44) between Brighton and Seaford it's an ideal place to start or end a day walk. Compass Travel's **bus** No 123 (Lewes–Newhaven) also stops here; see p47.

The excellent *YHA South Downs* (☎ 0345-371 9574, ☎ 01273-858780, 🖵 www .yha.org.uk/hostel/yha-south-downs; 4 x 2-, 2 x 3-, 3 x 4-, 2 x 5-, 4 x 6-, 1 x 8-bed rooms; Ⓛ) is housed in a converted farmhouse near Southease railway station. Dormitories won't be available until the end of the pandemic but are now being used as private rooms. Some rooms are en suite and where facilities are shared they are now either allocated on a private basis or time slot basis. Rates start from £29 (for a 2-bed room) but vary a lot so check the website for details. There's **camping** (from £14pp; 🐾), although only room for two tent pitches so booking is recommended, plus: four heated **camping pods** (from £39/49 for 2/4 people;

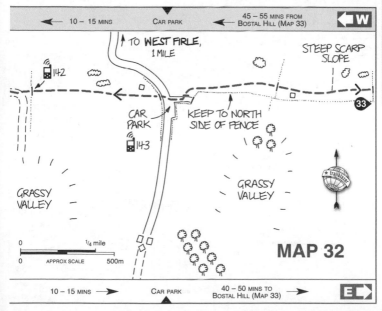

← 10 – 15 MINS   CAR PARK   ← 45 – 55 MINS FROM BOSTAL HILL (Map 33)   ◄W

↑ TO WEST FIRLE, 1 MILE

STEEP SCARP SLOPE

📶 142

33

CAR PARK
📶 143

KEEP TO NORTH SIDE OF FENCE

★ trailblazer

GRASSY VALLEY

GRASSY VALLEY

0   ¼ mile
0   APPROX SCALE   500m

MAP 32

10 – 15 MINS →   CAR PARK   40 – 50 MINS TO BOSTAL HILL (Map 33)   E►

🐾); two **land pods** (from £39; up to four in double bunks; 🐾) with table, bench and BBQ firepit outside but no heating inside; and two **bell tents** (up to four; £50-100; 🐾; Easter to end Sep). Bedding is provided for the pods and bell tents. Other facilities include a self-catering kitchen (closed at the time of research), drying room and bike shed. The on-site Courtyard **café** (daily 10am-4pm but later for guests) is licensed and is open to the public unless the hostel is booked for sole occupancy.

E→ SOUTHEASE TO ALFRISTON   MAPS 31-35

Continuing along the crest of the escarpment, with the high point at **Firle Beacon** (Map 33), this stretch affords easy walking for **7¾ miles (12.5km, 2½-3½hrs)** with fine views to the coast and across the lowlands to **Mount Caburn** (see p156), probably the most grandiose name for any hill of 150 metres' altitude.

Once past **Bostal Hill** the Way passes pathways that lead to **Alciston** (see p166) and **Berwick** (both off Map 34) before it drops steadily down to pretty, wee **Alfriston** (p167).

← 45 – 55 MINS FROM CAR PARK (MAP 32)   BOSTAL HILL ◀ W

↑VIEWS TO FIRLE TOWER BUILT IN 1819 AS A GAME-KEEPER'S LOOK-OUT

FIRLE BEACON

STEEP SIDED 'BOWL'

VIEWS OVER LOW WEALD OF SUSSEX

32

KEEP TO NORTH SIDE OF FENCE

MAP 33

TRIG POINT 📱144

VIEWS SOUTH TO CUCKMERE HAVEN ↓

TO BO-PEEP FARMHOUSE B&B, 250M ↗

BO-PEEP

📱145

BOSTAL HILL

DEW POND

34

0   ¼ mile
0   APPROX SCALE   500m

40 – 50 MINS FROM CAR PARK (MAP 32) →   BOSTAL HILL E ▶

WEST FIRLE   off MAP 32, p163

This small village among the trees lies at the foot of the Downs escarpment. **Firle Stores & Post Office** (☎ 01273-858219; **fb**; Mon-Sat 9am-5.30pm, also June-Aug Sun 11am-4pm), offers plenty of choice for your lunchbox.

The Ram Inn (☎ 01273-858222, 🖳 raminn.co.uk; 4D/2D or T, all en suite; ▼; 🐾; WI-FI) charges £50-97.50pp (sgl occ £90-195) for luxurious B&B rooms. **Food** (main dishes £13-24) is served in three rooms, one of which was formerly the Court Room where judges once passed sentence on misbehaving villagers. The real ales are worth the detour and the kitchen is open daily from 9am to 9.30pm.

About a 2½-mile walk from the pub is **Charleston** (☎ 01323-811626, 🖳 charleston.org.uk; Wed-Sun & Bank hol Mon 10am-5pm; house £14.50, exhibitions £9, combined ticket £20) which houses a gallery of work by the Bloomsbury group of artists (see box p162). There is now a timed entry system and booking is essential.

Charleston is a stop on Compass's No 125 **bus** service (Lewes to Eastbourne); Cuckmere Community Bus operates the limited-frequency No 40 service. See p46.

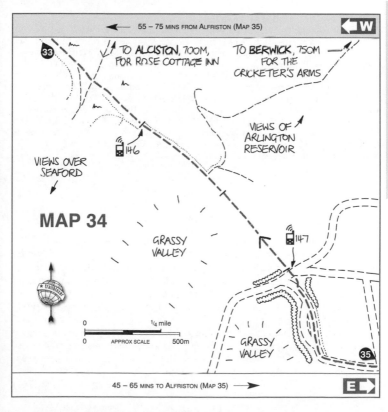

55 – 75 MINS FROM ALFRISTON (MAP 35) ◄ W

33

TO ALCISTON, 700M, FOR ROSE COTTAGE INN

TO BERWICK, 750M FOR THE CRICKETER'S ARMS

VIEWS OF ARLINGTON RESERVOIR

📱146

VIEWS OVER SEAFORD

MAP 34

GRASSY VALLEY

📱147

★ trailblazer

0   ¼ mile
0   APPROX SCALE   500m

GRASSY VALLEY

35

45 – 65 MINS TO ALFRISTON (MAP 35) ──► E ►

Around Bostal Hill There's **B&B** at *Bo-Peep Farmhouse* (off Map 33; ☎ 01323-871299, 🖥 bopeepfarmhouse.co.uk; 2D/1Tr, all en suite; 🛏; WI-FI; ⒧), about half a mile from the trail, on your right; they charge £65-70pp (sgl occ room rate).

ALCISTON   off MAP 34, p165

Alciston is yet another beautiful but tiny downland village with little to draw the walker here apart from *The Rose Cottage Inn* (☎ 01323-870377, 🖥 therosecottagealciston.co.uk; 🛏; WI-FI; 🐾; ⒧), formerly a country pub that had been around for over 350 years but now under new ownership and offering self-catering in some very charming self-contained flats. The two larger apartments (2Qd) boast kitchens, the smaller one (1D) has a microwave and kettle and even one of the smaller cabins (2D), known as Hikers' Rests, has a microwave. Rates start at £35/47.50pp (sgl occ room rate) in the cabins/apartments, with breakfast £12pp.

Alciston is a stop on Cuckmere Community Buses' infrequent Nos 40, 42 and 44 **bus** services; see p46.

BERWICK   off MAP 34, p165

Berwick is famous for the Bloomsbury Group of Victorian artists which included Vanessa Bell, Roger Fry and Duncan Grant. Some of Vanessa Bell's work can be seen in the small **church** (St Michael and All Angels) on the edge of the village.

Berwick is a stop on Southern's **railway** line (see box p44).

Compass's No 125 (Eastbourne–Lewes) **bus** service calls here. Cuckmere Community Bus's (CCB) No 126 (Mon-Sat), and their limited frequency No 47 (Cuckmere Valley Rambler) and Nos 40, 42, 43 & 44 services also call here. See p168 for details. Many of these bus services connect with train arrivals, making it a good place to start or end a day walk.

For **food** head to *The Cricketer's Arms* (☎ 01323-870469, 🖥 cricketersberwick.co.uk; **fb**; food Mon-Sat noon-9pm, Sun to 5pm; WI-FI; 🐾 on lead). Their menu generally includes pub favourites such as ham, eggs & chips (£13).

W ← ALFRISTON TO SOUTHEASE   MAPS 35-31

It's not easy to tear yourself away from Alfriston. It's not just the pull of the place itself, but the steep ascent out of the village that begins this **7¾-mile stage (12.5km, 2½-3½hrs)**. The villages of **Berwick** and **Alciston** (both off Map 34) provide reasons to drop right back down again, but if you're staying on the trail you'll find the walking does get easier, at least once you get over **Bostal Hill** (Map 33) and as you hike around the stage's high point at **Firle Beacon** (Map 33).

Your destination on this stage, **Southease** (Map 31), lies hidden in a valley but you can get an approximation of its location by drawing a line south from **Mount Caburn**, the isolated hill to the north of the trail and a near-permanent presence on this stage.

[*Next route overview p161*]

ALFRISTON

Alfriston is another candidate for 'prettiest village on the South Downs Way'. However, this small collection of Tudor wood-beamed buildings slung higgledy-piggledy along a narrow main street is far from a well-kept secret. In high season coachloads of tourists come to 'ooh' and 'ahh' at the sights and have cream teas. Nevertheless, it is worth planning on spending a few hours to take it all in at a leisurely pace. Whilst here make sure you take a look around the **church** and the **Clergy House** which is by the church and the village green.

Services

The **post office** (Sat 2-4pm) has recently moved into the Old Chapel Centre and now has much-reduced opening hours. Its former home was the **village store/deli** (☎ 01323-870201; daily 10am-5pm), where it's worth a visit just to take in its almost authentic 'Olde Worlde' atmosphere. The now-forgotten 'Lamson' system of moving cash to a single cashier, whereby cannisters containing the money were shot along wires and tubes, is still in place though no longer used. The deli here is a great place to pick up the ingredients for a top-class picnic.

There's an excellent independent bookshop, **Much Ado Books** (☎ 01323-871222, 🖳 muchadobooks.com; Mon, Tue & Fri noon-5pm, Sat & Sun 11am-5pm, Wed & Thur open by appointment) with an interesting stock of old and new books, maps and guides. Another good place to browse is **Music Memorabilia**, a record and CD shop.

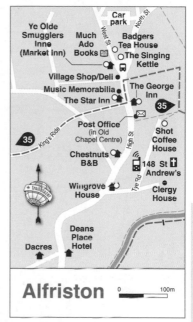

Alfriston   0   100m

Compass's Nos 119 & 125 **bus** services (to Seaford) call here as does the Cuckmere Community Bus (CCB) Nos 25, 26, 47 (seasonal, Sun/bank hol Mon only) & 126, as well as their limited frequency No 42. See p47.

For **information** about the village look at the website: 🖳 alfriston-village.co.uk. However, note that getting a wi-fi signal can be a problem in the village.

(cont'd on p170)

❑ ALFRISTON CHURCH AND CLERGY HOUSE

The **14th-century flint church** of St Andrew by the river sits in the middle of a well-groomed lawn and is worth a look, as is **Clergy House** (☎ 01323-871961, 🖳 nation altrust.org.uk/alfriston-clergy-house; £6, National Trust members free) nearby. However, at the time of research the house was open limited days and hours and advance booking was essential; check the website for details. This beautiful 14th-century, timber-framed thatched house was the first property the National Trust bought thanks to the local vicar who, in 1896, suggested the building be safeguarded for the nation. Apart from anything else it's a good spot for a picnic lunch.

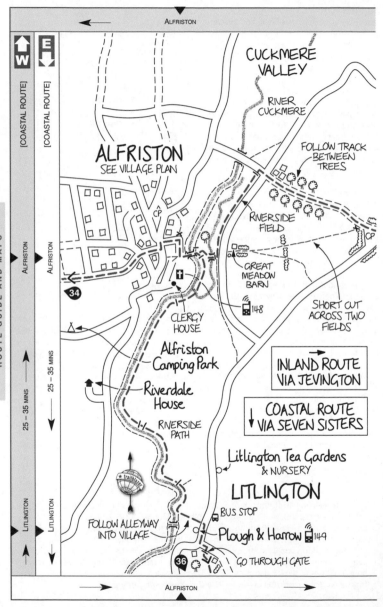

ALFRISTON

[COASTAL ROUTE]   [COASTAL ROUTE]

W   E

ALFRISTON   ALFRISTON

25 – 35 MINS   25 – 35 MINS

LITLINGTON   LITLINGTON

CUCKMERE VALLEY

RIVER CUCKMERE

FOLLOW TRACK BETWEEN TREES

ALFRISTON
SEE VILLAGE PLAN

CP

RIVERSIDE FIELD

CP

34

GREAT MEADOW BARN

148

SHORT CUT ACROSS TWO FIELDS

CLERGY HOUSE

INLAND ROUTE
VIA JEVINGTON

Alfriston Camping Park

Riverdale House

COASTAL ROUTE
VIA SEVEN SISTERS

RIVERSIDE PATH

Litlington Tea Gardens
& NURSERY

LITLINGTON

trailblazer

BUS STOP

FOLLOW ALLEYWAY INTO VILLAGE

Plough & Harrow   149

36

GO THROUGH GATE

ALFRISTON

ROUTE GUIDE AND MAPS

❑ THE LONG MAN OF WILMINGTON   Map 35, above

No-one is quite sure when or why this large chalk figure appeared on the side of Windover Hill above Wilmington.

Best viewed from the lane leading out of the village, he stands 70m tall and holds a vertical rod in each hand. Although it was only in 1969 that the white blocks were placed along the lines of the figure, suggestions as to when the original was made range from the prehistoric era or the Roman age to just a few hundred years ago.

As for the question of why, well that is even harder to answer. Some say he is a fertility symbol robbed of his genitalia; others claim he was carved out for fun by monks from the nearby Wilmington Priory. Or could it be that a real giant collapsed and died on that very spot?

Though the site is easily accessible on the Inland Route, those who took the Coastal trail will miss out. However, there is the Cuckmere Community **Bus** (CCB) No 26 that stops at Wilmington village, at the foot of the Long Man, as well as the limited frequency Nos 40 & 44; see p46.

Where to stay   [see map p167]

For the latest information on accommodation check the village websites (see p167).

Campers will find plenty of room at the family-friendly *Alfriston Camping Park* (Map 35; ☎ 07591-880129, 🖥 alfris toncamping.com; WI-FI patchy at best; 🐾; officially open Mar-Oct, but walkers are seldom turned away at any time of year though it depends on the weather), situated in three large fields surrounded by woods, a couple of minutes' walk from the village centre. There's a laidback atmosphere, so it can get noisy, but it's a fun place to camp. They charge from £10pp, including use of the toilets and showers.

There are numerous **B&B** options, but it's advisable to book ahead. *Chestnuts* (☎ 01323-870959, 🖥 chestnutsalfriston.co.uk; 1D or T en suite, 1D/1T shared bathroom; ☛; WI-FI; Ⓛ; 🐾) is a cute *café* (see Where to eat) with rooms costing £37.50-45pp (sgl occ £50-65). Breakfast includes vegan and vegetarian options.

Dacres (Map 35; ☎ 01323-870447, 🖥 patsyembry@gmail.com; 1Tr en suite; WI-FI) charges from £50pp (sgl occ £60) for B&B. The room has its own entrance, is open plan and is more of a studio apartment with an electric hob and oven, fridge, toaster and microwave so guests can self-cater in the evening. The excellent organic cooked breakfasts are served here and the hospitable owner is more than happy to provide a vegetarian or vegan breakfast if preferred. There's also a lovely garden to relax in.

Riverdale House (Map 35; ☎ 01323-871038, 🖥 riverdalehouse.co.uk; 3D/1D or T/1Tr, all en suite; ☛; WI-FI; 🐾) is peacefully located on the edge of the village, off Seaford Rd. It's a very comfortable B&B with lots of options for sleeping as they can put aero-beds in most rooms so they can accommodate families with up to three children. Rates range from £47.50 to £72.50pp (sgl occ rates on request). Luggage transfer is available by prior arrangement: to/from Lewes and Eastbourne (£20 per trip).

Wingrove House (☎ 01323-870276, 🖥 wingrovehousealfriston.com; 16D, all en suite; ☛; WI-FI) is a restaurant with rooms in a 19th-century colonial-style building. The rooms are luxurious and the food good. B&B costs £50-125pp (sgl occ room rate).

The villages' historic **pubs** also have rooms. *The George Inn* (☎ 01323-870319, 🖥 thegeorge-alfriston.com; **fb**; 5D, all en suite; ☛; WI-FI; Ⓛ; 🐾) is a magnificent old building with oak beams. B&B costs £55-75pp (sgl occ from £75). There is a minimum two-night booking policy at the weekend. *Ye Olde Smugglers Inne* (aka **The Market Inn**; 🖥 www.smugglersalfriston .co.uk; 1T/2D/1Tr, all en suite; ☛; WI-FI; 🐾) charges from £47.50pp (sgl occ £85) inc continental breakfast. The name is derived from a famous gang of smugglers who once used the pub to plan smuggling ventures at Cuckmere Haven. Note, they only take accommodation bookings through the 🖥 booking.com website.

The third in the triumvirate of great, ancient pubs in Alfriston, *The Star Inn* (☎ 01323 870495, 🖥 thepolizzicollection.com /the-star; 30D or T inc 4 'junior suites', all en

---

📖 SMUGGLING

Smuggling of wool, brandy and gin was rife along the Sussex coast with Cuckmere Haven and Birling Gap being favourite places for gangs of smugglers to load and unload their contraband in the late 18th and early 19th centuries. One of the most infamous groups was the Alfriston Gang who would smuggle goods to and from Cuckmere Haven along the Cuckmere River.

The leader of the Alfriston Gang was Stanton Collins who owned the now aptly named Ye Olde Smugglers Inne from where the group plotted their exploits. These included a raid on a Dutch ship wrecked at Cuckmere Haven. The figurehead of the ship, a red lion's head, still stands next to the Star Inn in the village. Stanton Collins was eventually arrested in 1831 for sheep rustling and was shipped off to Australia.

suite; ➾; WI-FI; 🐾) re-opened in 2021 after extensive refurbishment. Some rooms connect to provide accommodation for families/groups and many are in a building, dating from the 1960s, that is behind the inn. B&B costs from £70pp (sgl occ room rate).

At the southern end of the village is the large **Deans Place Hotel** (☎ 01323-870248, 🖥 deansplace.co.uk; 3S/30D or T/4Tr, all en suite; ➾; WI-FI; 🐾), a smart 14th-century country house hotel set in a big garden with manicured lawns and an open-air (heated) swimming-pool (May-Sep). B&B costs £50-100pp (sgl/sgl occ from £70/90); contact them also to enquire if they have any special deals.

Where to eat and drink

For such a small village Alfriston does well for pubs and cafés, many of which have long histories.

Badgers Tea House (☎ 01323-871336, 🖥 badgersteahouse.com, **fb**; Tue-Sun 9.30am-4pm, food until 3pm; 🐾) is a traditional English tearoom. Housed in a building dating back to 1510, the café has long been a favourite of walkers thanks to its delicious scones and with a pleasant walled garden to sit in. However, it has now changed hands; the new owners are keen to keep the standards of food and service of their predecessors. A cream tea costs from £8.95 and afternoon tea from £19.95.

Just off the trail and occupying an enviable location across the green from the church, **Shot Coffee House** (**fb**; daily 10am-4pm) sells soup, toasties, pastries, cakes and hot drinks.

Right in the centre of the village, **The Singing Kettle** (☎ 01323-870723; **fb**; daily 9am-5pm; 🐾) does a good range of breakfasts, plus sandwiches, cakes and good strong coffee. Down the road, **Chestnuts Tearoom** (see Where to stay; Tue-Sat 10.30am-4pm) does good-value breakfasts, including numerous egg options, plus soups, toasties and cream teas (£4.25).

One of the best **pubs** is undoubtedly **The George Inn** (see Where to stay; food daily noon-9pm but sometimes the kitchen is closed 3-6pm on Mon & Tue), which was first licensed way back in 1397. The menu changes seasonally but mains tend to start from £12. The pub also serves some cracking real ales.

Ye Olde Smugglers Inne (☎ 01323-870241; see also Where to stay; food Mon-Sat noon-2.30pm & 6-8.30pm, Sun noon-7pm; WI-FI; 🐾) has friendly staff and an attractive conservatory at the back. They serve good-value pub grub (most mains cost £11-14) with daily specials, Harvey's ales and Long Man Brewery beer (see box p22).

Wingrove House (see Where to stay; Mon-Sat noon-4pm & 6-9pm & Sun noon-3pm & 6-8pm) is a stylish **restaurant** and the contemporary British menu top notch. Mains will set you back £17-25. The wine list is extensive, and there's garden and terrace seating. Non-residents can eat here but booking is recommended.

ROUTE GUIDE AND MAPS

E➔ALFRISTON TO EASTBOURNE (COASTAL ROUTE VIA CUCKMERE)   MAPS 35-39

These **10¾ miles (17.5km, 4¼-5¾hrs)** to the end of the Way – plus another **1½ miles (2.4km) to Eastbourne**; see Map 42) are arguably the highlight of the whole walk, including a stretch through the beautiful **Cuckmere Valley** (Maps 35 & 36) which culminates in wide meanders leading to what is one of the few undeveloped river mouths in the South-East.

The final assault on Eastbourne is a spectacular roller-coaster ride over the **Seven Sisters** (Map 37), a line of chalk cliffs that are less famous than The White Cliffs of Dover, but far more spectacular and, ironically, given the names, far whiter due to more constant erosion.

If that was not enough the path continues, past the popular shingle beach at **Birling Gap** (Map 38), to reach the final high point of the whole walk: **Beachy**

Head (Map 39), a spectacular chalk cliff jutting into the English Channel with 360° views. Even the sprawling mess of Eastbourne is worth admiring from here.

The path finishes at the foot of the hill where it meets abruptly with Eastbourne's suburbs. There are both accommodation and refreshments in the neighbourhood of **Meads Village** (see p178), but if you want to go into Eastbourne there is a bus from there or a half-hour coastal walk along pavements to the town centre.

LITLINGTON   MAP 35, p168

Sitting on the eastern bank of the Cuckmere River, Litlington is yet another oh-so-charming downland village complete with flint cottages. On the other side of the valley is a chalk-horse figure carved into the hillside in 1924.

Litlington is a stop on Cuckmere Community Bus's limited No 47 and No 40 **bus** services; see pp46-7 for details.

The local pub is *Plough and Harrow* (☎ 01323-870632, 🖥 ploughandharrowlit lington.co.uk; **fb**; food daily noon-8pm; WI-FI; 🐾) which serves a variety of bar meals ranging from sandwiches (£7.50) to classic

pub-grub mains (from £11.50) as well as wood-fired pizzas (from £9). The bar is open all day and there's a beer garden at the back.

The village is also home to the delightful *Litlington Tea Gardens & Nursery* (☎ 01323-870222; **fb**; Apr-end Oct Tue-Sun & bank hols 11am-5pm; 🐾), which claims to have been around since 1870. Their lovely tree-shaded garden is the perfect spot for a cream tea (£4-9.50). They also do sandwiches (£4.50), jacket potatoes (£7) and soups (£5.50). Note they accept cash only.

WESTDEAN & EXCEAT   MAP 36

On the northern side of the small wooded ridge of chalk is the wonderfully secluded and secret **Westdean**, a tiny collection of

beautiful cottages complete with duck pond, nestled in a wooded fold.

On the other side of the ridge is **Exceat**, more a collection of tourist facilities than a

---

❏ SEVEN SISTERS COUNTRY PARK

This extensive country park of rolling coastal downland includes the spectacular Seven Sisters chalk cliffs over which the South Downs Way passes.

Apart from the obvious attraction of the chalk cliffs and downland the park also includes Cuckmere Haven and estuary, one of the only river mouths in the south-east of England that has not been spoilt by development. That is not to say that the estuary is untouched. The natural meanders of the river, seen so spectacularly from the ridge above Exceat, have been left to sit as idle ponds thanks to the man-made channel that diverts the flow of the river more swiftly to the sea. Plans were underway to restore the Cuckmere Estuary to its natural state by filling in the man-made channel and allowing the blockade to gradually deteriorate. This would have restored the flow of the river through the meanders and encouraged the natural restoration of the salt-marsh and mudflats. However, by 2006 this plan had been suspended after a 'modelling miscalculation' by the project's environmental consultant was found.

The country park covers an area steeped in history. Some of the most fascinating stories involve the numerous shipwrecks that litter the seabed below the Seven Sisters' cliffs. The most significant of these is that of the Spanish ship *Nympha Americana* which, in 1747, ran aground halfway along the line of chalk cliffs, resulting in the deaths of 30 crewmen.

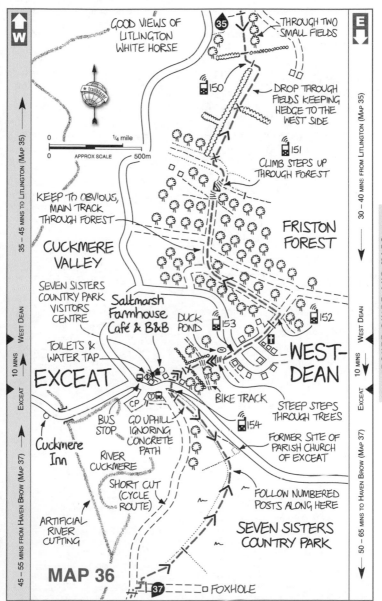

W

GOOD VIEWS OF
LITLINGTON
WHITE HORSE

THROUGH TWO
SMALL FIELDS

35

E

150

DROP THROUGH
FIELDS KEEPING
HEDGE TO THE
WEST SIDE

151

CLIMB STEPS UP
THROUGH FOREST

KEEP TO OBVIOUS,
MAIN TRACK
THROUGH FOREST

FRISTON
FOREST

CUCKMERE
VALLEY

0   ¼ mile

0   500m
APPROX SCALE

SEVEN SISTERS
COUNTRY PARK
VISITORS CENTRE

Saltmarsh
Farmhouse
Café & B&B

DUCK
POND

153

152

TOILETS &
WATER TAP

WEST-
DEAN

EXCEAT

BIKE TRACK

BUS
STOP

CP

GO UPHILL
IGNORING
CONCRETE
PATH

STEEP STEPS
THROUGH TREES

154

FORMER SITE OF
PARISH CHURCH
OF EXCEAT

Cuckmere
Inn

RIVER
CUCKMERE

SHORT CUT
(CYCLE
ROUTE)

FOLLOW NUMBERED
POSTS ALONG HERE

ARTIFICIAL
RIVER
CUTTING

SEVEN SISTERS
COUNTRY PARK

MAP 36

37

FOXHOLE

35 – 45 MINS TO LITLINGTON (MAP 35)

WEST DEAN   EXCEAT

10 MINS

45 – 55 MINS FROM HAVEN BROW (MAP 37)

30 – 40 MINS FROM LITLINGTON (MAP 35)

WEST DEAN   EXCEAT

10 MINS

50 – 65 MINS TO HAVEN BROW (MAP 37)

ROUTE GUIDE AND MAPS

village but with a very good information and visitor centre (see opposite). This is the gateway to **Seven Sisters Country Park** and the spectacular Cuckmere Valley and

beach. If Exceat is an overnight stop on your walk, try to arrive here early in the day to give yourself time to enjoy the area around the beach.

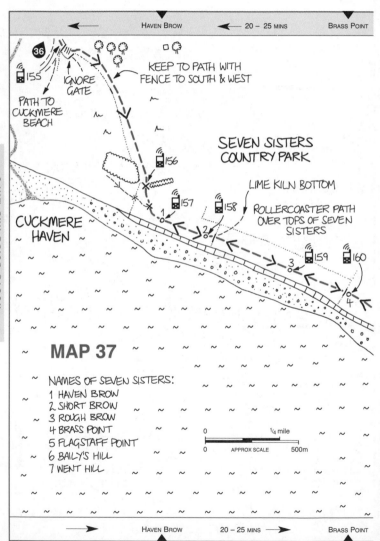

HAVEN BROW ← 20 – 25 MINS ← BRASS POINT

36

155

IGNORE GATE

KEEP TO PATH WITH FENCE TO SOUTH & WEST

PATH TO CUCKMERE BEACH

156

SEVEN SISTERS COUNTRY PARK

LIME KILN BOTTOM

157

158

ROLLERCOASTER PATH OVER TOPS OF SEVEN SISTERS

CUCKMERE HAVEN

1

2

159

160

3

4

MAP 37

NAMES OF SEVEN SISTERS:
1 HAVEN BROW
2 SHORT BROW
3 ROUGH BROW
4 BRASS POINT
5 FLAGSTAFF POINT
6 BAILY'S HILL
7 WENT HILL

0   1/4 mile
0   APPROX SCALE   500m

HAVEN BROW → 20 – 25 MINS → BRASS POINT

ROUTE GUIDE AND MAPS

Services

The excellent **Seven Sisters Country Park Visitors Centre** (🖳 sevensisters.org.uk; Easter-Oct daily 10.30am-4.30pm, Nov & Feb-Easter weekends & school hols only) has information on wildlife and conservation efforts in Seven Sisters Country Park. It also sells souvenirs, cold drinks and

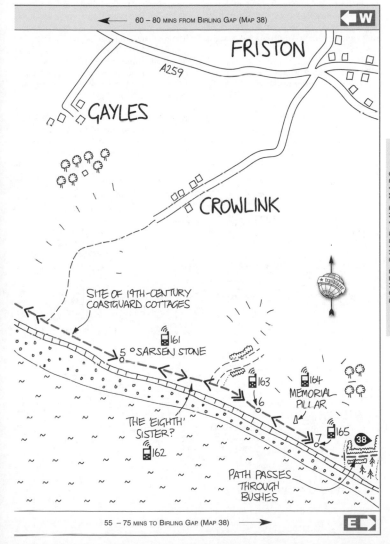

60 – 80 MINS FROM BIRLING GAP (MAP 38)

◀ W

FRISTON

A259

GAYLES

CROWLINK

SITE OF 19TH-CENTURY COASTGUARD COTTAGES

161

5 SARSEN STONE

163

6

164 MEMORIAL PILLAR

THE 'EIGHTH' SISTER?

162

7 165

38

PATH PASSES THROUGH BUSHES

55 – 75 MINS TO BIRLING GAP (MAP 38) ➡

E ▶

snacks; there's a **water tap** by the toilet block behind the visitors centre.

Brighton & Hove Buses' Nos 12A and 13X **bus** services provide regular links to Brighton and Eastbourne. Cuckmere Community Bus's No 47 stops at Seven Sisters Country Park (Mar-Oct Sun & bank hol Mon only) and their No 40 (Tue & Fri only) calls at both Westdean and Exceat; see also pp46-8.

Where to stay and eat

Saltmarsh Farmhouse (☎ 01323-870218, 💻 saltmarshfarmhouse.co.uk; 3D/1T/1Qd, all en suite; ✆; WI-FI) is an upmarket *café* (Mon-Fri 10am-4pm, Sat & Sun 9am-5pm but hours are weather dependent) with some courtyard seating. They also have extremely smart rooms (inc a £350-a-night, two-bedroom suite), but **B&B** in some

rooms can be from around £75pp (sgl occ room rate).

By the bridge, the large *Cuckmere Inn* (☎ 01323-892247, 💻 www.vintageinn.co.uk/restaurants/south-east/thecuckmere innseaford; **fb**; food daily noon-9.30pm; WI-FI; 🐾 designated area only) has a big garden overlooking the River Cuckmere. Their menu includes standard pub fare (mains £11.75-16.95). It gets very busy during the summer due to its great location. If staying at Saltmarsh and visiting the pub in the evening, take a torch as the road between the two is unlit.

BIRLING GAP   MAP 38

All that's in this gap is a small line of terraced houses that are falling into the sea, plus a visitor centre and café of sorts. Considering the beautiful position of the

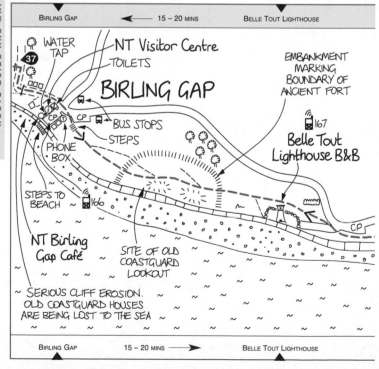

hamlet on a low saddle along the line of chalk cliffs, it's a shame that some of the buildings are so ugly and out of place. The huge steel staircase leading down to the stony beach is also an eyesore, although the beach is a popular spot on sunny summer days. For further information see 🖳 nation altrust.org.uk/birling-gap-and-the-seven-sisters.

Birling Gap is a stop on the 13X **bus service** (Sun & Bank hol Mon only) operated by Brighton and Hove Buses; see pp46-8.

At the time of research *National Trust Birling Gap Café* (☎ 01323-423197; daily 11am to 4pm) was only offering takeaway food (sandwiches and hot paninis, snacks, drinks, cakes and ice-creams) and the attached **visitor centre** and **souvenir shop**, were closed. However, the **toilets** were open (daily 10am-5pm) and there is a **water tap** outside.

A 15- to 20-minute walk from Birling Gap, *Belle Tout Lighthouse* (Map 38; ☎ 01323-423185, 🖳 belletout.co.uk; 6D, all en suite; ✓; WI-FI; mid Jan to mid Dec) is now a luxury B&B with incredible coastal views. They charge £97.50-137.50pp (sgl occ £136.50-233.75), with prices higher on Fri & Sat nights in summer. They don't accept children aged under 16 years old and there's a two-night minimum-stay policy but it's worth contacting them at short notice for a single-night stay.

BEACHY HEAD   MAP 39

Beachy Head is, thankfully, relatively unspoilt with just one large chain pub near the top: *The Beachy Head* (☎ 01323-728060, 🖳 vintageinn.co.uk/thebeachy

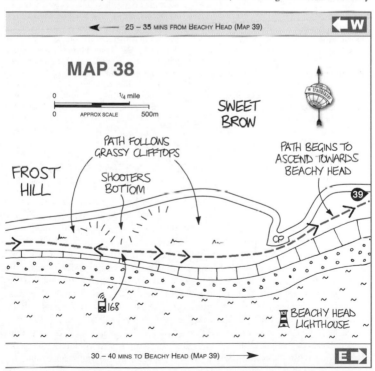

◄ — 25 – 35 MINS FROM BEACHY HEAD (MAP 39)   ◄W

MAP 38

0   ¼ mile
0   APPROX SCALE   500m

SWEET BROW

PATH FOLLOWS GRASSY CLIFFTOPS

PATH BEGINS TO ASCEND TOWARDS BEACHY HEAD

FROST HILL

SHOOTERS BOTTOM

39

CP

📱168

BEACHY HEAD LIGHTHOUSE

30 – 40 MINS TO BEACHY HEAD (MAP 39) ⟶   E ▷

ROUTE GUIDE AND MAPS

headeastbourne; **fb**; food summer Mon-Sat noon-10pm, Sun to 9.30pm, winter daily noon-9pm; WI-FI; 🐾) isn't really the best place to celebrate the walk's end but is useful if you need to shelter from the weather, and does have a sun-trap beer garden. The food is good value too.

Brighton & Hove Buses' No 13X Sun/Bank hol-only **bus** service calls here; Stagecoach's Nos 3/3A/4 services call at the foot of Beachy Head (end of South Downs Way); see pp46-8.

MEADS VILLAGE   MAP 39
Meads Village is actually the most westerly suburb of Eastbourne. It is a quiet, well-to-do part of town with a genuine village feel.

More importantly for South Downs Way walkers, it is positioned right at the official end (or start) of the walk, making a stop here a more appealing prospect than the half-hour walk into the more hectic centre of Eastbourne. The village lies on Holywell Rd, to the north of the start/end of the trail.

Services
Everything you might need here is centred along one short stretch of Meads St. There is a **Co-op** (daily 7am-10pm) on the corner of Matlock Rd which also incorporates the **post office** (Mon-Fri 9am-5.30pm, Sat to 12.30pm), and has an **ATM** outside it. There's also a **Tesco Express** (daily 7am-11pm) and a **pharmacy** (Mon-Fri 9am-5.30pm, Sat to noon).

Stagecoach's No 3/3A/4 **bus services** (see p46) go to central Eastbourne from here as well as from the foot of the hill at the end of the South Downs Way.

Where to stay and eat
Beachy Rise (☎ 01323-639171, 🖳 beachy rise.com; 2D/1T/1Tr, all en suite; 🛏; WI-FI; Ⓛ), on Meads Rd, has **B&B** for £35-37.50pp (sgl occ £55-60).

The Pilot Inn (☎ 01323-723440, 🖳 pilot-inn.co.uk; **fb**; 4D, all en suite; 🛏; WI-FI; 🐾 bar only), on a bend on Meads St, is the first pub reached after leaving the end of the South Downs Way. The bar is open all day (Mon-Sat 11am-11pm, Sun to 8pm), which makes it convenient for a celebration drink. And the **food** (daily noon-9pm, Sun to 6pm) is well-priced (mains £12-18, warm-filled ciabatta rolls £7.50-8). **Room only** costs £42.50-57.50pp (sgl occ room rate); a cooked breakfast (£9.75pp) is available.

EASTBOURNE   For the guide to Eastbourne turn to p183.

W ← (EASTBOURNE TO ALFRISTON (COASTAL ROUTE VIA CUCKMERE)   [MAPS 39-35]

It is this initial **10¾-mile stage (17.5km, 4½-6hrs** – plus another **1½ miles (2.4km) from Eastbourne** station to the official start; see Map 42, p185) on the South Downs Way that perhaps provides the main reason why most people choose to walk the trail from west to east. For while they have left the best – and toughest – section to the end, having used the rest of the path to toughen up their feet and improve their fitness, those who begin at Eastbourne are instead plunged straight into the deep end, and have to tackle the hardest and most scenic stage first. It's true, too, that the best views are reserved for those who are looking east – so those walking from Eastbourne will often find themselves looking over their shoulder to glimpse the best of the panoramas.

Still, if you are walking the South Downs Way in this direction, at least you'll have the satisfaction of knowing that, once you've tackled **Beachy Head** (don't forget to look behind you for views of the lighthouse) and the

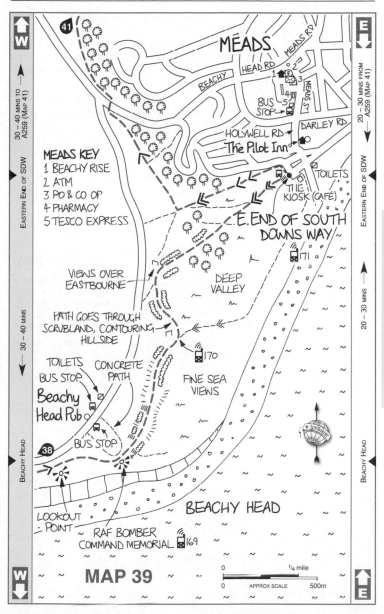

MEADS KEY
1 BEACHY RISE
2 ATM
3 PO & CO OP
4 PHARMACY
5 TESCO EXPRESS

MEADS

BEACHY HEAD RD

MEADS RD

MEADS ST

HOLYWELL RD
The Pilot Inn

DARLEY RD

TOILETS

THE KIOSK (CAFÉ)

E. END OF SOUTH DOWNS WAY

BUS STOP

VIEWS OVER EASTBOURNE

DEEP VALLEY

171

PATH GOES THROUGH SCRUBLAND, CONTOURING HILLSIDE

170

TOILETS
BUS STOP
Beachy Head Pub

CONCRETE PATH

FINE SEA VIEWS

38
BUS STOP

LOOKOUT POINT

RAF BOMBER COMMAND MEMORIAL 169

BEACHY HEAD

MAP 39

0 — ¼ mile
0 — APPROX SCALE — 500m

W
E

30 – 40 MINS TO A259 (MAP 41)

20 – 30 MINS FROM A259 (MAP 41)

EASTERN END OF SDW

EASTERN END OF SDW

30 – 40 MINS

20 – 30 MINS

BEACHY HEAD

BEACHY HEAD

ROUTE GUIDE AND MAPS

41

ever-undulating chalk cliffs of the **Seven Sisters Country Park**, you've got the toughest section of the trail out of the way, and will find the rest of the hiking, by comparison, a mere walk in the (National) park. What's more, the lovely villages of **Westdean** (Map 36) and **Litlington** (Map 35), and the views over beguiling Cuckmere Valley towards **Birling Gap** (Map 33), are all certainly easier on the eye than parts of Eastbourne.

[Next route overview p166]

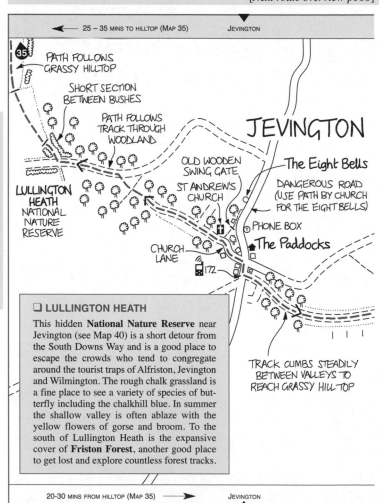

← 25 – 35 MINS TO HILLTOP (MAP 35)   JEVINGTON

PATH FOLLOWS GRASSY HILLTOP

SHORT SECTION BETWEEN BUSHES

PATH FOLLOWS TRACK THROUGH WOODLAND

OLD WOODEN SWING GATE

ST ANDREW'S CHURCH

JEVINGTON

The Eight Bells

DANGEROUS ROAD (USE PATH BY CHURCH FOR THE EIGHT BELLS)

PHONE BOX

LULLINGTON HEATH NATIONAL NATURE RESERVE

CHURCH LANE

The Paddocks

172

TRACK CLIMBS STEADILY BETWEEN VALLEYS TO REACH GRASSY HILLTOP

❑ **LULLINGTON HEATH**

This hidden **National Nature Reserve** near Jevington (see Map 40) is a short detour from the South Downs Way and is a good place to escape the crowds who tend to congregate around the tourist traps of Alfriston, Jevington and Wilmington. The rough chalk grassland is a fine place to see a variety of species of butterfly including the chalkhill blue. In summer the shallow valley is often ablaze with the yellow flowers of gorse and broom. To the south of Lullington Heath is the expansive cover of **Friston Forest**, another good place to get lost and explore countless forest tracks.

20-30 MINS FROM HILLTOP (MAP 35) →   JEVINGTON

E➜ALFRISTON TO EASTBOURNE (INLAND ROUTE VIA JEVINGTON) MAP 35, MAPS 40-41 & MAP 39

This inland **alternative route** is geared towards horse-riders and cyclists but walkers are welcome to use the bridleway too. Although these **8¼ miles (13.5km, 2¾-3¾hrs – plus another 1½ miles (2.4km) to Eastbourne** centre) are not as spectacular as the coastal route there are still plenty of fine downland

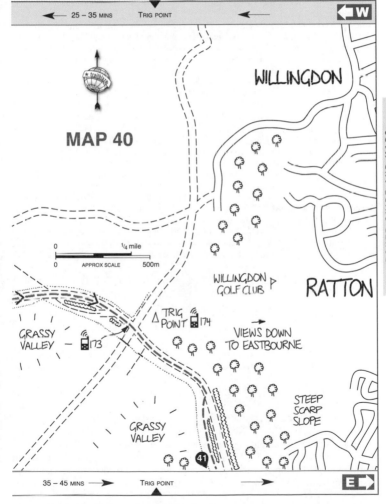

views to enjoy high up on **Windover Hill** (Map 35), while a detour to see the famous **Long Man of Wilmington** (see box p169) is strongly recommended and the sweet little villages/hamlets of **Milton Street** (Map 35) and **Jevington** (Map 40; p180) are right on the trail.

It is a good idea to keep an extra day spare for this section even if you have already walked the coastal route.

MILTON STREET   MAP 35, p169

Milton Street is nothing more than a small collection of scattered houses. There is, however, a good pub here; *The Sussex Ox* (☎ 01323-870840, 🖥 thesussexox.co.uk; **fb**; food Mon-Sat noon-2.30pm & 6-9pm, Sun noon-4pm & 5-8pm; WI-FI; 🐾). The menu is varied and changes daily but favourite mains might include the Ox beef burger (£12.50) or a roasted rack of lamb (£25), with the meat from their own farm in Jevington. Their draught lagers and ciders are all from Sussex including the Long Man Brewery at Wilmington and Burning Sky in Firle.

JEVINGTON   MAP 40, p180

Jevington, sitting comfortably in the Cuckmere valley, is another beautiful village that provides a potential alternative stop to the somewhat exploited streets of Alfriston. In the centre of the village is a plaque commemorating the former Hungry Monk Restaurant, which claimed to be the birthplace in 1971 of banoffee pie.

Where to stay and eat

For accommodation in the village there is *The Paddocks* (☎ 01323-482499, 🖥 paddockstables.co.uk; 1D/1T, both en suite; 🍺; WI-FI; ⓛ; 🐾), a comfortable B&B charging from £40pp (sgl occ £55). The only place to eat is at the village pub, *The Eight Bells* (☎ 01323-484442, 🖥 eightbellsjevington.com; **fb**; bar Tue & Sun 10am-8pm, Wed-Sat 10am-11pm; food Tue noon-3pm, Wed-Sat noon-3pm & 6-9pm, Sun noon-6pm; WI-FI; 🐾 on lead). It's a 5-minute walk up the lane; note the blind bend on the road is very dangerous as there is no pavement for pedestrians – it is safer to use the path by the church. They have a wide range of pub meals as well as a pleasant garden, with views over the Downs. It's a freehouse, so has a variety of ales.

W← EASTBOURNE TO ALFRISTON (INLAND ROUTE VIA JEVINGTON)   MAP 40, MAPS 39-8, MAP 35

It seems a shame to miss the most iconic, and certainly the most photographed, stage of the South Downs Way (I'm pretty sure, for example, that the Seven Sisters or Beachy Head has featured on the cover just about every edition of this guide, though I'm writing this before I know what photograph will be used on the front of this edition). But the truth is that if you're tackling the walk from east to west, you may simply not feel ready to do the toughest section straight out of the starting blocks. Thankfully there is a picturesque **8¼-mile alternative (13.5km, 2¾-3¾hrs** plus another **1½ miles (2.4km) from Eastbourne centre** where most people will start their walk, that is easier – though, it must be said, still fairly challenging.

There is interest aplenty on this route too, including a couple of cute villages (**Jevington**, Map 40) & **Milton Street** (Map 35), the views from **Windover Hill** (Map 35) and, if you take the recommended detour, a visit to the **Long Man of Wilmington** (see box p169).   *[Next route overview p166]*

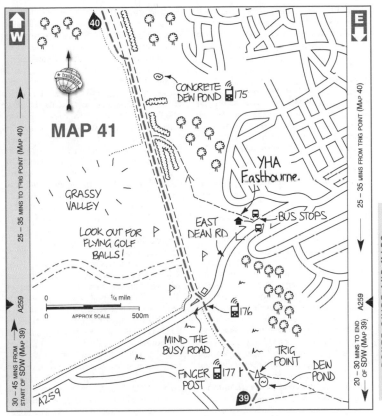

MAP 41

W E

40

CONCRETE
DEW POND 175

MAP 41

GRASSY
VALLEY

LOOK OUT FOR
FLYING GOLF
BALLS!

YHA
Eastbourne.

EAST
DEAN RD

BUS STOPS

0   ¼ mile
0   APPROX SCALE   500m

176

MIND THE
BUSY ROAD

FINGER 177
POST

TRIG
POINT

DEW
POND

A259

39

25 – 35 MINS TO TRIG POINT (MAP 40)

30 – 45 MINS FROM
START OF SDW (MAP 39)

A259

25 – 35 MINS FROM TRIG POINT (MAP 40)

A259

20 – 30 MINS TO END
OF SDW (MAP 39)

ROUTE GUIDE AND MAPS

EASTBOURNE   MAP 42, p185

Eastbourne is a typical English seaside resort, complete with a grand Victorian pier, though it does have something of a reputation as a retirement town.

Having received a lot of criticism over the years as being one of the least adventurous resorts, particularly when compared to its upbeat neighbour Brighton, Eastbourne has undergone something of a revival. The signs on the edge of town shout out 'Welcome to the Sunshine Coast' and certainly this is one of the sunnier corners of the UK. However, parts of the centre, particularly the area around the railway station, are far from appealing, and not the sort of places to linger. It certainly doesn't have the history and charm of Winchester at the other end of the South Downs Way, although nearby Beachy Head, at least, makes for a fitting end to a long walk.

You can walk along the long, stony **beach** on either side of the 300m-long **pier** which was built between 1866 and 1872 on stilts sitting in cups on the sea-bed allowing it to shift a little in stormy weather. In July 2014 the central domed building was destroyed by fire, but the pier is open again and is a good spot for arcades, fish & chips, coffee and ice-cream.

Towner (☎ 01323-434670, 🖳 towner eastbourne.org.uk; Tue-Sun & Bank Hol

Mons 10am-5pm; free) is an interesting contemporary art gallery on College Rd.

Wish Tower is a Martello Tower, one of a number built along the coast to counter an invasion threat from Napoleon.

Services

Terminus Rd is both the commercial and tourist centre, with most of the shops up at the railway station end of the road, and the restaurants, cafés and souvenir shops at the beach end. It's about 30 minutes' walk from the foot of the South Downs and the end of the Way.

The smart new purpose-built **Visitor Centre** (☎ 01323-415415, 🖥 visiteastbourne.com; Mon-Sat 9am-5pm, Sun 10am-4pm) is called The Welcome Building and is on Compton St. There is plenty of free information here, not only for Eastbourne but also the rest of South-East England and London too.

The **post office** (Mon-Fri 9am-5.30pm, Sat to 12.30pm) is inside WH Smith, on Terminus Rd, where you'll also find several **banks**. There's a **pharmacy**, Boots, in the Arndale Centre (Mon-Sat 8.30am-6pm & Sun 10.30am-4.30pm), as well as a big Sainsbury's **supermarket**. Other supermarkets include a Premier and Tesco Express on Seaside Rd, a Co-op on Cornfield Rd and Spar on Terminus Rd. Most open daily from around 7am to 11pm. Staying on Terminus Rd you'll also find branches of the **outdoor shops** Millets and Blacks (both open Mon-Sat 9am-6pm, Sun 10am-4pm), a Waterstones **bookshop** (Mon-Sat 9am-5.30pm, Sun 10am-4pm). Rainbows **Launderette** (Mon-Fri 8.30am-5.30pm, Sat 9am-5.30pm, Sun 9am-3pm) is on Seaside Rd, while back near the Visitor Centre is Hudson's (**fb**; Tue-Fri 8am-5.30pm, Sat 8am-2pm), a quality **deli** with great-value made-to-order sandwiches for around £3.

For sticks of rock, jars of humbug mints, boxes of Eastbourne fudge and other traditional teeth-rotting souvenirs, head to **Ye Olde Fashioned Humbugge Shoppe** (Mon-Sat 9am-5pm, Sun 10am-4pm, but stays open until 9pm in summer), a family-run business that's been here for more than 70 years.

Public transport

Eastbourne is connected by Southern Railway's **train** (see box p44) services to places along the south coast as well as to Gatwick Airport and London Victoria.

Stagecoach's **bus** No 3/3A/4 runs to Meads Village at the end of the South Downs Way. Brighton & Hove Buses go to Brighton (12A, 12X & 13X; the Sunday/Bank Hol Mon-only 13X calls at Birling Gap and Beachy Head). Compass Travel's No 125 goes to Lewes on weekdays while the Cuckmere Community bus No 25 covers the same route on Saturday. The CCB No 26 Sunday service goes to Seaford. CCB also run Nos 43 & 44 which call here on certain days of the week; see pp46-8.

Try Eastbourne 720 Taxis (☎ 01323-720720, 🖥 720taxis.com) for a **taxi**.

Where to stay

As a major seaside resort Eastbourne is overflowing with hotels and guesthouses. Note that for most hotels rates vary depending on whether there are any events on and also for places on the seafront whether you have a seaview or inland room.

YHA Eastbourne (Map 41, p183; ☎ 0345-371 9316, 🖥 www.yha.org.uk/hostel/eastbourne; 1 x 2-, 1 x 3-, 2 x 4-, 1 x 5-bed room, 1 x 6-bed female dorm, 1 x 7-bed male dorm, all en suite; WI-FI) was closed at the time of research but should re-open in Easter 2022. Whether their dorms will be able to reopen then is another matter but they do have private rooms too. The hostel always offered self-catering accommodation only but tea and coffee are available at the hostel for guests to use for a small donation. Welcome features include a drying room, laundry facilities and a bike shed. As with all YHA hostels the rates can vary a lot but expect to pay £29-49 for a two-bedded room and £15-25 for a dorm bed; they accept card payments. There is 24 hour access; a door code is given on arrival. Note that check-in times need to be adhered to as hostel staff go home at 9pm and nobody will be able to check-in after this time as ID needs to be seen by staff. The hostel is housed in a modern building by the A259 near the golf course on the western edge of

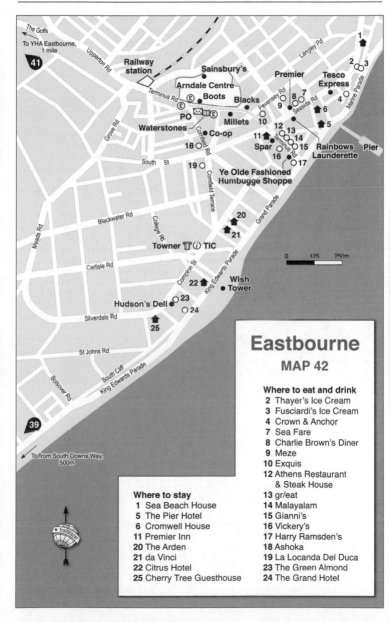

Eastbourne

MAP 42

Where to eat and drink
2 Thayer's Ice Cream
3 Fusciardi's Ice Cream
4 Crown & Anchor
7 Sea Fare
8 Charlie Brown's Diner
9 Meze
10 Exquis
12 Athens Restaurant
   & Steak House
13 gr/eat
14 Malayalam
15 Gianni's
16 Vickery's
17 Harry Ramsden's
18 Ashoka
19 La Locanda Del Duca
23 The Green Almond
24 The Grand Hotel

Where to stay
1 Sea Beach House
5 The Pier Hotel
6 Cromwell House
11 Premier Inn
20 The Arden
21 da Vinci
22 Citrus Hotel
25 Cherry Tree Guesthouse

Eastbourne, about a mile from the town centre. Brighton & Hove Buses No 12/12X & 13X services stop outside the hostel.

As for more upmarket accommodation, well *Citrus Hotel* (☎ 01323-722676, 🖳 www.citrushoteleastbourne.co.uk; 50 rooms; all en suite; 🐾; WI-FI; 🐕) describes itself as a 'limited-service' hotel. Rooms range from single, double and triple to 'studios' (with self-catering facilities) sleeping up to six people; their suites have a sea view. Using the business model of the nationwide chains, the hotel is packed with facilities including a recreation area with table tennis, dartboard and pool table; there's also a bar serving snacks. And as with the nationwide chains, the prices can be very reasonable starting at £40pp (sgl/sgl occ from £65/75) including a cooked breakfast. If not requested at the time of booking breakfast costs £7.99.

Near here you'll find three good B&Bs. *Cherry Tree Guesthouse* (☎ 01323-722406, 🖳 cherrytree-eastbourne.co.uk; 3S/2T/5D/1Tr, all en suite; 🐾; WI-FI; 🐕) is at 15 Silverdale Rd; it's an Edwardian townhouse with B&B for £45-60pp (sgl/sgl occ from £55). The place is very efficiently run and the breakfasts they provide are varied and delicious. They are also very dog-friendly, and even have towels by the front-door to use on any dogs caught in a downpour. Some of the rooms can sleep up to two children. Nearby, *da Vinci* (☎ 01323-727173, 🖳 davinci.uk.com; 4S/10D/5D or T/ 2Tr, all en suite; 🐾; WI-FI), on Howard Sq, has an **art gallery** downstairs and 'art-themed' rooms. It's a friendly, comfortable place and B&B is from around £40-55pp (sgl/sgl occ £40-60). Phone for the best prices. Some rooms sleep up to two children.

One block east, *The Arden B&B* (☎ 01323-639639, 🖳 www.theardenhotel.co.uk; 1S en suite but private toilet, 3T/3D/1Tr, all en suite; WI-FI; 🐕) is a fine family-run establishment on Burlington Place with some parking spaces (and discounts on on-street parking too). Rates are reasonable, starting at just £39.50-44pp (£44-58 sgl/sgl occ).

The chain *Premier Inn* (☎ 0333-321 9323, 🖳 premierinn.com; 65D, all en suite;

🐾; WI-FI) has a hotel on Terminus Rd. Book online rather than calling the high-rate phone number. Saver rates can be as low as £58.50 for the room (two people; a sofabed is available if you need separate beds) if booked and paid well in advance or more than twice that if booked last minute. The rooms have very comfortable beds and 40" flat-screen TVs. There's a restaurant: a cooked breakfast costs £8.99pp.

Right opposite the pier is the appropriately named *The Pier Hotel* (☎ 01323-728313, 🖳 thepierhotel.co.uk; 12S/11D/8T, all en suite; 🐾; WI-FI), a place that's not without its charms and is in a great location. Rooms cost £70-85pp (sgl £85-95, sgl occ rates on request). Also on the seafront, *Cromwell House* (☎ 01323-431066, 🖳 www.cromwell- house.co.uk; 2S/2T/1D/3D or T, all en suite; WI-FI), at 23 Cavendish Place, is a Victorian townhouse with B&B from £45pp (sgl/sgl occ £50).

Sea Beach House (☎ 01323-410458, 🖳 www.seabeachhouse.com; 5D/4T, all en suite; 🐾; WI-FI; 🐕) is at 39-40 Marine Parade. B&B costs £44-47pp (sgl occ £50-60); some rooms have sea views. Both Princess (later to become Queen) Victoria and Alfred, Lord Tennyson are said to have stayed here and the building dates from 1790, when Eastbourne was just a village.

Where to eat and drink

You'll find a surprisingly eclectic mix of restaurants and cafés on or around busy **Seaside Rd** and **Terminus Rd**.

Cafés & pubs On Terminus Rd, *Vickery's* (daily 9am-5pm) is a good-value café with all-day breakfasts. Almost opposite, the Greek café and deli *gr/eat* (🖳 www.gr-eat .co.uk; daily noon-3pm & 5.30-9.30pm, closed at times late Oct to early Jan) has a terrible name, but a good selection of Mediterranean fare.

On Seaside Rd, at No 54, *Charlie Brown's Diner* (☎ 01323-726588, 🖳 charliebrownsdiner.co.uk; Tue-Thur 6-10.30pm, Fri & Sat to 11pm; WI-FI) is good for burgers and the like.

For something more refined, and away from the holiday-maker hordes, *The Green*

Almond (☎ 01323-734470, 🖳 thegreen almond.com; **fb**; Wed-Sat 11.30am-4pm), 12 Grand Hotel Buildings, Compton St, is an award-winning vegetarian bistro with a nice line in curries and salads. Booking is recommended.

There are numerous **pubs**, some a lot rougher than others. *Crown & Anchor* (☎ 01323-642500, 🖳 crownandanchoreast bourne.co.uk; food daily 10am-9pm; WI-FI; 🐾), on the seafront at 15 Marine Parade, often has live music at weekends and is one of the more welcoming places.

As with any British seaside town, **ice-cream** is a big seller in Eastbourne. You can get it pretty much anywhere, but between Marine Parade and Seaside Rd are two particularly popular competing outlets; both very good. The cheaper of the two, *Thayer's Ice Cream*, (☎ 01323-641906; Mar-Oct Mon-Fri 1-9pm, Sat & Sun noon-9pm, generally closed in the winter) is a small family-run business with dozens of different flavours. Bigger, brasher *Fusciardi's* (🖳 fusciardiicecreams.co.uk; daily 9am-6pm), on the seafront, also has a sit-down café area.

Restaurants & takeaways At the seafront end of Terminus Rd, *Gianni's* (🖳 gianniseastbourne.co.uk; Wed-Mon 11am-6pm) is a friendly pizzeria that also sells Italian ice-cream, and there are various pizza chains around town. For something a bit classier, *La Locanda Del Duca* (☎ 01323-916011, 🖳 la-locanda-del-duca .com; daily noon-2.30pm & 5-11pm, Sun to 10.30pm), 26 Cornfield Terrace, is an authentic Italian place offering set menus

for £21.40/24.50 for two/three courses and traditional favourites à la carte.

Back on Terminus Rd there's *Athens Restaurant & Steak House* (☎ 01323-733278; daily noon-2.30pm & 6-10pm), at No 195. It's efficiently run by three generations of a hospitable Greek-Cypriot family and their moussaka is particularly good.

At 1 Pevensey Rd, *Exquis* (☎ 01323-430885; **fb**; Tue-Sat 6-11pm) is shabby outside but actually a delightful French bistro with a simple menu that's good value. Nearby *Meze* (☎ 01323-731893, 🖳 meze-restaurant.co.uk; daily noon-10pm), at 15 Pevensey Rd, is a good Turkish restaurant.

For decent Indian cuisine, head to *Ashoka* (☎ 01323-733344, 🖳 ashokaeast bourne.com; daily noon-2pm & 5.30-11.30pm), on Cornfield Rd. It's been in business nearly 30 years. The best Indian in town is probably *Malayalam* (☎ 01323-722227, 🖳 malayalamrestaurants.com; Tue-Thur noon-3pm & 5.30-9.30pm, Fri & Sat to 10.30pm, Sun noon-5pm) on Terminus Rd, serving South Indian fare with mains starting at just £6.25.

But for something more traditionally English, it has to be fish & chips. There are plenty of options here, including a branch of the *Harry Ramsden's* chain (☎ 01323-417454, 🖳 harryramsdens.co.uk/location/ eastbourne; summer Sun-Thur 11.30am-8pm, Fri & Sat to 8.30pm), on the seafront at the end of Terminus Rd. For a more down-to-earth chippy, try *Sea Fare* (☎ 01323-641893; **fb**; daily 11.30am-3.30pm & 4.30-10pm, winter days/hours variable), at 66 Seaside Rd.

ROUTE GUIDE AND MAPS

❏ AFTERNOON TEA AT THE GRAND

If your walk ends at about tea-time (or if you haven't started) and you wish to celebrate in style there can be no better place for a top-of-the-range cream tea than *The Grand Hotel* (☎ 01323-412345, 🖳 grandeastbourne.com). You should phone ahead to book. It's served daily from 2.45pm to 5.30pm when for £26-28.50 you get a full spread including sandwiches, scones and cakes. You can push the boat out even further with the Grand Champagne Tea (£34.50-37).

The hotel is easy to find: you walk right past it on the way into Eastbourne from the end of the South Downs Way. Splash out – you deserve it!

APPENDIX A: GPS WAYPOINTS

Each waypoint was taken on the route at the reference number marked on the map as below. This list is also available to download from 🖥 trailblazer-guides.com.

MAP	REF	GPS WAYPOINT		DESCRIPTION
Map 2	001	N51° 03.228'	W01° 16.749'	Road junction
Map 2	002	N51° 02.862'	W01° 16.146'	Tarred road ends/starts
Map 2	003	N51° 03.006'	W01° 15.865'	Path/track junction
Map 2	004	N51° 02.813'	W01° 14.842'	Road crossing (A272)
Map 2	005	N51° 02.997'	W01° 14.437'	Gate (Cheesefoot Head)
Map 3	006	N51° 03.433'	W01° 14.089'	Track junction at farmyard
Map 3	007	N51° 02.955'	W01° 12.769'	Cross road
Map 4	008	N51° 02.727'	W01° 12.399'	Gate to field
Map 4	009	N51° 02.346'	W01° 12.081'	Cross A272 road
Map 4	010	N51° 01.586'	W01° 11.793'	Path junction
Map 5	011	N51° 01.041'	W01° 11.358'	The Milbury's
Map 5	012	N51° 00.821'	W01° 10.521'	Gate
Map 5	013	N51° 00.580'	W01° 09.631'	Track passes houses
Map 6	014	N51° 00.059'	W01° 08.913'	Beacon Hill car park
Map 6	015	N50° 59.555'	W01° 08.413'	Kissing gates to cross fields
Map 6	016	N50° 59.342'	W01° 08.227'	Track between stiles
Map 6	017	N50° 59.040'	W01° 07.728'	The Shoe Inn, Exton
Map 7	018	N50° 59.252'	W01° 07.208'	Bridge over River Meon
Map 7	019	N50° 59.196'	W01° 06.725'	Cross disused railway
Map 7	020	N50° 58.854'	W01° 05.328'	Hill fort, Old Winchester Hill
Map 7	021	N50° 59.009'	W01° 04.712'	Turn off/onto track
Map 7	022	N50° 59.279'	W01° 04.827'	Car park
Map 7	023	N50° 59.443'	W01° 04.934'	Gate at fork in road
Map 7	024	N50° 59.238'	W01° 04.546'	Join/leave track
Map 7	025	N50° 59.296'	W01° 04.200'	Farmyard
Map 8	026	N50° 59.446'	W01° 03.153'	Tree-lined avenue
Map 8	027	N50° 59.066'	W01° 03.085'	Road crosses track
Map 9	028	N50° 58.079'	W01° 02.373'	South Downs Eco Lodge
Map 9	029	N50° 57.939'	W01° 01.698'	Road junction
Map 9	030	N50° 58.051'	W01° 00.110'	Homelands Farm
Map 9	031	N50° 58.026'	W00° 59.794'	Junction with Hogs Lodge Lane
Map 10	032	N50° 58.465'	W00° 59.274'	Butser Hill car park
Map 10	033	N50° 57.891'	W00° 58.866'	Gate by A3 road crossing
Map 10	034	N50° 57.450'	W00° 58.658'	Track into/out of woods
Map 10	035	N50° 58.095'	W00° 57.775'	Track junction
Map 10	036	N50° 58.372'	W00° 57.375'	Road crossing
Map 10	037	N50° 58.206'	W00° 56.456'	Track junction
Map 11	038	N50° 58.153'	W00° 55.787'	Road junction
Map 11	039	N50° 57.980'	W00° 54.137'	Road crossing
Map 11	040	N50° 57.611'	W00° 53.213'	Car park, B2146 road crossing
Map 11	041	N50° 57.435'	W00° 52.672'	Car park, B2141 road crossing
Map 12	042	N50° 57.659'	W00° 51.469'	Turn-off to East Harting
Map 12	043	N50° 57.547'	W00° 51.119'	Trig point, Beacon Hill
Map 12	044	N50° 57.535'	W00° 50.447'	Junction of several paths
Map 12	045	N50° 57.267'	W00° 49.981'	Track junction
Map 12	046	N50° 56.760'	W00° 49.665'	Track crossroads
Map 13	047	N50° 56.999'	W00° 48.587'	Track crossroads
Map 13	048	N50° 56.873'	W00° 47.494'	Path junction, Cocking Down

MAP	REF	GPS WAYPOINT		DESCRIPTION
Map 13	049	N50° 56.759'	W00° 47.002'	Track crossroads
Map 13	050	N50° 56.660'	W00° 46.360'	Junction near chalk boulder
Map 14	051	N50° 56.571'	W00° 45.338'	Car park at A268 crossing
Map 14	052	N50° 56.544'	W00° 45.002'	Water tap
Map 14	053	N50° 56.440'	W00° 44.226'	Fork in track
Map 14	054	N50° 56.463'	W00° 43.706'	Track junction
Map 14	055	N50° 56.466'	W00° 43.258'	Turn-off to Heyshott
Map 14	056	N50° 56.457'	W00° 42.857'	Path junction
Map 15	057	N50° 56.378'	W00° 42.375'	Track junction
Map 15	058	N50° 56.353'	W00° 42.128'	Track junction
Map 15	059	N50° 56.239'	W00° 40.938'	Signpost with memorials
Map 15	060	N50° 56.016'	W00° 39.082'	Track junction
Map 15	061	N50° 55.902'	W00° 39.598'	Track crossroads
Map 16	062	N50° 55.307'	W00° 38.925'	Cross A285 road
Map 16	063	N50° 54.803'	W00° 38.488'	Track junction
Map 17	064	N50° 54.441'	W00° 37.926'	Track junction
Map 17	065	N50° 54.402'	W00° 37.319'	Track junction
Map 17	066	N50° 54.464'	W00° 36.968'	Bignor Hill car park
Map 17	067	N50° 54.587'	W00° 36.157'	Memorial to Toby 1888-1955
Map 17	068	N50° 54.470'	W00° 35.814'	Track junction
Map 18	069	N50° 53.884'	W00° 34.403'	Cross A29 road
Map 18	070	N50° 53.837'	W00° 33.310'	Cross country lane
Map 18	071	N50° 53.952'	W00° 32.927'	Bridge over River Arun
Map 18	072	N50° 54.025'	W00° 32.358'	Cross B2139 road
Map 18	073	N50° 54.195'	W00° 31.927'	Road junction
Map 18	074	N50° 54.188'	W00° 31.839'	Leave/join road
Map 19	075	N50° 54.158'	W00° 31.215'	Gate
Map 19	076	N50° 54.190'	W00° 30.413'	Join/leave track
Map 19	077	N50° 54.145'	W00° 29.540'	Track junction
Map 19	078	N50° 54.111'	W00° 28.747'	Track junction
Map 19	079	N50° 54.051'	W00° 28.347'	Turn-off to Storrington
Map 20	080	N50° 53.656'	W00° 26.641'	Barn
Map 20	081	N50° 53.755'	W00° 26.032'	Gate on track
Map 20	082	N50° 53.791'	W00° 25.812'	Washington path junction (alt route)
Map 20	083	N50° 54.262'	W00° 25.039'	Join/leave track (alt route)
Map 21	084	N50° 54.251'	W00° 24.885'	Road/track meet (alt route)
Map 21	085	N50° 54.304'	W00° 24.306'	Frankland Arms, Washington (alt route)
Map 21	086	N50° 54.189'	W00° 24.382'	Road junction, Washington (alt route)
Map 21	087	N50° 53.807'	W00° 24.344'	Steep section of track
Map 21	088	N50° 53.617'	W00° 23.643'	Track junction
Map 21	089	N50° 53.757'	W00° 23.351'	Gate on track
Map 21	090	N50° 53.779'	W00° 22.928'	Chanctonbury Ring
Map 21	091	N50° 53.637'	W00° 22.612'	Gate on track
Map 21	092	N50° 53.409'	W00° 22.421'	Track junction
Map 21	093	N50° 53.269'	W00° 22.001'	Track junction
Map 22	094	N50° 53.219'	W00° 21.675'	Turn-off to Steyning
Map 22	095	N50° 52.669'	W00° 20.972'	Track junction
Map 23	096	N50° 52.403'	W00° 17.958'	A283 road
Map 23	097	N50° 52.430'	W00° 17.094'	Car park
Map 23	098	N50° 52.881'	W00° 15.991'	Road by YHA Truleigh Hill
Map 23	099	N50° 52.919'	W00° 15.461'	Communications tower
Map 24	100	N50° 53.063'	W00° 13.763'	Turn-off to Fulking

MAP	REF	GPS WAYPOINT		DESCRIPTION
Map 24	101	N50° 52.937'	W00° 13.213'	Gate
Map 24	102	N50° 53.092'	W00° 12.744'	Devil's Dyke pub
Map 24	103	N50° 52.978'	W00° 12.254'	Gate on path
Map 25	104	N50° 53.309'	W00° 11.663'	Road crossing (A281)
Map 25	105	N50° 53.349'	W00° 11.466'	Gate by woodland
Map 25	106	N50° 53.410'	W00° 10.968'	Gate on path
Map 26	107	N50° 53.743'	W00° 10.001'	Gate by road
Map 26	108	N50° 53.923'	W00° 09.837'	Crossroads, Pyecombe
Map 26	109	N50° 54.056'	W00° 09.593'	Car park at golf club
Map 26	110	N50° 54.026'	W00° 08.687'	Track crossroads
Map 26	111	N50° 54.227'	W00° 08.718'	Track junction
Map 26	112	N50° 54.027'	W00° 07.845'	Gate by Keymer signpost
Map 26	113	N50° 54.146'	W00° 07.327'	Dew pond
Map 27	114	N50° 54.046'	W00° 06.278'	Car park, Ditchling Beacon
Map 27	115	N50° 53.940'	W00° 05.814'	Turn-off to Ditchling
Map 27	116	N50° 53.910'	W00° 04.709'	Track between gates
Map 27	117	N50° 53.876'	W00° 04.387'	Turn-off to Plumpton
Map 28	118	N50° 53.759'	W00° 03.198'	Junction with path to Lewes
Map 28	119	N50° 53.259'	W00° 03.666'	Gate at track junction
Map 28	120	N50° 53.000'	W00° 03.295'	Gate at track/path junction
Map 28	121	N50° 52.505'	W00° 02.808'	Through gate by stile
Map 28	122	N50° 52.426'	W00° 03.190'	Small hut and pylon
Map 29	123	N50° 51.977'	W00° 03.268'	Steps
Map 29	124	N50° 51.977'	W00° 03.487'	Bridge over A27 road
Map 29	125	N50° 51.872'	W00° 02.952'	Path cuts under railway
Map 29	126	N50° 51.548'	W00° 03.227'	Through gate
Map 29	127	N50° 51.224'	W00° 03.463'	Through gate
Map 29	128	N50° 51.025'	W00° 03.266'	Through gate, follow fence
Map 29	129	N50° 51.278'	W00° 02.526'	Gate by dew pond
Map 30	130	N50° 51.032'	W00° 01.876'	Path joins/leaves track
Map 30	131	N50° 50.673'	W00° 01.557'	Track, Swanborough Hill
Map 31	132	N50° 50.086'	E00° 00.479'	Leave/join track through gate
Map 31	133	N50° 50.009'	E00° 00.149'	Track between gates
Map 31	134	N50° 49.566'	E00° 00.315'	Through gate onto/off track
Map 31	135	N50° 49.795'	E00° 01.061'	Road junction, Southease
Map 31	136	N50° 49.805'	E00° 01.562'	Bridge over River Ouse
Map 31	137	N50° 49.888'	E00° 01.849'	Level crossing
Map 31	138	N50° 49.804'	E00° 02.228'	Gate on track east of bridge over A26
Map 32	139	N50° 49.875'	E00° 03.090'	Trig point & dew pond
Map 32	140	N50° 50.092'	E00° 03.667'	Gate onto track
Map 32	141	N50° 50.063'	E00° 04.114'	Telecom masts, Beddingham Hill
Map 32	142	N50° 50.069'	E00° 04.468'	Gate on path
Map 32	143	N50° 50.018'	E00° 04.987'	Car park, Firle Beacon
Map 33	144	N50° 50.029'	E00° 06.497'	Trig point, Firle Beacon
Map 33	145	N50° 49.527'	E00° 07.208'	Gate, Bo-Peep
Map 34	146	N50° 49.108'	E00° 07.823'	Gate on path
Map 34	147	N50° 48.659'	E00° 08.550'	Gate by track junction
Map 35	148	N50° 48.405'	E00° 09.581'	Church, Alfriston (coastal route)
Map 35	149	N50° 48.689'	E00° 09.581'	Plough & Harrow, Litlington
Map 36	150	N50° 47.440'	E00° 09.628'	Path goes round the hedge
Map 36	151	N50° 47.098'	E00° 09.471'	Steps through forest
Map 36	152	N50° 46.707'	E00° 09.699'	Track junction

MAP	REF	GPS WAYPOINT		DESCRIPTION
Map 36	153	N50° 46.398'	E00° 09.559'	Crossroads, Westdean
Map 36	154	N50° 46.499'	E00° 09.244'	Road crossing, Exceat
Map 37	155	N50° 45.905'	E00° 09.085'	Track end
Map 37	156	N50° 45.909'	E00° 09.508'	Stile on path
Map 37	157	N50° 45.376'	E00° 09.578'	Haven Brow
Map 37	158	N50° 45.310'	E00° 09.793'	Short Brow
Map 37	159	N50° 45.198'	E00° 10.139'	Rough Brow
Map 37	160	N50° 45.143'	E00° 10.376'	Brass Point
Map 37	161	N50° 44.995'	E00° 10.792'	Sarsen stone
Map 37	162	N50° 44.957'	E00° 11.020'	The 'Eighth' Sister
Map 37	163	N50° 44.910'	E00° 11.284'	Baily's Hill
Map 37	164	N50° 44.570'	E00° 11.462'	Memorial pillar
Map 37	165	N50° 44.766'	E00° 11.667'	Went Hill
Map 38	166	N50° 44.585'	E00° 12.075'	Car park, Birling Gap
Map 38	167	N50° 44.302'	E00° 12.901'	Belle Tout Lighthouse
Map 38	168	N50° 44.112'	E00° 13.870'	Path near Shooters Bottom
Map 39	169	N50° 44.335'	E00° 15.220'	RAF Bomber Command Memorial
Map 39	170	N50° 44.634'	E00° 15.478'	Fork in path
Map 39	171	N50° 45.113'	E00° 16.027'	Eastern end of SDW

(see overleaf for Inland Route)

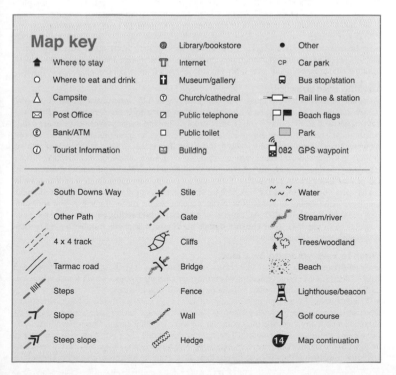

Map key

		@	Library/bookstore	●	Other
♠	Where to stay	🕮	Internet	CP	Car park
O	Where to eat and drink	🏛	Museum/gallery	🚏	Bus stop/station
△	Campsite	☉	Church/cathedral	▬□▬	Rail line & station
⊠	Post Office	☑	Public telephone	⊓⊨	Beach flags
⒠	Bank/ATM	□	Public toilet	▢	Park
ⓘ	Tourist Information	▥	Building	📟082	GPS waypoint

	South Downs Way		Stile		Water
	Other Path		Gate		Stream/river
	4 x 4 track		Cliffs		Trees/woodland
	Tarmac road		Bridge		Beach
	Steps		Fence		Lighthouse/beacon
	Slope		Wall		Golf course
	Steep slope		Hedge	14	Map continuation

MAP	REF	GPS WAYPOINT		DESCRIPTION
Inland route from Alfriston to Eastbourne via Jevington				
Map 40	172	N50° 47.518'	E00° 12.825'	Crossroads, Jevington
Map 40	173	N50° 47.222'	E00° 14.083'	Turn-off to Willingdon
Map 40	174	N50° 47.196'	E00° 14.162'	Trig point
Map 41	175	N50° 46.658'	E00° 14.575'	Concrete dew pond
Map 41	176	N50° 45.901'	E00° 14.776'	Road crossing (A259)
Map 41	177	N50° 45.729'	E00° 15.000'	Finger post
Map 39	171	N50° 45.113'	E00° 16.027'	Eastern end of SDW

APPENDIX B: WALKING WITH A DOG

WALKING THE WAY WITH A DOG

Many are the rewards that await those prepared to make the extra effort required to bring their best friend along the trail. However, because the South Downs is a prime sheep-farming area your dog may have to be on a lead for much of the walk.

And you shouldn't underestimate the amount of work involved. Indeed, just about every decision you make will be influenced by the fact that you've got a dog: how you plan to travel to the start of the trail, where you're going to stay, how far you're going to walk each day, where you're going to rest and where you're going to eat in the evening etc.

If you're sure your dog can cope with (and, just as importantly, *enjoy*) walking 10 miles or more a day for several days in a row, you need to start preparing accordingly. Extra thought needs to go into your itinerary. Study the town & village facilities table on pp30-1 (and the advice below), and plan where to stop and where to buy food.

Looking after your dog

To begin with, you need to make sure that your dog is fully **inoculated** against the usual doggy illnesses, and also up to date with regard to **worm pills** (eg Drontal) and **flea preventatives** such as Frontline – they are, after all, following in the pawprints of many a dog before them, some of whom may well have left fleas or other parasites on the trail that now lie in wait for their next meal to arrive. **Pet insurance** is also a very good idea; if you've already got insurance, do check that it will cover a trip such as this. On the subject of looking after your dog's health, perhaps the most important implement you can take with you is the **plastic tick remover**, available from vets for a couple of quid. These removers, while fiddly, help you to remove the tick safely (ie without leaving its head behind buried under the dog's skin). Being in unfamiliar territory also makes it more likely that you and your dog could become separated. All dogs now have to be **microchipped** but make sure your dog also has a **tag with your contact details on it** (a mobile phone number would be best if you are carrying one with you).

When to keep your dog on a lead

● **On cliff tops** It's a sad fact that, every year, a few dogs lose their lives falling over the edge of the cliffs. It usually occurs when they are chasing rabbits (which know where the cliff-edge is and are able, unlike your poor pooch, to stop in time).

● **When crossing farmland**, particularly in the lambing season (March to May) when your dog can scare the sheep, causing them to lose their young. Farmers are allowed by law to shoot at and kill any dogs that they consider are worrying their sheep. During lambing, most farmers would prefer it if you didn't bring your dog at all. The exception is if your dog is being attacked by cows. Some years ago there were three deaths in the UK caused by walkers being trampled as they tried to rescue their dogs from the attentions of cattle. The advice in this instance is to let go of the lead, head speedily to a position of safety (usually the other side of the field gate or stile) and call your dog to you.

● **On National Trust land,** where it is compulsory to keep your dog on a lead.

● **Around ground-nesting birds** It's important to keep your dog under control when crossing an area where certain species of birds nest on the ground. Most dogs love foraging around in the woods but make sure you have permission to do so; some woods are used as nurseries for game birds and dogs are only allowed through them if they are on a lead.

What to pack
You've probably already got a good idea of what to bring to keep your dog alive and happy, but the following is a checklist:

● **Food/water bowl** Foldable cloth or collapsible silicon bowls are popular with walkers, being light and taking up little room in a rucksack. You can get also get a water-bottle-and-bowl combination, where the bottle folds into a 'trough' from which the dog can drink.

● **Lead and collar** An extendable lead is probably preferable for this sort of trip. Make sure both lead and collar are in good condition – you don't want either to snap on the trail, or you may end up carrying your dog through sheep fields until a replacement can be found.

● **Medication** You'll know if you need to bring any lotions or potions.

● **Bedding** A simple blanket may suffice, or you can opt for something more elaborate if you aren't carrying your own luggage.

● **Tick remover** See opposite.

● **Poo bags** Essential.

● **Hygiene wipes** For cleaning your dog after it's rolled in stuff.

● **A favourite toy** Helps prevent your dog from pining for the entire walk.

● **Food/water** Remember to bring treats as well as regular food to keep up the mutt's morale. That said, if your dog is anything like mine the chances are they'll spend most of the walk dining on rabbit droppings and sheep poo anyway.

● **Corkscrew stake** Available from camping or pet shops, this will help you to keep your dog secure in one place while you set up camp/doze.

● **Raingear** It can rain!   ● **Old towels** For drying your dog.

When it comes to packing, I always leave an exterior pocket of my rucksack empty so I can put used poo bags in there (for deposit at the first bin reached). I always like to keep all the dog's kit together and separate from the other luggage (usually inside a plastic bag inside my rucksack). I have also seen several dogs sporting their own 'doggy rucksack', so they can carry their own food, water, poo etc – which certainly reduces the burden on their owner.

Cleaning up after your dog
It is extremely important that dog owners behave in a responsible way when walking the path. Dog excrement should be cleaned up. In towns, villages and fields where animals graze or which will be cut for silage, hay etc, you need to pick up and bag the excrement.

Staying (and eating) with your dog
In this guide we have used the symbol 🐾 to denote where a place welcomes dogs. However, this always needs to be arranged in advance and some places may charge extra. Many B&B-style places have only one or two rooms suitable for people with dogs; hostels (both YHA and independent) do not permit them unless they are an assistance (guide) dog; smaller campsites tend to accept them, but some of the larger holiday parks do not – however, in either case it is likely the dog will have to be on a lead. Before you turn up always double check whether the place you would like to stay accepts dogs and whether there is space for them. When it comes to eating, some cafés accept dogs and most landlords allow dogs in at least a section of their pubs, though few restaurants do. Make sure you always ask first and ensure your dog is on a lead and secured to your table or a radiator so it doesn't run around.   **Henry Stedman**

	START Winchester	Chilcomb	(Cheriton +1½)	Exton	(East Meon + 1)	(Buriton + ½)	(South Harting + ½)	(Cocking + ½)	(Heyshott + ½)	(Graffham + 1)	(Sutton/Bignor + 1)	(Bury + 1)	Houghton Bridge	Amberley	(Storrington + 1½)	(Washington + ½)	(Steyning/Bramber/Upper Beeding + 1)
START Winchester	0																
Chilcomb	2																
(Cheriton +1½)	6½	4½															
Exton	12	10	5½														
(East Meon + 1)	17	15	10½	5													
(Buriton + ½)	24½	22½	18	12½	7½												
(Sth Harting + ½)	28	26	21½	16	11	3½											
(Cocking + ½)	35	33	28½	23	18	10½	7										
(Heyshott + ½)	37	35	30½	25	20	12½	9	2									
(Graffham + 1)	38½	36½	32	26½	21½	14	10½	3½	1½								
(Sutton/Bignor + 1)	42½	40½	36	30½	25½	18	14½	7½	5½	4							
(Bury + 1)	45	43	38½	33	28	20½	17	10	8	6½	2½						
Houghton Bridge	46	44	39½	34	29	21½	18	11	9	7½	3½	1					
Amberley	47½	45½	41	35½	30½	23	19½	12½	10½	9	5	2½	1½				
(Storrington + 1½)	50½	48½	44	38½	33½	26	22½	15½	13½	12	8	5½	4½	3			
(Washington + ½)	53½	51½	47	41½	36½	29	25½	18½	16½	15	11	8½	7½	6	3		
(Steyning/U Bd + 1)	57½	55½	51	45½	40½	33	29½	22½	20½	19	15	12½	11½	10	7	4	
(Fulking + ½)	64	62	57½	52	47	39½	36	29	27	25½	21½	19	18	16½	13½	10½	6½
(Poynings + ½)	66	64	59½	54	49	41½	38	31	29	27½	23½	21	20	18½	15½	12½	8½
Pyecombe	68	66	61½	56	51	43½	40	33	31	29½	25½	23	22	20½	17½	14½	10½
(Clayton + ½)	69	67	62½	57	52	44½	41	34	32	30½	26½	24	23	21½	18½	15½	11½
(Ditchling + 1½)	70½	68½	64	58½	53½	46	42½	35½	33½	32	28	25½	24½	23	20	17	13
(Plumpton + ½)	72½	70½	66	60½	55½	48	44½	37½	35½	34	30	27½	26½	25	22	19	15
(Lewes + 3)	73½	71½	67	61½	56½	49	45½	38½	36½	35	31	28½	27½	26	23	20	16
(Kingston + 1)	78½	76½	72	66½	61½	54	50½	43½	41½	40	36	33½	32½	31	28	25	21
Rodmell/Southease	82½	80½	76	70½	65½	58	54½	47½	45½	44	40	37½	36½	35	32	29	25
(West Firle + 1)	86	84	79½	74	69	61½	58	51	49	47½	43½	41	40	38½	35½	32½	28½
(Alciston/Bwk + 1)	88½	86½	82	76½	71½	64	60½	53½	51½	50	46	43½	42½	41	38	35	31
Alfriston	90½	88½	84	78½	73½	66	62½	55½	53½	52	48	45½	44½	43	40	37	33
[via IR] Jevington*	*93*	*91*	*86½*	*81*	*76*	*68½*	*65*	*58*	*56*	*54½*	*50½*	*48*	*47*	*45½*	*42½*	*39½*	*35½*
[via IR] End (E+1½)*	*97*	*95*	*90½*	*85*	*80*	*72½*	*69*	*62*	*60*	*58½*	*54½*	*52*	*51*	*49½*	*46½*	*43½*	*39½*
Litlington	91½	89½	85	79½	74½	67	63½	56½	54½	53	49	46½	45½	44	41	38	34
Exceat/Seven Sstrs	93	91	86½	81	76	68½	65	58	56	54½	50½	48	47	45½	42½	39½	35½
Birling Gap	96	94	89½	84	79	71½	68	61	59	57½	53½	51	50	48½	45½	42½	38½
Beachy Head	99	97	92½	87	82	74½	71	64	62	60½	56½	54	53	51½	48½	45½	41½
END (Eastbrn +1½)	100	98	93½	88	83	75½	72	65	63	61½	57½	55	54	52½	49½	46½	42½

* Inland (Alternative) route from Alfriston

South Downs Way
DISTANCE CHART

Winchester – Eastbourne

miles (approx) – 1 mile = 1.6km

Note: Where a place name is shown in (brackets) on this chart the distance to the turnoff to this place is shown. Add the (+) number in the brackets to calculate the total distance to that place. Most villages lie below the South Downs.

(Fulking + ½)	(Poynings + ½)	Pyecombe	(Clayton + ½)	(Ditchling + 1½)	(Plumpton + ½)	(Lewes + 3)	(Kingston near Lewes + 1)	Rodmell/Southease	(West Firle + 1)	(Alciston/Berwick + 1)	Alfriston	[via inland route*] Jevington	[via inland route*] End [Eastbourne + 1½]	Litlington	Exceat/Seven Sisters	Birling Gap	Beachy Head	END (Eastbourne + 1½)
2																		
4	2																	
5	3	1																
6½	4½	2½	1½															
8½	6½	4½	3½	2														
9½	7½	5½	4½	3	1													
14½	12½	10½	9½	8	6	5												
18½	16½	14½	13½	12	10	9	4											
22	20	18	17	15½	13½	12½	7½	3½										
24½	22½	20½	19½	18	16	15	10	6	2½									
26½	24½	22½	21½	20	18	17	12	8	4½	2								
29	27	25	24	22½	20½	19½	14½	10½	7	4½	2½							
33	31	29	28	26½	24½	23½	18½	14½	11	8½	6½	4						
27½	25½	23½	22½	21	19	18	13	9	5½	3	1							
29	27	25	24	22½	20½	19½	14½	10½	7	4½	2½	—	—	1½				
32	30	28	27	25½	23½	22½	17½	13½	10	7½	5½	—	—	4½	3			
35	33	31	30	28½	26½	25½	20½	16½	13	10½	8½	—	—	7½	6	3		
36	34	32	31	29½	27½	26½	21½	17½	14	11½	9½	—	—	8½	7	4	1	

INDEX

Page references in **red** type refer to maps

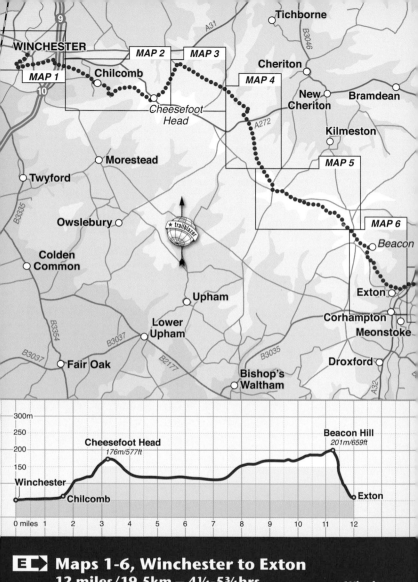

Maps 1-6, Winchester to Exton
12 miles/19.5km – 4¼-5¾hrs

Maps 6-10, Exton to Buriton
12½ miles/20km – 4½-6hrs

Note: Add 20-30% to these times to allow for stops

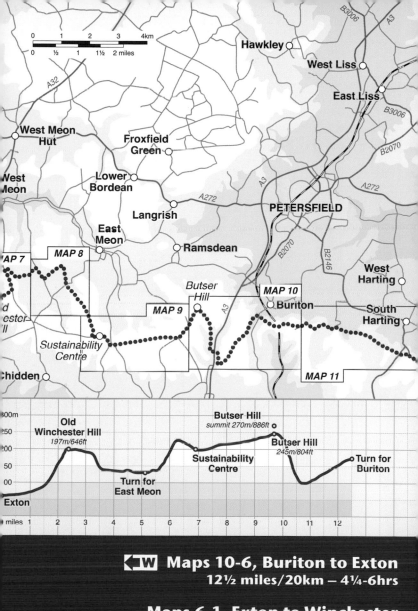

← W Maps 10-6, Buriton to Exton
12½ miles/20km — 4¼-6hrs

Maps 6-1, Exton to Winchester
12 miles/19.5km — 4¼-6hrs

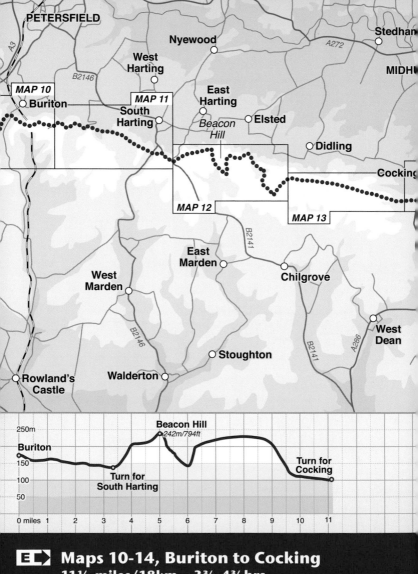

PETERSFIELD

Nyewood

Stedha

West
Harting

A272

MIDHU

B2146

MAP 10

Buriton

MAP 11

East
Harting

South
Harting

*Beacon
Hill*

Elsted

Didling

Cocking

MAP 12

MAP 13

B2141

East
Marden

Chilgrove

West
Marden

B2146

B2141

A286

West
Dean

Stoughton

Walderton

Rowland's
Castle

250m

Beacon Hill
242m/794ft

Buriton

150

**Turn for
Cocking**

**Turn for
South Harting**

100

50

0 miles 1   2   3   4   5   6   7   8   9   10   11

Maps 10-14, Buriton to Cocking
11¼ miles/18km — 3¾-4¾hrs

Maps 14-18, Cocking to Amberley
12 miles/19.5km — 3¾-5¼hrs

Note: Add 20-30% to these times to allow for stops

Wincheste

Bu

Cock

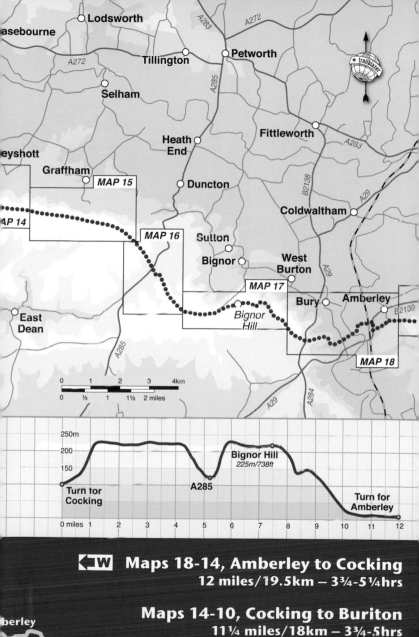

Lodsworth

asebourne

A272

A283

A272

Petworth

Tillington

A285

Selham

Fittleworth

A283

Heath
End

eyshott

Graffham

MAP 15

Duncton

B2138

Coldwaltham

A29

AP 14

MAP 16

Sutton

Bignor

West
Burton

A29

MAP 17

Bury

Amberley

B2139

East
Dean

A285

*Bignor
Hill*

MAP 18

A29

A284

A29

0   1   2   3   4km

0   ½   1   1½   2 miles

250m
200
150

Bignor Hill
225m/738ft

Turn for
Cocking

A285

Turn for
Amberley

0 miles 1   2   3   4   5   6   7   8   9   10   11   12

◀☰W **Maps 18-14, Amberley to Cocking**
12 miles/19.5km – 3¾-5¼hrs

Maps 14-10, Cocking to Buriton
11¼ miles/18km – 3¾-5hrs

berley

Eastbourne

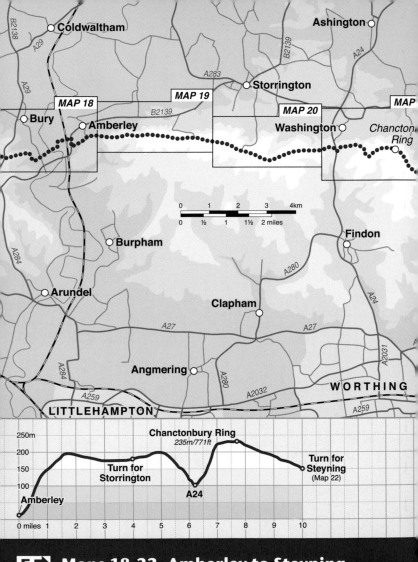

Maps 18-22, Amberley to Steyning
10 miles/16km − 3¼-4¾hrs

Maps 22-26, Steyning to Pyecombe
10¼ miles/16.5km − 4-5½hrs
Plus 20-30mins from Steyning to South Downs Way

Note: Add 20-30% to these times to allow for stops

Maps 26-22, Pyecombe to Steyning
10¼ miles/16.5km – 4¼-5¾hrs
Plus 25-35mins to Steyning from South Downs Way

Maps 22-18, Steyning to Amberley
10 miles/16km – 3¼-4¾hrs
Add 20-30% to these times to allow for stops

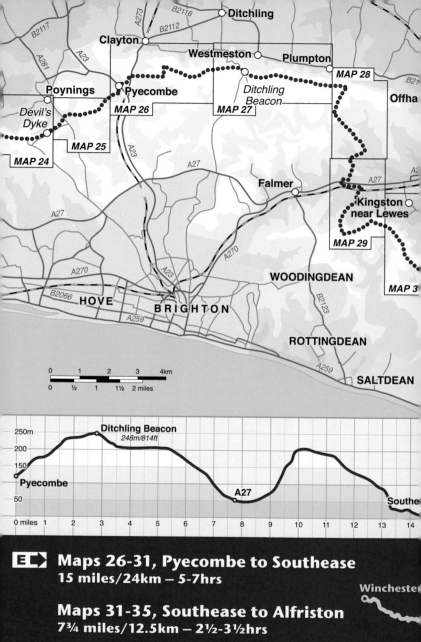

Maps 26-31, Pyecombe to Southease
15 miles/24km – 5-7hrs

Maps 31-35, Southease to Alfriston
7¾ miles/12.5km – 2½-3½hrs

Note: Add 20-30% to these times to allow for stops

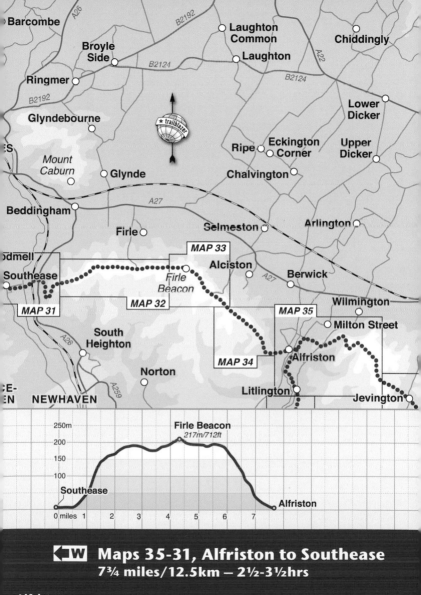

Maps 35-31, Alfriston to Southease
7¾ miles/12.5km – 2½-3½hrs

Maps 31-26, Southease to Pyecombe
15 miles/24km – 5-7hrs

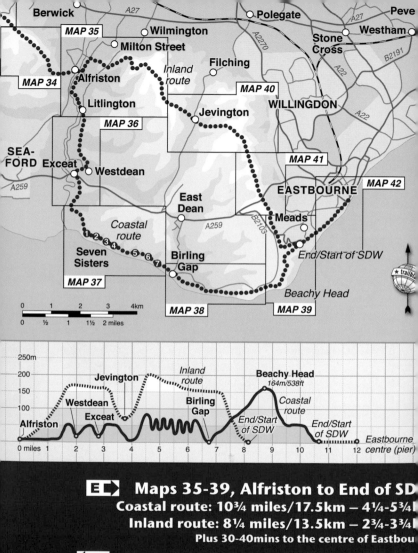
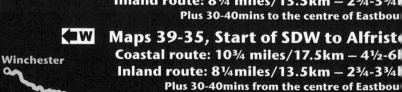

TRAILBLAZER TITLE LIST

Adventure Cycle-Touring Handbook
Adventure Motorcycling Handbook
Australia by Rail
Cleveland Way (British Walking Guide)
Coast to Coast (British Walking Guide)
Cornwall Coast Path (British Walking Guide)
Cotswold Way (British Walking Guide)
The Cyclist's Anthology
Dales Way (British Walking Guide)
Dorset & Sth Devon Coast Path (British Walking Gde)
Exmoor & Nth Devon Coast Path (British Walking Gde)
Great Glen Way (British Walking Guide)
Hadrian's Wall Path (British Walking Guide)
Himalaya by Bike – a route and planning guide
Iceland Hiking – with Reykjavik City Guide
Inca Trail, Cusco & Machu Picchu
Japan by Rail
Kilimanjaro – the trekking guide (includes Mt Meru)
London Loop (British Walking Guide)
London to Walsingham Camino
Madeira Walks – 37 selected day walks
Moroccan Atlas – The Trekking Guide
Morocco Overland (4x4/motorcycle/mountainbike)
Nepal Trekking & The Great Himalaya Trail
Norfolk Coast Path & Peddars Way (British Walking Gde)
North Downs Way (British Walking Guide)
Offa's Dyke Path (British Walking Guide)
Overlanders' Handbook – worldwide driving guide
Pembrokeshire Coast Path (British Walking Guide)
Pennine Way (British Walking Guide)
Peru's Cordilleras Blanca & Huayhuash – Hiking/Biking
Pilgrim Pathways: 1-2 day walks on Britain's sacred ways
The Railway Anthology
The Ridgeway (British Walking Guide)
Scottish Highlands – Hillwalking Guide
Siberian BAM Guide – rail, rivers & road
The Silk Roads – a route and planning guide
Sinai – the trekking guide
South Downs Way (British Walking Guide)
Thames Path (British Walking Guide)
Tour du Mont Blanc
Trans-Canada Rail Guide
Trans-Siberian Handbook
Trekking in the Everest Region
The Walker's Anthology
The Walker's Anthology – further tales
West Highland Way (British Walking Guide)

For more information about Trailblazer and our
expanding range of guides, for guidebook updates or
for credit card mail order sales visit our website:

www.trailblazer-guides.com

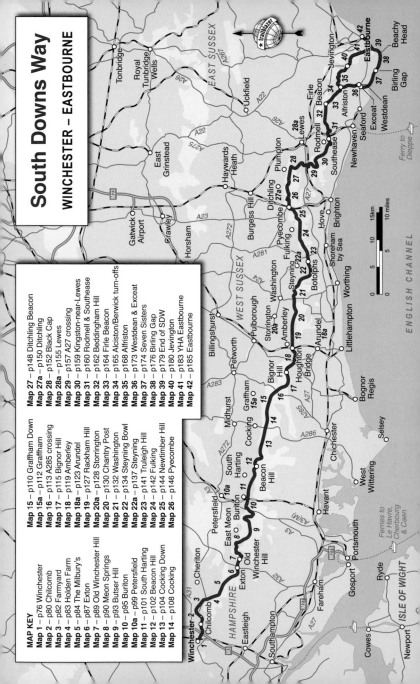

South Downs Way

WINCHESTER – EASTBOURNE